Praise for *To See You Again*

'Out of a disaster with too few miracles comes a miracle of unrequited love that would have challenged Shakespeare. *To See You Again* is a powerful memoir of tragedy, love and – in the end – familial responsibility, which proves once again that the Holocaust had no happy endings'
Alan Dershowitz

'This is disturbing, inspirational and a shocking lesson in human nature – from both a positive and unspeakably evil perspective'
Heat **magazine**

'The Betty Schimmel story is not just another gripping account of the victory of the human spirit over Nazi bestiality although that alone would make it compulsive reading. It is also the most moving true life story one could wish to read'
Jewish Telegraph

'*To See You Again* is a wrenching true story of love during the unspeakable horror of the Holocaust. It touches many emotions on many levels and opens a window into the heart of the human spirit'
Linda Howard, author of *Now You See Her*

'Set in a period of unspeakable horror, *To See You Again* is a memoir of the human heart. It is a drama of the highest order as well as an important document of twentieth century history'
Faye Kellerman, author of *Jupiter's Bones*

'Betty Schimmel has given us a great gift, a powerful and heartbreaking memoir. A fifteen-year-old girl in war-torn Europe, she had the courage to fall in love. The lives of all readers will be enriched when they take Betty's hand and make the journey through this tragedy and triumph and celebration of life'
Alicia Appleman-Jurman, author of *Alicia: My Story*

'A fascinating journey into love, war and betrayal'
Catherine Coulter, author of *The Edge*

To See You Again

A TRUE STORY OF LOVE
IN A TIME OF WAR

By Betty Schimmel

With Joyce Gabriel

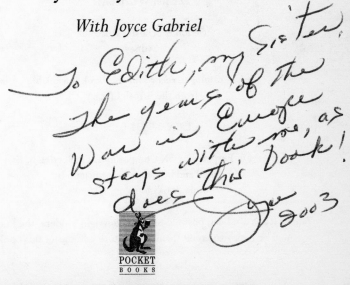

*To Edith, my Sister,
The years of the
War in Europe
stays with me, as
does this book!*

2003

POCKET
B O O K S

LONDON · SYDNEY · NEW YORK · TOKYO · SINGAPORE · TORONTO

First published in Great Britain by Simon & Schuster UK Ltd, 1999
This edition first published by Pocket Books, 2000
An imprint of Simon & Schuster UK Ltd
A Viacom Company

1 3 5 7 9 10 8 6 4 2

Simon & Schuster UK Ltd
Africa House
64–78 Kingsway
London WC2B 6AH

Simon & Schuster Australia
Sydney

A CIP catalogue record for this book is available
from the British Library

ISBN 0-7434-0388-6

Typeset in Perpetua by SX Composing DTP, Rayleigh, Essex
Printed and bound in Great Britain by
Omnia Books Limited, Glasgow

dedication

This book is dedicated to many people who helped shape and sustain my life.

To the memory of my mother Ethel, for her encouragement at a time when I wanted to give up. She held us together as a family through unspeakable horror and loved us more deeply than I ever thought possible.

To the memory of my father Jacob, for his foresight in leading our escape from Czechoslovakia at such an early hour. We would not be alive today if he had not. He saved us as he saved so many other men and women.

To my sister Rose, who was and is my friend, and to my brother Larry who, as the youngest, needed our mother's love the most.

To my children, Robert, Sandy and Jeffrey, who have suffered because I had a tortured soul.

To my grandchildren, Jessica, Aliyah, Alexsandra, Sarah, Jacob Isaac and my late beloved Derek. I love and appreciate them all more than life itself.

To the memory of my mother-in-law Sari, my sister-in-law Irene and brother-in-law Rudi who were victims of the Holocaust, and to all the people who suffered and died at the hands of the Nazis.

Most of all, to Otto, for all he has endured.

A black man whose name I don't recall, best expressed the way I have tried to live my life: 'I shall allow no man to belittle my soul by making me hate him.'

acknowledgments

A special thanks to my friend and Hollywood film agent, Daniel Ostroff, who encouraged me to write this book and introduced me to my New York literary agent, David Hendin. And to my editor, David Highfill, for his belief and support.

    . . . BS

For my husband, Peter, who always believed, and for my sons, Justin, Benjamin and Matthew, who printed endless drafts of the manuscript. And a special thanks to Catherine Coulter, for her friendship and support.

    . . . JG

chapter *One*

*M*y father threw back his head and pounded the piano keys in a rousing song about the carefree soldier's life. It had my mother singing and swaying and my aunts and uncles clapping and dancing. Had there ever been a better entertainer, I wondered as I watched him? Even without his dashing Czech army captain's uniform, Jacob Markowitz was the most stunning man I had ever seen.

'Rose, Larry, Baby,' he called to my younger sister, brother and me. 'Come and sing and dance.'

We didn't hesitate. We threw ourselves into the raucous circle, adults and children laughing and singing. My father's entire family was there, brothers, sisters, nieces and nephews. He revelled in it, the adored 'baby' of the family, the one his mother, my doting late grandmother, called *liebling* (dear one). He grabbed hold of my tiny, beautiful mother, Ethel, and danced her around the room, while his brothers kept the song going with their violins.

He smiled, but I could see the shadows in his eyes. I knew he was sad. It was early 1938. It was a wonderful party, but it was also goodbye. And everyone in that room knew it.

I tried to look as happy as he was, linking my arms with my brother and sister as we twirled, pretending to be gypsies. But I couldn't shake the sadness behind my smile. I wished I could see this evening as a child like my sister Rose and brother Larry. For them, moving away was a great adventure and I had promised not to tell them otherwise. But at nine I was too old for such a fantasy. I had heard my parents whispering in the night. I knew we had to leave because an evil man named Hitler was about to invade our country and my father, as an intelligence officer and a Jew, did not want to be here when it happened. Besides, it was my own fault that I knew the real reason why we had to leave our lovely house in the middle of a meadow, why it could be a long time before I saw again the majestic peaks of the Carpathian Mountains that ringed my tiny world.

'Baby, come and dance with me,' my father commanded again, using the nickname my friends and family often called me. As always, I ran to him and he swung me around as easily as he had swung my mother. 'No long faces,' he leaned down and whispered. 'I am counting on you, Baby. Besides, we're about to start a journey. Uzhgorod is all well and good, but it is not the world. Now Bratislava, where we are going, is a real city. Think of what you will discover.'

I smiled up at my father, hoping the smile would show in my eyes. It wasn't that difficult. I did long to see more of the world than this market town along the border of Czechoslovakia and the Ukraine. I was unhappy that we had to leave, but I knew we did.

As the music swirled around me, my fear of such a great change fought with my longing for adventure. I knew that Bratislava, a city in Czechoslovakia, would be far more exotic than the town of Uzhgorod that I'd lived in all my life. I dearly loved to travel, even then, and had inherited that wanderlust from my father, who travelled all over the world on military missions. On the other hand, it was frightening to leave behind all I knew.

'I don't want to stay here and fight either the Russians or the Germans,' I'd overheard my father tell my mother when he thought we were asleep.

I heard him telling her we would need something called 'new papers'.

'In order to lose ourselves, we need to change our names,' he had said. Then he'd paused, as if he was struggling to find the right words. 'In fact, Mamika,' he said, using his affectionate nickname for my mother, which meant 'little mother', 'we would be far safer if we pretended to be Christians.'

My mother's answer had been loud and clear. 'Never,' she said. 'I will live and die as a Jew. I will never deny my faith or my heritage.'

My father had sighed. There had been these kinds of disagreements between them before – never any unkind words, but arguments about the importance of being Jewish. My father, who was tall, over six feet, with light brown hair and even features, looked more Czech than Semitic. He had been raised nominally Jewish, but his family was far from devout, seeing themselves as Czechs first and Jews second. With his looks and his upbringing, he was, for all intents and purposes, assimilated into the society around him, and this had greatly helped advance his army career. Although he would never have denied his religion in ordinary times, it was definitely not at the centre of his life, and he would have given it up to keep his family safe.

In a way, it was ironic that he should have fallen in love with my mother, the devout daughter of an orthodox Jewish patriarch for whom religion was the essence of life. In fact, when my father first asked my grandfather for my mother's hand, my grandfather refused, saying he was not devout enough to be her husband. But my father loved my mother enough to become more observant, at least during the courtship, and to accept the rules of her orthodox upbringing. Even when she cut off her beautiful jet-black hair when they were first married, wearing a wig or scarf when she went out, as was the custom for married women, he didn't complain.

Throughout our childhood, they had accommodated each other's point of view. She had let her hair grow when they moved from my mother's tiny village of Zeteny to Uzhgorod. He would prepay the ice-cream vendor so that he could buy us all ice cream on our Saturday afternoon walks, because my mother believed that no money could change hands on the Sabbath.

But an outright denial of her heritage was not possible for my mother. Her faith was as simple and as absolute as a child's. And nothing, not even what happened to us later, would shake her abiding belief in God. I wish I could say the same.

'We cannot deny who we are,' she had calmly told my father.

Things had moved quickly after that. My parents gathered us together and told us we would be moving to Bratislava. 'Hopefully, only for a little while,' my tiny mother said in her usual calm way, her dark brown eyes looking straight into ours. 'But we cannot tell anyone our real names or that Papa was in the army, do you understand?' she asked, looking at each of us in turn. My eight-year-old sister and my five-year-old brother nodded, although I don't really think they fully understood what she was asking of them. Even I, at nine, didn't stop to think about how lonely and isolating it would be to keep so much to ourselves. But we had no choice.

My father left for a day, and when he came back he told us he had rented a beautiful furnished apartment in Bratislava. But the hardest part was yet to come: telling his brothers and sisters that we had to go. That was why he had invited them all tonight. I looked around at them, my handsome uncles and pretty aunts and their lively children, who were my cousins and my playmates, and I felt tears come, knowing how much I would miss them and our life together here. They had understood why we had to go, why my father's position in the army would make it unsafe for us to stay. They had no such fears for themselves. Their family had lived here, in peace, for generations. But, for all their understanding, I could see sadness in their eyes as they looked at their baby brother. I was sure they would miss his easy laughter, his love of fun and adventure, and the beautiful music he made.

'I am just glad Mama did not live to see this day,' his oldest brother, Josef, had said sadly. I was afraid that my father might cry, something I had only seen him do once, a couple of years before, when my grandmother had died.

It was my mother who had helped us get through that moment. She was as gay as she was pious, and she loved to sing, as so many Hungarians do, especially when they're sad, because they believe that the music chases away grief. She knew all the old Hungarian and Czech songs, having lived in a border town all her life, and all the gypsy songs because they are so much a part of both cultures. Almost every night, after dinner was over, she and my father would make music together, he at the piano, or violin, and she with her lilting, beautiful voice. They would fill our house with song, and often my sister and brother and I would fall asleep to those haunting melodies, secure in our soft feather beds, down comforters tucked under our chins.

To break the mood of gloom, my mother had proposed one last night of song. Gaily, she'd pushed my father to the piano and ordered him to play a funny Hungarian folk song about a goose who gets loose and runs through the mud, and about Bazmare, the little peasant girl who chases him. This song always made the children laugh, and tonight was no exception. After a while, the adults laughed, too.

I watched my father's hands caress the piano keys and I felt sad, because he couldn't take the piano to our new home. I could hear wistfulness in his voice as he drew my mother closer to him and started singing her favourite song, 'The Pale Yellow Rose'. He sang the melody to her harmony, and the words touched my soul: 'Yellow Rose, if you could only talk, I could tell you that I have no reason to live now; without you, my life is filled with pain, so Yellow Rose I would die for you.'

The love between them was there for us all to see.

There wasn't a dry eye when they finished, for we all knew this party would be our only farewell. We needed to sneak away, like thieves in the night, so that no one would know where we had gone. The harsh truth was that, once my father shed his uniform and left his post, he would be a deserter and the Czechs would be looking for him. I tried to fix all their faces in my mind. We all tried so hard to be happy that night, all caught up in the music, even the children. I can still see them today in my mind's eye. But, apart from a brief, secret meeting a year later, we never saw any of them again. We fled to survive. They stayed, sure that their risk was not so great, and disappeared under the crush of the Nazis' boots, exterminated as if they were vermin.

It never occurred to me then that I would be separated from this part of my family for ever. I had grown up surrounded by certainty. I knew, every Friday night, that there would be the weekly ritual celebrating the beginning of the sabbath. My mother would light the candles and cut the challah bread she had baked that day, and she would say the blessing that would begin the sabbath feast. Afterwards, we would sing or sometimes we would have company. I knew that every day my father would go off at dawn to the barracks where his regimental office was and return in the evening. Unless, of course, he was travelling on an important military or diplomatic mission, and there were many of those when I was a little girl. Once he took my sister with him and bought her a beautiful Persian lamb fur coat to travel in. I remember I was so jealous over that coat and wanted to know why I couldn't have one too. My father gently explained that it was one the furrier had made for someone else who had never picked it up, and since it had fitted my sister perfectly and was an excellent price, my father had bought it for her. Another time he returned from a trip to Germany with chocolate for us all – a chocolate ball for my brother and chocolate dolls for my sister and me.

I knew that God watched over each and every one of us – my mother's gift of faith to her children. Each day was bound by prayer. In the evening we said a prayer when the sun went down; at bedtime we said a prayer before we closed our eyes. In the morning we had to wash our hands and say a prayer; and when we sat down to have our bread we said another prayer.

I knew that every few months we would go to my grandfather's farm in Zeteny, a small farming village several hours by train from Uzhgorod, where we would live in the midst of his huge family – eleven children in all – and work alongside his tenant farmers, the eighteen peasant families who had worked for his family for generations. The farm was filled with all kinds of animals to delight town-bred children like us – chickens, geese, sheep, goats, horses, dogs and cats. From the moment we arrived, we were immersed in farm life, but the excitement began to build up long before we got there.

My sister and I would press our faces up against the windows of the train, looking at the cherry trees and the fields ablaze with bright red poppies and brilliant blue cornflowers as the train cut through the rich farmland between Uzhgorod and Zeteny. Even as a baby, my brother would sense the excitement and try to crawl up the window frame as my father restrained him with a chuckle. As he got older, he would bounce with excitement, asking a thousand times, 'When are we going to get there?'

The farm was a series of fields which stretched out behind a U-shaped compound of houses, with my grandfather's large farmhouse at the centre. The houses of his tenant farmers surrounded it. There was a large single-storeyed outbuilding made of stucco with a clay-tiled roof, where much of the harvesting of the farm produce was done. There the sheep were shorn, the goose feathers sorted by grade from coarse to fine, and the lamb's wool spun into yarn on the ancient spinning wheel. The wool was then dyed with vegetable dyes and woven on the large hand loom in one corner to create chair cushions and table covers.

My grandfather would come out to greet us, his regal white beard reaching to his chest, making him look every bit the patriarch he was. But when he saw me, he would open his arms wide and I would fly into them, to be enveloped by his hug. He was an imposing man, and though not terribly tall, he was larger than life in stature and character. He had fathered eleven children from two wives (his first wife, my mother's mother, had died young). I adored him.

He would begin each day with prayer, his side curls swaying gently as he dovened, his fringed prayer shawl in place, a look of absolute absorption on his face. He was uncompromising about his faith. He prayed, he kept kosher and kept all God's laws as handed down to him through the generations. He took great care to bring up children who did the same. He had passed on this simple, abiding faith to my mother, who embraced it absolutely and forced us to believe. Many times, in the years to come, it was all the protection we had. Miraculously, it was enough. Nothing could dislodge her trust in God and, I believe to this day, He kept us safe.

My grandfather was the greatest cook, better even than my mother, whom he had taught and who was a legendary cook herself. Grandfather loved to make us cold soups – berry and cherry were favourites – so sweet and refreshing that they seemed to capture summer itself. He made the best fried chicken in the world. He would grab a very young chicken from the yard, take it to the kosher schochott to kill the chicken properly, and bring it home, where we would all help to pluck it. Then he would salt the chicken, letting it stand for an hour in the salt before soaking it in water for half an hour. Next, he'd cut it up into pieces and dip each piece first into flour, then into salted beaten eggs, then breadcrumbs, before browning it in a huge frying pan greased with goose fat. Finally, he would cook the whole dish in a giant wood-burning stove in the kitchen.

At harvest time, my mother and I worked side by side with my aunts and the wives of the tenant farmers, plucking and separating goose feathers, removing the husks of the corn, collecting the eggs and shearing the lambs. We also made the brightly coloured Ukrainian eggs produced from eggs that have been hollowed out then carefully and intricately hand-painted. The women would spin and weave and sew and dye fabric. And, as they worked together, they would sing, my mother's voice joining with theirs in songs that had been passed down for generations – Hungarian and Czech songs and the plaintive yet passionate songs of the gypsies. It was through this communal singing that I learned to love this music, a love that has stayed with me all my life. To this day, I know all the words of the most obscure folk songs, and I revel in them.

We lived an idyllic life of town and country, an odd mix of cosmopolitan and rural, secular and religious. My sister and I vied for my father's affection, although I believe she was clearly his favourite, as the younger and the one who was most like him in temperament. My brother was the baby and my mother doted on him. We had grandparents who loved us, and we were well-to-do, with all the material things we needed. In Uzhgorod, although my mother did her own cooking and baking, we had a maid called Joli who did the housework. We were comfortable and secure. We did what generations had done before us.

Then the threat of war came to our door, and we left that world behind.

When the party came to an end, I saw my father and his oldest brother embrace, crying, as they grasped each other's shoulders. I could see my mother using all her self-control to keep smiling as she waved them all away, promising to write, as if we were going on a short holiday.

The next morning, my mother carefully and lovingly packed her china and the delicate hand-embroidered linens she had brought from Grandfather's farm as part of her dowry, and got them ready to be transported by train to Bratislava. We were careful to tell no one, other than our family, our plans because our secret could cost us our lives. Once the house and furniture had been sold and everything had been packed up, we took the nearly 200-mile train ride from Uzhgorod to Bratislava in southern Czechoslovakia. We had a compartment just for our family, so we were able to eat and sleep and sing our way to our new home, feasting on the individual picnic meals my mother had prepared. When we stopped at stations my father left the train and brought back drinks, chocolate and even fresh fruit from a stand. Rose, Larry and I looked out of the windows, watched the trees go by and tried to count the telephone poles. We even made up songs to go with the rhythmic clickety-clack of the train's wheels.

My parents had done a good job of distracting us. We were fleeing our old life, leaving behind the certainty and the affluence and the comfort. In a sense, we were a new family, with our new names printed on new identification papers. Our family history, as it had existed before, was gone. My father the dashing army officer was now my father the travelling men's and ladies' silk imported underwear salesman, although even that was not the truth. It seems clear to me, looking back at the people who came through our apartment in Bratislava and later in Budapest, and we suspected then, that my father was helping people escape from central Europe, and that he was working for the Czech Underground. But he never really told us anything, probably to protect us. This journey marked the beginning of confiding in no one, of living a lie to protect our family.

It was to continue for the rest of my childhood.

chapter *Two*

Bratislava, the Slovakian capital of what was then the merged country of Czechoslovakia, is a picturesque city on the west bank of the River Danube, nestled in the foothills of a valley where the Little Carpathian Mountains cut across from Austria. It lies near the place where the borders of Austria, Hungary and Czechoslovakia meet. Its geography would prove significant.

We took a taxi from the station to our new house, and even my mother was amazed at the size of the city. The buildings were tall in comparison to the ones in small towns and villages we had known. The city seemed endless.

Our new home was in a lovely Jewish neighbourhood of winding, hilly streets filled with shops and apartments, nestled in the shadow of the medieval castle that dominates the city's tallest hill, 300 feet above the banks of the river. The pastel buildings brought to mind a kinder, gentler time, when art, not war, flourished, where artisans created delicate pieces of handblown glass, as they had for centuries. Whether Slovaks, Hungarians or Czechs ruled, the city and its people had prospered ever since the eighth century.

Our third-floor apartment was large and airy, with lovely furnishings. My mother clapped her hands and laughed happily when she saw it. 'This will do, this will do very nicely,' she said, nodding her head as if to reinforce that it would be all right. My father had bought all the beautiful furniture from the Jewish family who had lived there before us. They had left to go to the United States. My mother made lovely new curtains for all the windows and unpacked the boxes of china, silver and linens that helped to make this new place home. Lovingly, she placed the silver candlesticks that had been her mother's on the dining-room table, topping them with ivory candles, ready to be lit for the Sabbath blessing. She unpacked the challah plate and placed it in the corner cupboard, ready for use on Friday night. She sang as she worked, dusting and polishing and rearranging. If she missed our old house or our old life, she never mentioned it, even though we no longer had a maid and she now had to do the housework. My mother was never one for looking back. She was a survivor.

Our first Friday night dinner in the new apartment was special, even more festive than the usual Sabbath dinner. We were celebrating our new home. My mother, knowing what it felt like to be a newcomer, invited two single Jewish men from our new synagogue, who had no family in Bratislava, to join us. And from then on, if it was a holiday or Friday night dinner, we always had a guest. Both my parents were very generous people, and they liked to share the good things that God had given them.

My mother was the kind of religious person who had the goodness that comes from believing in God. My father disappeared each working day, but whether he was selling men's underwear or taking people across the border, we never knew. Money seemed to be no problem, but we were no longer well-to-do. My parents had saved the money from the sale of their house and furniture, and someone was paying my father a salary, so we were, once again, comfortable.

My sister and I went to a Jewish school in the neighbourhood. My mother got involved in the synagogue and found the kosher butcher shop so that she could continue to keep a scrupulously kosher home. My parents tried to make our lives as normal as possible, even with our assumed names, new address and the thunder of Hitler's tanks in the distance.

My father had always taken in stray animals – cats, dogs, even birds. Once he brought home an exotically coloured bird which he had been told could talk. When the bird got wet, all the 'exotic colouring' wore off and we saw that it was just an ordinary parakeet who would never talk. But my father loved him all the same. Everything else may have changed, but his adoption of strays had not. He brought home a cat who turned out to be pregnant. She had her litter of kittens in the apartment and everyone, especially my mother, became very attached to them, talking to them and feeding them titbits of food.

She began to bottle preserves, in glass jars with parchment paper on top, stacking them neatly in the glass-fronted dark oak cabinet that held our china and silver. When the sun's rays struck them, the brightly coloured jars were lit like so many jewels, and it seemed to give her much satisfaction. Perhaps she felt she was preserving our home as well.

At nine, I was a skinny little girl, about average height
with long, wavy brown hair that shone with red highlights whenever the sun hit it. I had inherited my
mother's small nose and dark brown eyes. My sister was
even thinner than I was, always a somewhat frail child,
with long dark hair and my father's amber cat's eyes.
People always told my parents how pretty we both were
and, although my mother never approved of vanity, she
had exquisite taste and loved to make clothes for us,
dressing us in identical outfits that were beautifully made
and often richly embroidered.

My sister and I immersed ourselves in school and
made new friends. My mother would take my brother to
the park in the centre of town, where he made new
friends too. There was no piano, but my father still had
his violin and his harmonica. Some nights, he and my
mother would play and sing as they had in Uzhgorod,
especially when people he introduced as 'old friends' of
his came to stay for a night or two, on their way to who
knows where.

We began to feel at home in Bratislava, putting down
the roots all families do when they move somewhere
new. The year went by fast and we were living well,
although there were rumours of war and of increasing
Jewish hatred in Germany. Hitler had invaded Austria in
March 1938 and was petitioning for the annexation of
the Sudetenland, a region at the northern border of
Czechoslovakia mostly inhabited by Germans, which had
once been part of Bohemia. This was widely believed to
be the first step in Hitler's takeover of Czechoslovakia,
where struggles among minority groups, particularly
the Slovaks, led many of them to long for the kind of
nationalistic state that Hitler would later install there.
The Nazis were now to the north and south of us.

One day in late September, everything changed. Once again, Hitler was about to disrupt our lives. With the agreement of England and France, at the Munich Conference in 1938, he forced the Czech president Eduard Benes to yield the Sudetenland to Germany in exchange for his agreement to leave the rest of Czechoslovakia alone. Hitler rolled his army across Austria, to the borders of Czechoslovakia. One day, we saw him, halfway across a bridge spanning the Danube which separated Austria from Czechoslovakia, riding arrogantly in the back of an open touring car as he surveyed Bratislava. And so did all the Fascists. Although he did not invade the rest of Czechoslovakia at that time, my father was sure invasion would come, and quickly. The Hlinka Guards, the Slovakian army's equivalent of the SS, were emboldened by Hitler's appearance and began to persecute Jews.

From that day on, Jews were not safe. The Hlinka Guards targeted Jewish businesses, broke shop windows and came into our neighbourhood to throw rocks through our windows.

My father knew we had to leave, but where to go, and how to pay for it? I heard my parents whispering in the night and I heard my mother crying softly.

'I will make a plan,' I heard my father promise her. 'I will keep us safe.'

In the meantime, my father took precautions. He boarded up our windows, making our light, airy apartment as dark and isolated as a tomb, and we were taken to school and picked up afterwards. A new tension filled the house. My mother was ill at ease and worried about our safety.

Then events made it even more urgent that we leave.

About a week after we saw Hitler on the bridge across the Danube, as I walked home through the peaceful streets of my neighbourhood, I saw a group of Hlinka Guards beating a young Jewish man with side curls. They pulled at his beard and his side curls until the skin came off his face and he passed out. It was such a terrible sight that I ran home screaming and crying. I could not understand why anyone would be so heartless as to beat a seemingly innocent man.

'What kind of crime did he commit to deserve such punishment?' I demanded of my mother. She stood there, silent, shocked, her face pale and her lips white, as I asked question after question – questions to which, of course, there were no answers except the inescapable.

'They attacked him because he is Jewish,' my mother said quietly, all the sadness in the world in her voice.

The answer terrified me because I was Jewish, and that meant that I, too, could be attacked and beaten. My father was out of town, which made me frantic.

'I want Papa to come home now,' I cried. 'We need him to protect us from the Hlinka Guards.'

My mother said nothing; she just hugged me and soothed me, and tried to reassure me that everything would be all right. I didn't believe it, and I don't think she did, either.

When my father came home a couple of days later, he confirmed my worst fears.

'It's time to move on,' he said, looking as sad and angry as I had ever seen him. 'You see, the Germans have given the Slovakian Fascists permission to act against the Jews, and there is no one who will go against them, as the whole country is practically collapsing, with no outside support from France or England.'

He covered his eyes with his hands, and for the first

time in my life I saw my father standing less than straight, as if this was too much, even for him. But then he threw his shoulders back and when he uncovered his eyes, he was smiling and looked liked my old, confident Papa who could solve anything.

'We will leave soon, but in the meantime we must be very careful,' he said. 'And that means you and your sister can no longer go to school, and Mama can no longer take Larry to the park.'

'But Papa,' I protested, 'I like school. I want to go.'

'It wouldn't be a good idea,' my mother answered gently.

'It's just not safe,' my father said. And that was the end of that.

So we waited while my father made plans. Every day, rocks were thrown. We could hear them through the boarded-up windows, but we were rarely allowed outside. My father had a new problem. If we were to go to Hungary (and it seemed the most reasonable choice of country to go to), my father needed new papers, saying he was a Hungarian citizen. At the same time, he needed to have a different surname from my mother's and ours, so that if anything happened to him, whoever arrested him would not know we were his family. He was desperate to make sure that no harm came to us because of him.

Unfortunately, with the new atmosphere of violence and anti-Semitism in Bratislava, those papers proved impossible to obtain, so my father decided we would leave without them, while we could still leave at all.

'Just pack a bag with a few things for all of you, as if we're going on a short trip,' my father told my mother one morning about a week later.

She looked up at him, wide-eyed. 'But what about everything else? The cat, the kittens, all my lovely china and linens, all my beautiful jars of preserves?'

My father closed his eyes. 'We'll have to leave it here.'

That was the first time I saw my mother cry, when she realized that everything we owned was being left behind, even her precious cat and her kittens. But it couldn't be helped. My father just stood there calmly and let her cry. He knew there was nothing else he could do. My mother packed up all the food we could carry into a picnic basket and my father ordered a taxi to come to the house. He didn't say another word to any of us about where we were going.

The taxi ride through Bratislava was a nightmare. As part of the attack against the Jews, it had been declared illegal for any Slovakians to transport Jews, but our taxi driver took the risk anyway, eager for the large amount of money my father agreed to pay him. He was a dark, tense man who seemed to be constantly looking over his shoulder while he drove. As we passed the railway station, the platform was crowded with people waiting for the next train anywhere. While a crowd of Jewish families waited, many of them were beaten, their possessions stolen. I closed my eyes. I did not want to see more. I could not bear it.

When the driver reached the outskirts of the city, he took back roads that were not well used, probably hoping to avoid any guards who might be looking for escaping Jews. My father directed the driver to a route through a forest, where we picked up a man my father knew, who was going to ride with us as far as Kotchov Kosice, a town across the border in Hungary. When we got to the outskirts of Kotchov Kosice, one of the car's wheels broke, and the driver asked my father for more money.

'I've already paid you a fortune,' my father said sharply.

The driver shrugged his shoulders. 'The price did not include the car breaking down. It is going to cost me a lot of time and money to have it fixed.'

My father stared at him for a long minute, and I could see anger and contempt in his eyes, but in the end he reached into his pocket and paid the extra money.

Then we went on foot, carrying our bags, to a Jewish orphanage in Kotchov Kosice, where we slept that night. The next morning, we got on a train. It was then my father told us we were going back to Uzhgorod, but only for a visit. He was hoping he might be able to get papers there, through his old contacts.

I smiled when I looked out of the train window and saw the station at Uzhgorod come into view, the quaint town spread out behind it and out there, just beyond sight, the sweet house we used to live in, set in the middle of a meadow. Things seemed quiet here and safe after the chaos in Bratislava. But I knew the scenery was deceptive.

'You've got to leave here as soon as possible,' my father's brother Josef told him. 'The Czech army has been looking for you.' He looked grim. 'If they find you, they'll hang you for deserting.'

My father nodded. I'm sure he knew that and also that he didn't want it mentioned in front of his wife and children, but he didn't say so to his brother.

Instead, he asked, 'Can you help me get new papers? It's likely we'll have to leave the country and I can't do that with the papers I have now.'

Josef helped him get the papers and we saw our aunts, uncles and cousins one last time, in secret, before leaving the very next day. It seemed so cruel to come back only to have to leave again, but my parents explained calmly that there was no choice. Besides, my mother said with a smile, we are going to visit Grandfather's house. At that, everybody smiled.

The next morning, we were once again on the train, this time headed for Kiraly Helmec, the town closest to Zeteny in what was then Czechoslovakia. From there, we sent word to my grandfather that we had arrived. He was surprised by our visit, but relieved to know we were safe, because he had heard about all the violence in Bratislava. He picked us up in the familiar horse-drawn carriage and drove us to his farm several miles away.

He was so angry with my father that he could barely contain himself. I saw my mother's face pale and her hands clench when she looked back and forth between the two of them. But my grandfather said nothing until we arrived at the farmhouse.

'Do you have any idea how reckless you've been?' he shouted at my father. They were behind closed doors, but it hardly mattered. 'First you desert the army and dishonour your name, then you leave Bratislava without most of your worldly goods, including my daughter's dowry. At least the first time you ran away you managed to salvage some of your possessions, although even that wasn't much.' My grandfather was a decorated veteran of the First World War and had no sympathy for my father's decision to leave the Czech army as it faced its greatest challenge. But he was even more upset at the spectacle of his daughter and grandchildren arriving at his door, practically destitute, with nowhere to go, and his son-in-law wanted by the army.

'I always thought you were a playboy, a soft Mama's boy who never finished anything,' I heard my grandfather tell my father. My mother looked as if she might walk out through the door, but she stopped herself, apparently thinking better of it. 'Whenever my daughter truly needed you, you were never there. She even had to come home to have Betty, because you were off somewhere. Even coming here shows a basic lack of judgement. You've now put my entire family, probably the entire village, at risk. The Czech authorities have already come here once looking for you. If they were to come back and find you here, they would probably hang you and deport or imprison the rest of us. Is that what you want to happen?'

We could hear my father murmuring softly in response. How he must have wanted to yell and shout, but he didn't. He probably knew he needed my grandfather's help. And maybe he agreed with some of what Grandfather was saying. But when they walked out of that room, they had made peace, at least a peace of sorts. It had been decided that we would stay for a couple of days; then my father would leave by train for Budapest and we would follow.

And that is what we did. When my grandfather drove us back to Kiraly Helmec, in the carriage, he made one last appeal to my mother.

'I think this handsome husband of yours is taking you on another wild-goose chase. It would be far better and safer for you and the children to let him go, since he's the one who is wanted by the authorities. Then you could stay here with us until this madness is over.'

But my mother shook her head. She would never think of leaving my father. But more than that, she was afraid to stay anywhere near the Nazis because she had seen their brutality and their hatred, and she knew they would soon occupy all Czechoslovakia.

'You didn't see what they did to the Jews in Bratislava,' she told my grandfather. 'It is not safe to be Jewish any more in Czechoslovakia, at least not obviously so. You might want to cut off your beard until all this is over.'

But my grandfather just laughed at her. 'Everyone knows me here. With or without a beard, they know I'm a Jew, and I won't deny who or what I am. You should know that by now.'

They looked at each other, and both were crying. My grandfather was seventy-eight then. Perhaps he sensed he would never see my mother or the rest of us again. He hugged me close. I cried, but he told me we would see each other soon, although I don't think he believed it.

When the train pulled into the station, we got on it, helping my mother with the five suitcases that held all we had left in the world.

My grandfather stood there, straight and dignified, watching us go, still a powerful figure even at his advanced age, beloved by children and the Gentile peasants who worked his fields. But none of this helped him when the Nazis finally came.

I still remember my last glimpse of him, looking like an Old Testament prophet, his right hand shading his eyes as he watched the train pull out of the station. I looked back at him for as long as I could see him, until the train went around a bend in the track, and he was gone from my view.

My grandfather had given us three parting gifts: some money, a picnic basket filled with food for the five-hour journey to Budapest, and his prayers.

chapter *Three*

*W*hen we arrived in Budapest, it was dark. The west train station was so huge and imposing that we thought at first it was a mansion. We stood on the crowded platform looking for my father and marvelled at the fairy city spread before us. The lights of the suspension bridges spanning the Danube sparkled like diamonds strung across a black velvet sky. The colourful, ornate buildings that formed the skyline of Buda on one side of the Danube and Pest on the other made an elegant frame for the majestic river. We stared wide-eyed. Perhaps this truly was little Paris, as we'd heard my father describe it. It was certainly the grandest city any of us had ever seen. Even Mama said so.

At the time we barely had the energy to enjoy it. My sister, brother and I had slept for most of the journey, our bellies full from the picnic my grandfather had given us. After hours of riding, we wanted to be safe in our new home. But we had to settle for the already-crowded apartment of one of my father's friends.

'I wanted to have our new home ready and waiting for you, but there just wasn't enough time,' Father explained, introducing us to a couple of his friends, who had come along to help with our luggage. The good news, he said, was that he had found us a wonderful apartment and in a week or so we would be able to move in. In the meantime, as we crowded into the one room he'd managed to rent for us, we explored our new city. And what a city it was. Budapest, the merged city formed by the joining of the two ancient cities of Buda and Pest, was a showcase of the rococo architecture the Habsburgs had made famous throughout the Austro-Hungarian Empire. There were buildings along the cobblestoned streets of Old Buda that proudly traced their origins back to the Renaissance. And, although there were churches everywhere, each more elaborate than the other, their stained-glass windows and plaster friezes celebrating Jesus and all the saints, there were also many synagogues, attesting to the relative freedom and acceptance Hungarian Jews had enjoyed for almost a hundred years. It was a freedom that had stood in stark contrast to the rest of Eastern Europe and Russia, where anti-Semitism often erupted in regular violence against Jews, including pogroms and even resettlement.

Although Jews had been seen as a race and religion apart in Hungary, for almost a century they had been welcomed into the worlds of commerce and government and were able to live free and full lives alongside their Gentile countrymen. Some of that freedom and tolerance had been eroded over the last decade and a half by the rising tide of Fascism. By the time we arrived in Hungary at the end of 1938, there were already in place a number of restrictive laws against Jews. But no one was being beaten in the streets. We all felt relieved. And safe, at least for the moment.

We eagerly explored our new city, my mother enthusiastically and tirelessly leading the way. We walked or we took the trolleybus which ran throughout the districts on the Pest side of the Danube. We explored the hills of Buda, the ancient Roman ruins on the outskirts of the city, the elegant, still bustling shopping district and the nobly built Parliament, not to mention the Regent's Castle on the Castle Hill, overlooking the Danube.

But my mother's greatest joy, I think, came when we joined the Dohany synagogue, the largest synagogue in Eastern Europe, located in the heart of what was later to become part of the Jewish ghetto. This was a wealthy, powerful, thriving religious community until the Nazis arrived in 1944, and the Hungarian Holocaust began. After it was over, barely a fraction of those Jews remained alive, and most of those had lost everything of value to them except their lives, and some of them the lives of their children.

But all I knew at the time we arrived was that the synagogue was beautiful and larger than any I had ever seen. Its beige brick and fine mosaic tiles made it look majestic and immutable. My mother was happy to be involved in such a robust and devout Jewish community. Even with some of the anti-Semitic restrictions already being enforced against Jews, Budapest in 1939 was still the freest and safest place to be in Eastern Europe if you were Jewish. And this was a far larger and more affluent Jewish community than my mother had ever been a part of, although she had always participated in the life of the synagogue. She had always done charitable work, and here there were even greater opportunities for her to do so, and she relished it.

A week after we arrived, our apartment was ready —
and, even better, it was located in the same building that
we were already staying in. We were all happy about that.
The building, one of two 'twin' buildings that stood side
by side in a good neighbourhood just two blocks from
the Danube, was very elegant. It even had a lift. As was
the custom in most of these luxury buildings, the apartments were arranged around an inner courtyard with
beautiful potted plants, chairs and outdoor furniture.
The building was seven storeys high, connected to its
twin building by another courtyard, this one cobblestoned and protected by a wrought-iron gate and fence.

Our first-floor apartment was spacious and lovely,
with twelve-foot ceilings and ornate mouldings. It had
three bedrooms, a large living room and dining room
connected by French doors, a spacious bathroom with a
separate toilet, and central heating, as opposed to the old
ceramic stove we'd had in Bratislava. Best of all, it had a
kitchen large enough for my mother to cook to her
heart's content, which was great news for the rest of us.
The first things she baked for us were her famous poppy
seed and raisin rolls. We watched the butter yeast rise as
my mother cooked the poppy seeds with raisins, milk,
rum and sugar to make the delicious filling. We helped
her roll out the dough and spread the thick filling on top,
then rolled up the dough and waited, impatiently, for it
to rise again. When it was ready, she brushed the tops
with egg and milk and put them in the oven to bake.
Later, as we stood around the kitchen eating the first
batch, we all smiled at our good fortune. We thought we
were in heaven.

Our next task was to furnish the apartment. Once
again, my parents produced enough money for us to buy
furniture, probably a combination of what was left from

the sale of our house in Uzhgorod, whatever money my father had made either from the Czech Underground or from selling men's underwear and the money from my grandfather. They scoured antiques and second-hand shops, managing to buy some lovely pieces of furniture for the apartment, as well as china, linens and some silverware — all things we had been forced to leave behind in Bratislava. There was, however, no money for a piano, which was probably just as well, since my father had decided he needed to keep as low a profile as possible.

In fact, we were told never to bring anyone home when he was there, and never to tell anyone he was our father. He did not want us linked to him as family, for our safety. If we were asked, we were to say our father was a travelling salesman who was rarely home. This man who truly was my father was to be introduced as a 'friend', not a relative. My father was a man who strode through life, but now he had to sneak around corners and could not even publicly claim his wife and children. He was still a deserter and a former Czech intelligence officer. His past could get us deported or killed if it was known that we were related. The fact that my mother kept her maiden name on her papers and on ours was my father's only means of protecting us, he said. The Hungarian government was Fascist-leaning and allied with Nazi Germany. Every able-bodied man between the ages of eighteen and fifty-two had to serve in the army. My father could produce no proof that he had ever served in the Hungarian army, and he didn't want to be drafted now. At that time, in early 1939, everybody had to register with the police and give their religion. This policy had been in place in Hungary since the early 1920s. But my father never registered with the police. He wanted to be an invisible man so that he could stay with us and protect us, while working with the Underground.

During the day, he left the apartment and hid at what he called a 'safe house' owned by the Czech Underground, located somewhere in Buda. We thought he still worked for the Czech Underground, but none of us ever really knew, not even my mother. This was my father's choice. He felt that only true ignorance could save my mother. He knew that, with her inherent honesty, if anyone were to try to torture the truth out of her, she would tell. It was better for her not to know.

We learned then, if we hadn't realized it during the months in which we lived in Bratislava, that we were to trust no one with information about our lives. No one could know we had false papers and weren't really Hungarian citizens, because non-Hungarians could be deported or worse. And no one could know that my father, still a strikingly handsome, fit former Czech army officer, was hanging about the city, probably working for the Czech Underground. It was from that experience, forged so early in my life, that I learned to be a loner, to keep my business to myself. It was a habit that made it impossible for me to have a true confidante, even later in life when I would have liked one. I was constitutionally unable to seek this kind of friendship because I was afraid to share all the 'secrets' of my life. On the other hand, keeping quiet in those years probably saved our lives, and certainly spared my father.

My mother put together a home, lovingly making new curtains, including beautiful sheer ones for the glass-paned French doors that separated the living room from the dining room. To bring in extra money, she cooked and baked for people and was so extraordinarily good at it that she was much in demand. Although my father was scarcely around during the day, people still came to our apartment and even stayed for a day or two, just as they had in Bratislava, and for the same reason, I suspect; I believe my father was helping illegal aliens escape from Hungary.

If my mother ever resented all the moves we had made, or blamed my father, I never heard her say so. Unbelievably, through all the changes in our lives, through all the people and things we left behind and missed later, I never heard my parents argue. My mother told me often that she found my father irresistible from the first time she saw him – a tall army officer patrolling the streets of Kiraly Helmec. She still seemed to find him so, even though having to stay inside to hide so much made him restless.

Sometimes, he would use the three of us as a diversion, making us 'fight' one another, as if we were soldiers under his command.

'Betty, tackle Rose – that's it, bring her down, but don't hurt her now,' my father would say, lounging back against a wall in the living room.

I would dutifully tackle Rose, and she would fight back, biting me or pulling my hair. Meanwhile, Larry would jump in on both of us. My father would watch for a while, see who could win and then call a halt to it. I suppose, looking back, that's a strange thing for a father to do, but I guess he thought he was teaching us how to be tough and survive. It did help me, later on. My mother would just watch and say nothing.

School became a priority. My mother wanted us to attend a Jewish school and Rose and Larry went dutifully, but I balked at the dowdy knee-length, long-sleeved dresses, knee socks and ugly black-laced shoes that were required. I wanted to go to public school, to the local gymnasium. My parents relented, so long as I agreed to go to religious instruction after school. My mother was still determined to raise us as good and practising Jews; she still kept a kosher home in spite of the war and all our moves, and my father still could not have cared less.

The first friend I made on the first day of school turned out to be a neighbour. Violet Storch, even at the age of eleven, was a breathtakingly beautiful girl, with ebony hair, a heart-shaped face and violet eyes. She was vivacious and funny and, from the moment I met her, we were friends.

She came up to me in the playground at breaktime. 'Hallo, you're new,' she said.

I introduced myself and she asked me where I lived. When I told her, she said, 'We're neighbours. I live across the street. What floor do you live on?'

'The first,' I answered.

She clapped her hands together. 'We do, too.'

I don't know what made me so stubborn about going to public school, but I suspect it was fate. If I had gone obediently to the religious school, I would never have met Richie Kovacs.

I'd been a tomboy all my life. Although I never grew beyond five foot one, I was always strong and well co-ordinated, unlike my sister, who was always thinner, more sickly and not at all athletically inclined. She had a spot on her lung from a childhood illness and my parents pampered her because of it. It makes sense now, but it annoyed me when we were children. I was the physically active one, so it was only natural that when I learned that the school had a gymnastics course, I was determined to try for it.

When I first took a good look at Richie Kovacs, I had

a reason to scrutinize him closely. In the pairing of the gymnastic teams of boy and girl partners, he'd been designated as mine. I looked him over. He was at least a couple of years older than I, which made him about twelve, and much taller. He had the kind of dark good looks that, even at my age, could take your breath away, and gorgeous blue eyes that you could lose yourself in. But I wasn't really interested in all that then. I just wanted to make sure he was strong enough to hold me when we did our stunts. It was his broad neck and shoulders that convinced me he was. I realized I was staring at him and, at that moment, he looked right into my eyes, gave a little smile and waved.

Each pair was asked to 'audition' and, while the rest of us were waiting, we were given the chance to climb a rope up the wall of the gym. We were all standing around, watching one another. When it came my turn to climb the rope, I found it a struggle. I had to work my short legs hard and pull myself upwards with arms that weren't as long or as strong as I would have wished. Behind me, I heard Richie's voice. 'Come on,' he said, not a trace of sympathy in his tone, 'pull that bottom up.'

I thought I might not like being his partner but, after the audition, he came up to me and gave me that smile of his again. 'Where do you live?' he asked.

'In the Fifth District,' I said.

'I don't live so far away,' he said. 'Just in the Eighth District. Would you like to walk home together?'

I remember nodding shyly, glad I'd made a new friend, and one who was as athletic as I was.

As we walked home, we talked.

'I'm going to stay in this new gymnastics class,' Richie said. 'It's good for my posture. Of course, I play football, too, but that's different. This is more disciplined, in a way.'

I nodded. 'I'm going to stay in the class, too, even though it's three days a week after school. I like it.'

'Do you play a musical instrument?' he asked me as we walked along the wide promenade on the high banks of the Danube. We looked down at the barges gliding slowly downstream.

'No,' I answered, 'although we used to have a piano but we sold it when we . . .' Here I hesitated, not sure of what to say and then decided to just say, 'when we moved.'

He smiled at me. 'We have a piano. My mother plays, and I play the piano and the drums. If you ever want to play, you can come over and use my piano,' he said.

I remember looking up and thanking him, thinking how generous his offer was, and how kind.

That was the beginning. We would go to those classes three days a week – every Monday, Wednesday and Friday – and he would either walk me home and then take the tram back to his house, or we would take the tram together, using our unlimited student passes, talking the whole time. Sometimes, the walk would take an hour or two. We would stop and look at the river or get something to drink – cocoa or a fizzy drink. Once, I remember, I was dying for one of the raspberry drinks sold by the street vendors. I didn't say anything because I didn't have any money to buy one, and I was embarrassed to tell him so.

As if he was reading my mind, he said, 'I'm so thirsty. I'm dying for a drink.' He steered us over to the vendor. 'Want one?' he asked. I just shook my head, too miserable to answer and too proud to tell him the truth. So I stood there and watched him drink the whole thing.

It didn't take many walks to learn that Richie's family were wealthy. They owned a large vineyard in the

countryside outside Budapest as well as Hungary's
largest liquor distributorship. Richie's father was also
editor and co-owner of *The People's Voice*, a daily newspaper in Budapest. My family barely had enough money
to live on. Although we ate regularly and had a nice
apartment, we were no longer affluent; we weren't even
anywhere near it.

Sometimes I was late getting home, the time forgotten as we walked and talked. When that happened, my
mother would get angry with me, especially on Friday
nights. They were still as sacred as ever to her. She would
prepare a large meal, itself a ritual. Early in the day, she
would go to the butcher to buy her kosher chicken, all of
which she used, feet included. We would start the meal
with a soup made of chicken broth, into which she put
her mouthwatering homemade noodles. Then she would
serve the chicken, accompanied by her homemade challah, followed by a pot roast or some other kind of roast,
accompanied by potatoes, carrots, beans and apple sauce
– whatever was in season. For dessert, there would be
stollen from the bakery and one of my mother's glorious
cakes. Her best was *varadi lepeny*, a cake with a walnut
pastry dough on the bottom and the top. It is made very
rich by the addition of a thick walnut filling with eight
egg whites and eight egg yolks, each beaten separately,
then mixed together with cocoa and sugar. To this day, it
is my children's favourite.

Before we could eat, my mother would put a beautiful lace mantilla over her head, light the five Shabbas
candles in the centre of the dining room table, and pass
her hands over the candles three times before covering
her eyes and saying her prayers. She ended the ritual with
the words 'Good Shabbas' and a kiss to each of us
children. At almost the same moment, my father would

arrive home from the synagogue, sometimes alone, but often with friends. We never knew whom he would bring home. Often these 'friends' would join us for dinner and then stay to play cards, even though the sabbath had officially begun, and my mother would complain to my father later, 'Couldn't you have waited until Saturday night to play cards?'

In some ways, we all wanted freedom in those days. My father had gloried in the freedom he had had in the military. As an intelligence officer he often worked independently and was used to his adventurous trips abroad. He loved to travel, and had been as far as Australia and New Zealand on military and diplomatic missions when most people had barely heard of them. When he went out during the day, he had to be careful to remain as 'invisible' as possible. My mother always worried when he didn't come home when he was supposed to, afraid that he had been picked up and she would never see him again. But he himself seemed more bored and frustrated by his captivity than afraid. As I got older I wanted more freedom myself to come and go, but my mother needed me at home during the day to watch over my brother when she went out to a cooking job.

No matter how much we wanted to broaden our horizons, my mother's were firmly bounded by the dictates of her religion. The Jewish dish cholent was a great example of this. You could not cook on Saturdays because it was the sabbath and such chores were forbidden. But you had to eat, so my mother and many other orthodox Jewish women would make Saturday's dinner on Friday afternoon. That dinner was cholent, a casserole reminiscent of cassoulet but so uniquely delicious in its own right, especially the way my mother prepared it, that I prefer to think of it as in a class by itself. As in so many

Middle European dishes, how this one is prepared depends on the country you're in. Cholent originated in Russia, where it is basically made with equal parts of barley and pinto beans. Made by Hungarians, it is three quarters beans and a quarter pearl barley. Austrians, on the other hand, use more barley than beans. My mother had her own special recipe that made our cholent truly heavenly. She put the beans, barley, garlic and onions in a heavy two-gallon pot. Then she took a goose neck and stuffed it with flour, goose fat, salt, paprika and a little water, and added it to the pot. The goose neck acted as a kind of stuffed skin, lending richness and flavour. Next she would add some smoked goose and some beef flank and fill the pot half full with water.

When the cholent was assembled, it was my job to carry the pot to the local baker, who would cook our pot, along with pots belonging to a couple of hundred other Jewish families in the neighbourhood, in his huge oven overnight, after the last of the challah loaves had been baked, when the oven's fires had been banked and the pots could cook among the smouldering coals. Each family would label the lid of their pot with their name, and make sure that a piece of parchment paper was inserted between the lid and the cholent. Throughout the night, the baker would add water to the casseroles as they cooked slowly. They would cook from Friday night to Saturday afternoon.

Whenever I was late carrying the heavy pot down to the baker, he would shake his head at me. 'You are not going to have cholent tomorrow,' he would say. 'You have come too late.'

I would beg and plead. 'You have to take this or my mother will kill me,' I would say with just the right amount of contrition and humility. And the kindly baker would relent and add my pot to all the others.

On Saturday afternoon at one o'clock, I would go back to the baker's to retrieve the fully cooked cholent, along with the freshly baked challah loaves, and we would have a big Saturday lunch of cholent, with challah and homemade pickles. The dish was so heavy and filling that my father would lie down on the living-room sofa after eating it and sleep for two hours. No one was allowed to talk or make the slightest sound while he napped. Afterwards, when he woke up with his usual smile, he would always say that the cholent had put him to sleep.

Sometimes, at night, after we children had done our homework and said our prayers and Mama had tucked us in, I would hear her and my father talking about what had now truly become a war. The news was not encouraging. The Nazis were winning, invading country after country. Poland had fallen at the end of 1939. By now, 1940, the rest of the free world, having done nothing to stop the Nazis when they could, was in a life-or-death struggle for its continued existence.

'At least,' my father said, 'England has come into the war, and I hear that a number of Polish pilots will be flying for the RAF.'

He never told anyone how he knew these things and we children never thought to ask. It was a confusing time, because, as the 'good Hungarians' we were supposed to be, we should be solidly behind the Nazis, because they were our allies. On the other hand, as both Jews and Eastern Europeans, it was frightening to see how the Germans were taking over everything, and the whispered conversations between my parents about what was happening to the Polish Jews made me wake up in the middle of the night in fear.

'Don't worry, Mamika,' I heard my father telling my mother one night. 'We are still safe here. And by the time the Germans get around to invading Hungary, the war will be over. Just wait and see.'

My father was always positive, and my mother always seemed calm, unless I was late home. She had come to depend on me more and more. And, although they never discussed it, money was always tight. We never got pocket money. There was never anything 'extra' left over, and the beautiful presents my father used to bring us – porcelain dolls and Swiss chocolates and fur coats and jewellery – were all things of the past. But my mother still dressed herself and us beautifully in clothes she designed and made by hand. And she continued to make my sister Rose and me identical outfits, even though we weren't twins.

Richie and I were still firm friends. In fact, we were together so much that my friend Violet complained to me about it many times.

'We used to walk home together every day after school until you met Richie,' Violet would say. 'Now you're always with him.'

There wasn't much I could say, and I certainly didn't want to give up my time with Richie or share that time with Violet.

Richie and I had both been chosen to perform in a marching group of twenty-four, with the school band, doing various kinds of exhibition routines. This was a great honour and a lot of fun. We had uniforms – navy-blue trousers for the boys and navy-blue pleated skirts worn with navy-blue polka dot shirts and a bow tie for the girls. Richie and I were good at this, he twirling a baton as if he was born to it because of his practice with

drum sticks and me proudly carrying the Hungarian flag
as I stepped through an intricate routine. I wish I could
say the same for our performance on the gymnastic
team, but I can't.

We did a lot on the trapeze, but I wasn't very good at
it. Richie was supposed to hold me up while I made a
human bridge. On one occasion, there we were, with
him holding me, and we were swinging back and forth,
and I was so afraid that he was going to drop me that I
grabbed his hands so hard that he couldn't move or
manoeuvre. Perhaps it was then that I began to fall in
love with him, because he never blamed me for our less
than stellar performance – which was really quite something, because Richie tended to be a perfectionist at
whatever he did.

It was around this time that our friendship took a new
turn. Richie began inviting me to his home for dinner,
and I would invite him to mine. Richie was one of the
few people who knew that my father was my father.
Although we weren't supposed to tell anyone, I had
introduced him as my father at the beginning. In a way,
that was for the best because, even though I couldn't
invite anyone else over in the evening, I could invite
Richie since he already knew about my father. When
Richie began coming to dinner, my father found it highly
entertaining and used to tease me about it mercilessly.

Richie would walk in and my father would raise an
eyebrow, as if to say, 'Another date?'

I would look away and Richie would catch my eye and
wink at me, part of our special 'language' for communi-
cating when others were around. I knew he was laughing
with me, not at me.

I would try to remain dignified, but my father was not
to be denied his fun.

'Ah,' he would whisper as he passed by me. 'I see your special friend is once again a dinner guest. Should I call the rabbi? Should I hire the hall?'

I would blush furiously. I was not yet twelve years old, and Richie and I were just friends, although I had to admit, at least to myself, that we were very special friends. He was the closest person to my heart and one of my two best friends, along with Violet. But I still didn't dare tell Richie all my secrets – that my father had deserted the Czech army, that he was not Hungarian – because I knew my father, or all of us, could be punished for them, especially now that the government was deporting many people, many of them Poles and Czechs who were not Hungarian nationals. We all tried to protect my father in those days, even as he tried his best to protect us.

Dinner at Richie's home was lovely and elegant. The Kovacs' apartment, situated at the top of the large building that housed both the liquor distributorship and a small orthodox synagogue that had been built by his great-grandfather, was huge, and tastefully and expensively furnished with priceless antiques and polished mahogany furniture. His father was handsome, but very dignified and remote. He would speak to me politely at dinner, then disappear afterwards into his study. Richie's mother was much more friendly. She was a beautiful woman, slim and petite, whose dark hair and ivory skin rivalled my mother's. In those days, before the German Occupation, she would dress for dinner, her long, slender hands beautifully manicured, her nails shiny with a coat of light polish. She had elegant jewellery and always wore pearls as well as diamond and pearl earrings; and she had an exquisite wedding ring and a large diamond engagement ring. She used her hands a lot

when she talked. Like Richie, she played the piano. I'm
sure he inherited his long-fingered, slender hands from
her — and her kindness, as well. Richie was one of the
kindest people I had ever met, and so was his mother.
Because she saw her family's wealth as a privilege and a
blessing, she felt it was her obligation to help those less
fortunate. She spent much of her time doing charity
work in Budapest, a job that became more and more
important as the war dragged on, the economy collapsed, there were food shortages and families were
without sons and fathers to help provide for them.

Although Richie's great-grandfather had built an
orthodox synagogue, Richie's parents were very modern
Jews, who had moved away from the strict dictates of
their religion. Like many affluent Jews of that time, they
saw themselves as 100 per cent Hungarian and 80 per
cent Jewish. They were assimilated — or so they thought.

chapter *Four*

Looking back, I suppose it was inevitable that Richie and I would become boyfriend and girl-friend. Our bond had formed so immediately and so solidly that it had to be more than just friendship. The change began when I was just twelve. Richie had turned fourteen that year. He had grown taller and more hand-some, and had begun to play the drums in the school band. All the girls were crazy about him, but to my delight he had eyes only for me.

We were inseparable by then, together so much that my good friend Violet was by now disgusted with my attachment to him. I think she was jealous on a certain level, as well as resenting Richie because of the amount of time I spent with him; some of which at least she thought I should be spending with her. Sometimes, she would ask to come along with us on our walks or to the cinema, but I would always say no. I didn't want to share my time with Richie. When I was with him, at least for a time I could forget the war and just be young, be myself.

One day he looked at me and asked me solemnly, his blue eyes twinkling, 'Will you be my girlfriend?'

I remember the moment perfectly. It was a beautiful day and we had been walking along the Danube when Richie suggested we walk down the few steps from the wide promenade to sit under the bridge. We always brought along breadcrumbs to throw to the carp who swam by. I went totally still for a moment, a handful of crumbs still clutched in my hand, as my eyes searched his face.

'What, has the cat got your tongue, *kis pofa*?' Richie asked. That was his pet name for me, 'little face' in Hungarian, because, although I had got older and I was beginning to develop a woman's body, I was still only a little over five feet tall and everything about me was small, including my face.

I shook my head. 'No, you won't be my girlfriend?' Richie asked, but he was smiling now, so much so that I began to smile, too, and then to laugh.

'No, the cat does not have my tongue, but yes, I will be your girlfriend.'

And I was, from that moment on.

On our first date, Richie took me to the cinema and we sat in the balcony. I don't remember what we saw – some American film. We loved American films, and American music – show tunes, big band songs, jazz. Richie put his arm around the back of the seat and, halfway through the movie, he kissed my cheek, then turned my face and kissed my mouth, a chaste, innocent, closed-mouth kiss that was very gentle and very loving. I had stars in my eyes. No wonder I don't remember what film was being shown.

*

The Danube has always been at the heart of life in Budapest. It was a route of travel and commerce, a beautiful point of geographic interest, a body of water that neatly bisected and yet joined two proud and ancient cities. It was also the place to have fun and, beginning in the spring of 1941, Richie took me there every Saturday and Sunday.

The Kovacs owned a boat, which was kept in a row of narrow wooden boathouses on a small side street running perpendicular to the banks of the Danube in Buda. The boat was a rowing boat, with oars with which you could row energetically upstream so that you could later drift lazily downstream. The boathouse itself was a tiny little space with room for only a single bed, a chair and a table. It had one small window.

The boat was to be our magic carpet, freeing us from the heat and humidity of the city and the prying eyes of parents and friends. The boat was to be our private adventure and escape.

Of course, my mother would never have allowed me to go out alone in a boat with any boy, even Richie, whom she had grown to like and trust. It was not proper. As it was, she was reluctant to let me go out in a boat on the river at all, afraid that I would drown. I was able to convince her that I was a strong enough swimmer to go, and I simply lied about being alone with Richie: I told her we were going with friends. I didn't feel good about lying to her, but I did it anyway, because I wanted the adventure and I really wanted to be alone with my boyfriend.

First I had to solve one more problem, for which I needed my friend Violet's help. I needed a bathing suit to go boating on the river, but I didn't own one, and I refused to ask my mother for one because she was so

strictly religious that it would have had legs and sleeves.
At that time, everyone in Hungary, everyone in Europe,
wore a bikini; even old women. But my religious mother
would never have permitted me to own such a costume,
so I had to ask Violet to loan me one of hers. She was as
tiny as I was, and we often borrowed clothes from one
another. Her parents could afford cupboards full of
clothes for Violet and her equally beautiful older sister,
including several bikinis. In no time, one of them was
mine.

My growing relationship with Richie was the beginning of my keeping secrets from my mother – a normal
enough development in the life of a teenage girl, even if
it was the middle of the Second World War. If my mother
had known I was seeing a boy alone on a boat, dressed in
a bikini, she would have forbidden me from ever seeing
Richie again.

It was a long, hot trip to the boathouse. We had to take
first a tram across to Buda, then another train, and then
we had a long walk across a meadow before we reached
the boathouse. But the walk served its purpose. The first
time Richie ever held my hand was when we were walking through this meadow, which was filled with flowers.
These fields were cultivated by Bulgarians who came to
Hungary hundreds of years before and were still the
major vegetable growers in the country. Richie took my
hand as we passed through the Bulgarians' fields and held
on to it, and I found myself hoping that he would never
let it go. The feel of his hand wrapped around mine felt
like electricity going through me. I think that he felt it,
too. He held on tightly to my hand and kept squeezing it,
but, of course, we didn't talk about it. We were both so
young and still shy in some ways, although, in most
things, Richie was one of the most self-confident, self-

assured people I had ever met, but quietly so. He would
never brag. He didn't have to, because he simply excelled
at everything he did. And, because he was the perfect
only child of adoring, affluent parents, he had never felt
the need to prove himself to anyone.

On that first boat trip, Richie had to teach me how to
row. I sat there, in the boat, dressed only in Violet's
bikini, with more skin bared than I had ever shown to
anyone in my young life. In order to teach me how to
row, Richie had to sit behind me, with his arms around
me, so that he could show me how to position the oar in
the water and then pull it through. He was so close to me
that his body touched mine. It was hard to concentrate
on the rowing, but somehow I learned the stroke and,
once satisfied that I'd mastered the technique, Richie
went back to his seat, without ever taking advantage of
our closeness or my near-naked body.

I had so many blisters on my hands after that first day
of rowing that my palms were raw. We didn't go very far
upstream. The ride downstream as we drifted along was
heavenly. I was able to lie down on my side in the boat,
the hot sun warming my skin. Richie looked over at me
from his seat, where he was gently guiding the boat back
to the dock. 'How beautiful you are, and how much I
love you,' he said quietly.

On many subsequent boat rides, we shared our
dreams. Richie wanted to go to university and become a
biochemist. My ambitions then were far more simple
and much closer to home: I wanted nothing more than to
be Richie's wife and the mother of his children. My
childhood had been so odd, distorted by the war and all
the moves and the secrecy, that I just wanted a quiet life
with Richie, far away from war and all it had done to
people. We would row all the way to the Czech border,

which would take about four hours up but only two back, since we'd be going downstream and didn't even have to row.

As we walked home later that day, I made Richie stop to watch the sunset from the banks of the Danube. It was breathtakingly beautiful, the bright orange sun slipping from view below the horizon. The sky was slashed with vivid arcs of fuchsia, purple and gold, a last flash of brilliance before night fell on the city.

Suddenly I felt a chill down my spine as the last of the light faded. 'Will you always love me just as you love me now?' I asked Richie, somehow needing to be reassured.

He cupped my face in his hands and lightly kissed my lips, soft as a whisper. 'Always,' he promised.

When we weren't boating or at school, we would go into antiques shops and browse together. Richie was already in his second year of secondary school and he knew many things I didn't. Patiently, he explained things to me about art: who Titian was and what and when he had painted; what triptychs were. I remember once we looked at a painting of a woman holding a rose and he described the variations of brushstrokes.

One January night in 1942 Richie came to pick me up to go the cinema. The snow was falling so fast and thick that it looked like a giant curtain.

'Maybe we shouldn't go to the cinema,' I said. 'By the time we get out, everything will be covered.'

Richie just smiled. 'It's not going to be covered, Baby. Besides, you're dressed warmly and so am I, so what does it matter?'

My eyes lit up. 'If you really don't mind the cold and the snow, let's go skating.' I loved to skate and ice dance on one of the artificial lakes near by, but I knew Richie didn't care much for it. Still, since he seemed to be enjoying the snow, it was worth a try to get him there.

By this time, we were already outside. Instead of answering me right away, he picked up some snow and began shaping a snowball. Without any warning at all, he threw it at me, hitting me smack in the face. 'So, you want to go skating, hey?' he asked, laughing as he scooped up more snow.

My surprise turned to fun in a second as I scooped up some snow of my own and threw a snowball back at him. We ran after each other, throwing snowballs, all the way to the cinema. Needless to say, by the time we got there we were indeed covered with snow. And then, as if we hadn't seen enough of the cold, white stuff, the American film playing was *Serenade in Sun Valley*, with ice skater Sonja Henie. At least someone got to skate that night.

We drifted through 1942 as the war blazed on. My father had to be more and more careful. He was still helping people to escape and my mother was still working, cooking for others, to supplement the money we had. She often brought home food for us as well.

One bright, sunny day in the summer of that year, when I was thirteen, my father asked me to go for a walk with him. I was both surprised and delighted because often recently he would avoid being seen with us.

I looked up into his face and saw him smiling, but only with his mouth, not with his eyes. In fact, his eyes looked incredibly sad.

'Is something wrong, Papa?' I asked.

He just shook his head and said, 'Come along.' We walked for a few blocks until we came to a beauty shop, where he surprised me by taking me inside. Before I

could even ask questions, he instructed the beautician to
cut off my long, wavy hair until it was little more than a
shoulder-length bob. Then he made her give me a perm,
one so ugly that people teased me about it for months
afterwards, until it finally grew out.

'I need you to look older, because you must be older
from now on,' he told me solemnly as he saw how sad I
was at the loss of my beautiful hair. 'You are the oldest
child and you must help your mother, and be her partner, her other pair of hands and set of eyes.'

He looked away from me for a long moment then
turned back, took my hand and led me out of the shop.
When we were halfway down the street, he looked down
at me from his great height, this dashing, golden man,
and said, 'I have to leave the country, Baby, on a secret
mission. I don't want to, but it's simply too risky to stay
here. They'll send me to the Russian front or to a forced
labour camp and then I'll be in no position to help you
and your mother and your sister and brother.' He wiped
a tear that had fallen from one of my eyes and was making its way down my cheek. 'You must be strong, Baby.
For you, and for me, but most importantly for your
mother.'

'But where will you go, Papa?'

He sighed, squeezing my hand. 'Some friends of mine
can get me out of the country on a mission that involves
smuggling refugees into the Foreign Legion. It's a risky
business and I could be gone for a while. I had hoped that
the war would be over by now, that we could all remain
safely here in Budapest, but it was not to be. I need to
make this mission and maybe others.' We walked for
another block or so, until we came to a millinery shop,
where my father bought me a plaid taffeta picture hat
that tied under the chin. It was supposed to make me

look older. With my new frizzy hair, I thought it made me look hideous, but I could hardly tell Papa so, not if he was truly leaving us for God knew how long.

I could not believe this was happening. My father was at the centre of our lives, just as surely as my mother was, even though he had to hide half the time and we hadn't been able to tell most people that he was our father. In all the ways that counted, he was the head of our family and our protector; I couldn't imagine our family without him. How I hated this dreadful war. 'But when will you come back, Papa?'

'As soon as I can,' was all he said.

My mother gasped when she saw my hair, and she got really angry at my father.

'What on earth have you done to my pretty Betty?' she demanded.

'She has to look older because she has to take my place for a while, and be your helper,' my father said quietly.

I saw from the shocked look on my mother's face that she had had no idea this was coming.

'What do you mean? Where are you going?' she gasped.

And then he told her that he had to leave on a mission, taking people out of the country, and that he would be gone for a while, perhaps months, on a journey to North Africa. He had never said much about the secret work he did, and he said little now.

Dinner was unusually quiet. My sister was too upset to eat; my little brother looked very confused. My mother barely spoke, even though my father tried to be gay and charming. Perhaps he wanted to remember the family that way, one last time. After dinner, he persuaded my mother to sing while he played the violin. At first, he played some mournful gypsy tunes that sounded the way

I felt: 'The frost decorated the windows with icy flowers at the time I met you, and it was spring when I left you . . .' I suppose he had a right to sing melancholy songs that night. He helped my mother tuck us into bed, lingering while she watched us say our prayers, perhaps wanting to remember that moment as well. Later, after we were supposed to be asleep, he played some lively, gay songs, even a csárdás that made me feel like dancing, although the rest of me was too sad to do so. I heard my mother laugh, once, and then heard my father answer with his.

When I got up the next morning, he was gone. A couple of weeks later, we received a postcard from him. It was a picture of my father on a boat near Constantinople. My mother explained that he had travelled there through a route long used by the Czech Underground, through Yugoslavia, whose underground movement was also very active against the Germans. From there, he had been smuggled into Turkey. From Turkey, she said, he and the refugees would most likely go by ship to Morocco, where these men would join the ranks of the French Foreign Legion, long the place of last resort for many unsavoury characters and now a haven for some refugees from eastern Europe. It was far from a perfect escape, according to my mother. She said that my father had once told her that when these refugees arrived in North Africa, they were given arduous jobs in the French Foreign Legion and many died there.

About four weeks later we got another postcard from my father. He was in Morocco. The picture was of him standing in front of a camel and smiling, the desert sands behind him. The message was brief and obscure, simply saying he was safe and the trip had been a success.

That was the last we ever heard of him.

*

None of us knew what to think as the months and then years went by with no word. There was no way we could find out where he was, although my mother did try to contact some of his refugee friends through our synagogue, but she could find no trace of them and, in any case, had limited ideas about where to look. Besides, my mother knew that my father knew where we were. She reasoned that if he was still alive, he would find us and come back to us. But that never happened. Our best guess, years later, when we never found him and he never found us, was that he had been killed returning from his mission.

Losing my father effectively ended any last vestiges of my childhood. I was forced to grow up before I was ready, to help my mother, and to be a 'parent' in his absence to my sister and brother. I took my responsibilities seriously, but I also resented them. I was young and I wanted to have fun. I was in love and wanted to be with my boyfriend. In some ways, losing my father pushed me closer to Richie. He was the man in my life. Now, when he came to Friday night dinner, my mother asked him to sit at the head of the table, in my father's place. He was barely more than a child himself, but he was older than I was, and very protective of me and my family.

While my father's disappearance ended my childhood, it devastated my sister, the child of his heart, who had always been extremely close to him. She even looked like him: she had his proud Roman nose and his golden cat's eyes. As a child, she was so attached to my father that when she crawled into his bed in the middle of the night after having a nightmare, she would tie the hem of her nightgown to the bottom of his pyjama top so that he couldn't get away from her. With him gone and with me so involved with Richie, I think Rose felt very much alone, injured suddenly by the war in a personal way.

My brother was still young enough not to truly comprehend that our father was gone, perhaps for ever. Most families no longer had husbands and fathers at home. All the Jewish men had been forced to work for the army, being made to place land mines before an enemy advance or act as human 'bullet catchers', running before the Hungarian army as it advanced on the eastern front. There was no escape, it seemed, for Hungarian Jewish men.

When my father left, we lost a lot more than emotional security; our financial security was gone as well. We had no real income any more, except for what my mother could earn cooking for people, and often that wasn't enough to support us. When she couldn't make ends meet, she would go out and pawn a piece of jewellery to keep us going, asking for only enough money for us to get by, so that she could retrieve the pieces which had sentimental as well as monetary value for her. Then, when she had gathered enough money, she would return to the pawnshop and buy back the pawned ring or necklace or bracelet for the same price she'd been paid, plus interest. The same piece of jewellery would go in and out of the pawnshop three or four times a year. Not that she had an abundance of jewellery. She had a ruby and diamond ring, a heavy gold chain with a cameo attached and a heavy gold bracelet, as well as a couple of other smaller rings. But she made these work for us, making sure we didn't starve and could always pay our rent. Her system worked for almost two years.

chapter *Five*

$\mathscr{N}$ineteen-forty-three wasn't a very good year for the Axis Powers – Germany, Italy and Japan, who signed an agreement in 1940 – and their allies. They had received stunning defeats in the Ukraine and at Stalingrad, which is why Hungary's pragmatic Prime Minister at the time, Miklos Kállay, decided to hedge his bets on the outcome of the war. Although Hungary outwardly remained a staunch ally of Germany's Third Reich, Kállay began to reorient his policies towards the extrication of Hungary from the Axis alliance.

But while the Prime Minister might have had second thoughts about remaining in the alliance, the anti-Semitic laws that he and a host of his predecessors had put in place were putting pressure on the Jews of Hungary, and taking their businesses and professions away from them through confiscatory legislation and racially restrictive quotas. Thousands of Jews were sent out to forced labour units at the Russian front.

At home, the effects of the war were being felt in increased shortages. All families were feeling the pinch of a war-time economy. We continued to hear awful rumours about the mass resettlement of Jews throughout the rest of Eastern Europe, but so far no such policy had been initiated in Hungary and, although Kállay wasn't a friend of the Jews, he wasn't a rabid Fascist either. Looking back on it, I understand that he was a realist and knew that it seemed likely now that the Allied forces (including Britain and the United States) would win, and he wasn't anxious to do something heinous that he would have to answer for later.

In spite of our hardship, I was the happiest I had ever been in my life. At fourteen I was madly, profoundly, irrevocably in love with a tall, smart, handsome, talented young man who loved me as completely as I loved him. Budapest is made for lovers. You see them today, on every street corner, at every turn of the Danube, kissing and embracing. You watch them staring at each other intently, as a gypsy violinist serenades them. Hungarians are passionate and intense by nature, and Budapest is a city as lush and tempting as paradise. When you put those passionate Hungarians into that paradise of a city you have love everywhere. Richie and I were in love in a city of lovers. While the war raged around us and food was scarce, while I raced home to help my mother and still missed my father, I was totally enveloped by a passion all my own.

And Richie was blossoming. Always a talented musician, he was now part of a dance band that played at afternoon tea dances at some of the best hotels in Budapest, such as the Hotel Royale. Every Wednesday and Saturday afternoon, at five o'clock, young men and women went there to meet and dance. The women had to be chaperoned, of course, brought along by a mother, a sister or a brother, so that they were not alone. But often I would go as part of the band, carrying Richie's drums for him. I would sit in a corner and watch him perform, so proud of him and so happy to be with him. I made him two stripes out of black felt for the front of the drum, then I spelled out Richie, making sure that the two 'i's' in his name fitted into the two vertical felt lines. We both thought it looked very smart.

The band was a lively group of four young musicians. There was Richie on the drums. Tommy, the piano player, had wavy blond hair and a very large nose. 'When I get on the tram, my nose gets on first,' he joked. Tibor, the clarinet player, was short with curly brown hair, and George, the trumpet player, was a big, good-looking guy and the only one in the group who wasn't Jewish. They were all full of life, and they all had a lot of fun playing together.

The songs they played were pure romance: 'Night and Day', 'Kiss Me Once', 'Sentimental Journey', 'For All We Know' – all the American big band songs and a lot of songs whose lyrics had been translated into Hungarian, such as 'Stardust'.

Of course, I could never dance at these tea dances. The couple of times I did, Richie gave me such a disapproving look that I didn't have the heart or the courage to do it again. He was clearly jealous, in a possessive sort of way. He had been the only man in my life, and that's the way he wanted it. That's the way I wanted it too, so even though I loved to dance, I never danced when Richie was playing in the band.

Richie had begun university in the autumn of 1943 – no easy feat, since the Jewish quotas for all the professional courses were so small as to make it virtually impossible for Jewish students to get on to a science course at university level. But Richie was exceptional and was from a family that, even in the increasingly anti-Semitic environment, was still prominent. He loved his classes, and we were both happy that our goals – his career in science and our marriage – seemed more possible every day.

At fourteen, I had blossomed into a pretty young woman, as had my sister, although we were both still tiny and could pass for much younger if we wanted to. But in early 1944, we both wanted to look older, not younger. Once, I put peroxide in my hair, wanting to bring out the red highlights that were already there. Unfortunately, I didn't have the faintest idea how to apply the peroxide, and it never occurred to me to ask. When I was rinsing my hair with it, my mother came into the bathroom and asked suspiciously, 'What are you doing?'

'Nothing,' I answered, quickly wrapping my head in a big towel. Then I forgot to rinse out the peroxide. My hair became lighter by the hour and when my mother saw the results, she was never angrier. 'What have you done to yourself?' she asked and, for the first time in my life, she slapped my face. I suppose she thought I looked like a hussy. I'm embarrassed now to think how stupid I was and how self-centred, to do such a thing in the middle of a war. But I paid for my sin of pride. My hair turned a sickly orange and had the consistency of straw until the peroxide wore off. Even Richie had to laugh when he saw it.

Richie and I still went out together in his boat, treasuring the time we spent alone, just the two of us. We did much of our planning for the future there.

One Saturday we got up at dawn and were out on the river by six o'clock. It was quiet and peaceful, with no one around us. As he always did, Richie told me over and over again how much he loved me, and I told him the same. And we talked about how one day, after he was through university, we would get married, as we had discussed so often before. Except that this time he said he wanted to get me a ring so that we could have a long engagement while I finished school; then we could get married, he said. By then, Richie assured me, the war would be over. We would have a big, beautiful wedding at the Hotel Royale, and all our friends and family would come, and we would have our honeymoon in Venice.

'You will love Venice, Baby,' he told me. 'I was there a few years ago and it was the most beautiful city I've ever seen. More romantic even than Paris or Budapest,' he said with a laugh. 'I want to get you alone in a gondola on one of the canals and kiss you while the gondolier serenades us with an Italian aria. Or, better still, I want us to walk arm in arm in St Mark's Square, feeding the pigeons and sharing kisses.'

I was speechless, looking up at him, my weaver of dreams. Richie spun dreams of a time and place in which there was no war and no fear, only our love for each other.

I remember going home that night, happy and glowing. Even my mother, who yelled at me because I was late, couldn't pierce the profound happiness I felt. Later, after dinner was over and my mother had calmed down, I told her I planned to be engaged at sixteen. My mother just looked at me for a long moment. God only knows what she was thinking. Perhaps that we would be lucky if we survived the war. Perhaps that I was only fifteen and things could change. Or perhaps she believed me and believed in our love, but wanted us to be cautious. At any rate, she finally smiled and said, 'We'll discuss it when you're sixteen.'

Another time, when we were talking about the future,

Richie said he thought we should move in with his parents for a while when we were first married, while he got his degree. Once he had, we could have a family, but not before then. And until we had children, he did not want me to stay at home; he wanted me to pursue my own career, if I wanted. But there was nothing I could do unless I got a degree myself. I wanted children right away, but he didn't want them until he had a profession. I didn't think that much of studying. I didn't want to go on to more studying, although I had done very well in secondary school. I just wanted to stay at home, to be content as the lady of the house.

Still, sometimes I was afraid. All around us, terrible things were happening. Already, all non-Hungarians had been deported. The anti-Semitism was getting worse and awful stories about atrocities against Jews in other countries continued to be whispered at the synagogue — forced labour, deportation, relocation, beatings, shootings. How I longed for the kind of reliable news my father had always been able to provide. We still had access to the outside world through our radios, but the Germans controlled the airwaves in Budapest, so there wasn't much objective information about the war. Even many of the newspapers were right-wing rags, but not the one owned by Richie's father and his partner: *The People's Voice* tried to tell the truth.

But Richie would always reassure me. 'We will survive this, *kis pofa*,' he would say. 'You and I will not die in this war. I promise you that.'

I know it sounds silly, but his simple words gave me hope and courage. I always believed him. He had grand plans for us, and I had confidence that nothing could stand in our way. Which just goes to show how foolish and foolhardy youth is.

How can I explain the connection Richie and I had to each other? Perhaps it is the kind of feeling one has to experience to understand, but to me, it was like meeting the other half of myself, the other part of my soul. I felt completed with him, and at peace. I knew there was nothing better for me in life than to be by his side. And he felt the same. Neither one of us ever looked at another person. It didn't even occur to us. And our relationship seemed almost sacred to both of us, something that was intensely private. My friend Violet always tried to find out if Richie and I had slept together, and I remember thinking, 'If we had, I would never tell you or anyone else.' It was simply too private, especially to share with someone like Violet, who saw sex as something to be done lightly. Richie and I thought of it as something you did only out of love.

One day, on our walk across the meadow to the boathouse, it started to pour with rain. In Hungary, it can rain at a moment's notice and stop just as quickly. The sun had been shining one minute and the next the skies darkened and the rain fell as if it would never stop. We were thoroughly soaked by the time we got to the boathouse. My lips were blue, my teeth were chattering and I was shivering as if I had pneumonia. Richie took one look at me and said, 'You have to get out of those wet clothes.' He could see me hesitating. 'Do it, *kis pofa*. Otherwise, you could catch cold. We'll stay here until our clothes dry and the rain stops.'

Cautiously, I began to remove my wet clothing – my blouse and skirt and finally my swimming costume. Richie had turned round so that I could have some privacy and I jumped under the covers on the small single bed.

'It's OK now,' I said to him. He turned round and looked at me.

'Baby, would it be all right if I took off my wet clothes, too? I'd leave my bathing suit on, and just get under the blanket with you and hug you to warm you.'

I slowly nodded, afraid to say anything, afraid of what might happen. We had been intimate in some ways before. Like the time when we were drifting downstream in the boat and I took off the top of my swimming costume. Richie had looked at me and caught his breath and said, 'I knew you would be that beautiful.' He had knelt beside me and so gently, so very gently, touched my breasts and kissed me over and over again. Then he had stood up abruptly and said, 'Put your top back on, Baby. Please.'

And I had. I knew that there were things we should not do together. My friend Violet, who was so beautiful, went out with lots of boys. She was a flirt, and she liked to have fun, and although she didn't sleep with them she didn't think there was anything wrong with sex. Richie and I loved each other, but we wanted to wait until we were married to sleep together. But as time went on, our kissing did lead to other things.

Once, my mother, who loved me and trusted Richie, said to us as we were on our way out, 'Don't do anything I wouldn't do.'

We promised we wouldn't, but I couldn't help thinking that we had probably already done things my mother never would have done at our age. It felt in some ways beyond our control – as if the relationship had a life of its own and rules of its own, and they were all that mattered.

Another time, we were kissing passionately at the front door of Richie's apartment and his mother suddenly opened the door and saw us. At first, she looked shocked, but then she started to laugh. I was so embarrassed that I blushed. Just the week before we were late getting home because Richie and I had been caught in the rain on the boat and my mother had yelled at me. I had told Richie's mother it would never happen again, but she had just laughed at me.

'Of course it will happen again,' she'd said matter-of-factly. 'I can tell when two people are in love. That's how I was with Richie's father. And Richie acts about you just the way his father acted with me. He is totally taken with you, totally in love. And when you love like that, you lose track of everything, including the time, so of course you will be late again.'

This time, having caught us in the act, she warned us playfully, 'Be careful where you kiss.'

The problem was that we kissed everywhere we could, taking every chance we could get. At his front door, under the stairs in my apartment building, along the outer wall of the Regent's Castle at the Castle Hill overlooking the Danube, on the boat, on the trolleybus, in the meadow, on street corners. We were quite shameless. The more the war raged on, the more desperate our love and our passion seemed to become.

So now, here we were in the boathouse, all alone, the rain pouring outside the tiny window, drumming on the shingled roof, enclosing us in a very private world of our own. I could feel the roughness of the blanket on my naked skin. I watched Richie strip off his wet shirt and trousers, standing there in only his bathing suit, the bulge of an erection clearly visible under the thin fabric. I swallowed, then held back the covers for him to join me.

We embraced, and I felt his naked chest against my breasts, his thighs against mine. It felt sinful. It felt forbidden. It felt wonderful. Richie looked deep into my eyes. 'Do you know how much I love you, Baby?' he asked softly.

'As much as I love you,' I said, reaching up to stroke his face. Then he kissed me, a long, passionate kiss that seemed to go on and on . . . I thought I would die from wanting him, from wanting more, and when I heard him groan I knew he felt the same way. I felt reckless, as if I wanted to do everything, and damn the consequences. But another part of me was scared. Suddenly, Richie pulled away from me and literally jumped out of the tiny, narrow bed, to stand across the room, his back towards me. He was shaking.

'Did I hurt you?' I asked, feeling the cold, empty bed.

'No, Baby, it's just that . . .' he looked over at me and began again. 'You see, when a man feels that strongly, that passionately about a woman, his . . . he has no control over . . . over certain organs and then, then the pressure builds up and there is an ache, a very real ache. But I don't want us to sleep together until we are married and if I hadn't moved away from you, clear across the room, I couldn't have promised myself that I wouldn't have taken you anyway, just because I love you so much and have wanted you for so long. Do you understand?'

'Yes,' I said, my voice hoarse. I suppose I did understand, but I was confused too.

Richie pulled a chair up to the bed, wrapped himself in a blanket from the foot of the bed, held my hand and began to talk to me about our future. We would be married and have three children, and each one would be more perfect than the other. Time passed, the rain stopped and our clothes dried. When it was time to go, we got dressed and went back home.

I never doubted that he wanted me; he just wanted me in the right way, the honourable way. But we hadn't counted on the surprises that war can bring. We thought we had seen it all, had suffered enough, but we had no idea. Unfortunately, we didn't have long to wait to find out just how bad things could get.

In March 1944, Hitler once again changed my life for the worse. He invaded Hungary.

chapter Six

Sunday, 19 March 1944. It was a clear, bright, sunny spring day, warmer than usual for that time of year. My mother had opened the windows to let in some fresh air as we sat around the kitchen table, eating a light breakfast of apples, cheese and bread. There was nothing unusual, nothing to warn us that a seminal event was about to occur, one that would signal the beginning of the worst days of our lives.

Suddenly, we heard the earthshaking rumble of tanks. We ran to the windows, craning our necks for a look. What was happening? We had seen a lot of troops and some armoured vehicles come through Budapest over the past couple of years, but nothing that had made this kind of noise. I grabbed my sweater and ran to the door, my mother running after me, yelling, 'Don't go out there. It's not safe. We don't know what's happening. Let's wait here.'

I didn't even pause. I raced down the stairs into the

lobby and out of the front door, following a large group
of people already heading for St Istvan Kor. Ut, a traffic
circle in downtown Budapest a couple of blocks from my
house. When we reached the corner, we saw tanks coming by, one after the other, as if they were part of some
kind of victory parade. As we stood there, people were
asking one another, 'What does this mean?' We knew, by
then, that Germany was losing the war. In fact, the
Hungarian Jewish community was hoping they would
lose, even though Hungary was still officially allied with
them, because of what we knew they were doing to the
Jews in other countries, although we didn't know anything about concentration camps.

Was this display now one last show of strength headed
for the Russian front? But that didn't make any sense,
because hundreds of us stood on the pavement from nine
o'clock in the morning until noon and, after about an
hour, I noticed the same serial numbers on the tanks that
I had seen before. The display, which was supposed to
make us think there were hundreds of tanks, was a sham,
with only about thirty of them circling round and round.
I mentioned this to my mother, who had joined me by
this time, bringing my sister and brother with her. By
then, the crowd had worked out what all the tanks and
troops meant. The Germans had arrived and they were
here to stay. Without any advance warning, Hungary had
been occupied.

I turned to my friend, Elizabeth, the daughter of the
superintendent of our building and a friend since we first
moved in, though she was a Gentile and I was Jewish.
Elizabeth, whose father didn't make much money, would
often borrow clothes from me and other Jewish tenants
in our building when she went out on a date, to make her
boyfriends think she was better off than she actually was.

Now I said to Elizabeth, 'This is awful, the Germans coming in.' And she looked at me in disgust and answered, 'Are you talking to me, you dirty Jew?'

I was stunned. 'You're calling me a dirty Jew? Only last night you borrowed my dress. I wasn't a dirty Jew then.'

She sneered at me, moving away. 'Yes, you were, but I couldn't tell you that then.'

I felt sick inside, not just because of Elizabeth's betrayal but because I realized that the Germans coming here would mean the same thing for the Jews that it had meant when they had arrived in Bratislava. We would be persecuted. The war, in all its ugliness, had finally come home to us.

I realized immediately that Elizabeth's father was probably a Nazi but, like most of the other Jew-haters in Hungary before the Germans came, he had kept his hatred to himself. Now all that hatred would be out in the open, and we would suffer, with no one to defend us. I was both terrified and angry.

We walked slowly back to our apartment, my mother with her arm around my shoulders, consoling me about everything – the coming of the Germans and Elizabeth's betrayal. 'Your father was right when he said more suffering would come before this war ends. He also said the Hungarians would never fight the Germans; that instead they would co-operate with them. It seems he was right about that, too,' she said quietly. But my mother was a fighter, and she knew that now the fight had just begun. 'Who knows what awaits us, my darlings? But, no matter what happens, we are going to stay together,' she promised, wrapping her arms around us as if, by that gesture, she could keep us safe.

That night, as a group of us gathered around the

expensive short-wave radio my father had bought when we'd first moved to Budapest, we heard officially that the Germans had occupied Hungary. Years later, I learned that this was Hitler's project called Operation Margarethe I — a code name for what he was then describing as a 'restricted occupation' of Germany's ally, Hungary. But it was more horrifying even than that. Hitler had added SS units to the occupation forces, and, under the direction of SS official Adolf Eichmann, they were to implement the so-called 'final solution' of the Hungarian Jews. Admiral Nicholas Horthy, the Regent of Hungary, and Miklos Kállay, its Prime Minister, were informed of the invasion the day before it happened, at an urgent meeting in Salzburg, Austria, arranged by Hitler. The meeting was a ploy to keep the leaders out of Hungary until the Germans had marched in. Once again, Hitler had taken over a country without a single shot being fired.

Luckily, none of us gathered around my father's radio in our apartment — my family as well as our neighbours who had no radio — had any idea then that anything so ominous lay ahead of us. Nonetheless, we were all worried about this new turn of events.

As it turned out, we had every reason to be. The Occupation forces would try to destroy the Jews of Hungary, and they would have the co-operation, how-ever reluctant, of Horthy's government, for once the more liberal Kállay resigned as prime minister a few days after the Occupation began, the Germans installed a rabid Hungarian Nazi named Dome Sztojay as Prime Minister and he, in turn, gave the Hungarian Arrow Cross, a militant Fascist group, free reign. Once the Sztojay government took power on 22 March, the fate of the Hungarian Jews was sealed.

As I lay in bed that first night, trying to fall asleep, all I could think about was Richie. I had to see him. But my mother didn't want me to go out of the house; she felt it wasn't safe. It took me two days to sneak out to meet Richie at our place at the Castle Hill. There, nestled in the bends of the old stone wall surrounding the ornate castle, where the Regent lived in isolated splendour, we could look down at Pest and the unchanging Danube spread before us. Here, we had some privacy. When Richie arrived that day, he didn't say anything, just came over and hugged me. 'Did you see the German tanks?' he asked.

I smiled up at him, trying to look brave and confident. 'They didn't look so monstrous.'

He smiled back, but I could see that his eyes were not smiling. 'You cannot tell from the faces of the German soldiers what kind of orders they will get and what they will do to us.'

He didn't say more, but I suspected he knew something he wanted to shield me from, at least for now. By then, Richie was helping the Hungarian Underground by carrying messages, and doing other jobs. But when I tried to question him, he changed the subject.

'Enough of the war, *kis pofa*,' he said with a laugh, hugging me more tightly. 'Wouldn't you rather kiss me? I've missed your kisses for the last two days and I intend to collect my full share before I let you go home.'

I leaned back in his arms and looked up into those eyes of his that were as deep and as blue as the sky. 'Let's not waste a single minute.'

The day was warm. Perhaps God was giving us a final gift of peace. Richie eased me down to the ground, on to the blanket he'd brought with him, and he planted kisses all over my face, starting first at my eyelids and then my cheeks and closer and closer towards my lips until he reached them. When Richie kissed me, all my fears, all the ugliness went away. I opened my mouth to him and he kissed me until I couldn't breathe. All I knew about making love I had learned from him, and we had learned it together, for he had never had another girlfriend. When we kissed, when we hugged, when he touched my breasts through my sweater or eased his hand up under my blouse, I could feel all his love and passion. And I could feel my own in response. But I could also feel how much he cherished me through his restraint. He would touch me and stroke me, but he would not sleep with me. That, he would always say, we would wait to do until we were married.

That day, on the hill, the sun warmed us and the walls hid us from view. We escaped the war, and took each other to the place where we only had to think about our future.

Soon, it was time to go. My mother worried about me being out and also because she often needed me to help watch Larry and Rose. Today I knew I couldn't keep her waiting because, now that the Germans were here, she would be frantic that something had happened to me if I didn't show up on time. I raised my lips to Richie's one more time, savouring the soft feel of his lips against mine, tasting the chocolate he had brought for us to share between kisses. I wanted to hold on to him for ever. Instead, I whispered, 'I have to go.'

'I know,' he said, hugging me as if his arms had a will of their own. But then, slowly, gently, he released me and got up, offering his hand to help me up. We half walked, half ran down the serpentine pavement that terraced the hill, separating at the base so that each of us could run across our respective bridges and race home.

*

For the first few days, nothing happened. We had heard rumours that the Jews were to be concentrated in several parts of the city and that they would be assigned to live in houses specially designated for them. But before that rumour became reality, we were subjected to the first of many humiliations. It was announced in the newspapers, on the radio and on placards posted all over the city that all Jews would have to wear yellow stars on their clothing to show the world that they were Jews.

I cringed at the thought. My mother had always had a great sense of style and we were pretty girls, well dressed, and used to receiving admiring glances. We had certainly never been the objects of scorn, but I understood immediately that now we would be, that Jews were to be identified so that they could be hated and punished. I couldn't stand the idea. My mother, calm and practical as always, found an old yellow linen dress that she could cut up into stars. The Germans had exact specifications for these stars – they had to be six inches across and sewn neatly, with small, even stitches, on to all outerwear – sweaters, jackets, coats. We were never to go out without the hated stars. These instructions were meticulously detailed with Germanic precision so that there could be no mistake.

My mother sat there cutting those stars, systematically and precisely, hemming them neatly so that there were no frayed edges.

'Why do they have to be so neat?' I asked, with all the anger and humiliation I felt.

My mother looked up at me and I could tell she understood my anger, but she would have no part in it because anger, at a time like this, could be dangerous. 'It should be neat,' she said simply.

I wanted to scream, and I knew my sister felt the same way. I could see it in her face. I had just turned fifteen, but in many ways I was still a child and that star embarrassed me; it marked me as clearly as if I'd been branded. How was I ever going to go back out on the street, knowing that from now on I would be seen only as a Jew, as someone to be despised, not as a pretty, vivacious young woman, not as a person. That night, as I looked at my pretty sweaters and my jacket now hideously defiled by those dreadful stars, I cried myself to sleep, but I made sure I was quiet about it. I didn't want to upset the rest of my family.

But as bad as the stars were, they were only the beginning. Next, we were told, Jewish children could no longer go to school. And then one more blow fell. It was another sunny morning, almost the last day of March, and we were sitting in the kitchen with my mother when we heard the pounding of many boots in the hallways and balconies. The courtyard reverberated with the sound. We heard a fist pounding on our door, and someone yelling, 'All Jews take what you can carry and only what you can carry and get out of this building.' They rang a bell continuously and kept repeating the message so that there could be no mistake.

We stared at each other, wide-eyed, but there was no time for shock, no time for pain. We grabbed what we could and stuffed it into pillowcases as Hungarian soldiers yelled and banged on doors and made sure all of us got out of the building. If people moved too slowly, the soldiers simply pulled them outside. They told us not to take our valuables and there was no time to hide them, although I saw some people trying to put them inside the airshaft between our twin buildings. My mother took with her what was left of her jewellery and a few other necessities and we got out.

When they had us all on the street, they lined us up
and divided us into groups, sending us to different
houses, now designated as Jewish 'star' houses. We had to
walk to our new house, and it was a long, humiliating
walk through the streets of a city that had once held so
much gaiety for me and now held only sadness and horror. This act of violation had been carried out by
Hungarians against Hungarians. I felt as if I had lost the
ground from under my feet because Hungarians were
doing this to me, as if I had fallen into a hole that would
never end and nothing could save me. But I didn't cry
because my mother would have had to comfort me and
that would have drawn the attention of the soldiers. We
did not want to draw their attention. We did as we were
told.

We walked through the streets, my mother carrying
my brother when the walk became too much for him,
my sister and I walking right ahead of them. 'Stay
together, stay together,' my mother kept repeating like
some sacred litany that would somehow make everything better. The walk seemed to take for ever, but finally
we arrived. That was the day our privacy ended.

We were shown to a single room in an apartment in a
building several blocks from where Richie lived. We were
made to share that room with three other families. The
people who had originally lived in the apartment were
nice enough. The father had already been taken to a forced
labour camp, and the mother and the two daughters
shared a bedroom with two other families. But some of
the other families who were moved into that house were
not the kind of people we were used to: they were rough
and tough, they yelled and swore. We could not escape
from them; on the contrary, we had to protect whatever
possessions we had left from some of them.

'Do you have to take so long in the kitchen?' a woman shouted at my mother as she carefully prepared our dinner. 'We all have to share, you know. No one can hog.'

I saw my mother close her eyes, struggling for control. It was our first night in this terrible star house and she was making us some soup after our long walk and after the shock of losing our home.

'We are almost finished,' my mother said quietly, giving me a warning look as she saw me open my mouth. Reluctantly, I closed it. I knew she didn't want me to make a scene. I could see how hard this was going to be. All around us that day people had lost control, crying or screaming, throwing tantrums, even in the star house. But it was stupid and dangerous, and we all knew it. My mother had made sure we all knew it.

'Just make it fast,' the woman said gruffly, sticking her chin out at her. 'You may think you're better than we are, but you're not. We're all here in this same stinking place and don't think you'll get any special privileges because you sound like a high and mighty lady. We're all just dirty, stinking Jews, just like the soldiers kept telling us.'

My mother shuddered as she turned her back on the woman, ostensibly to take the soup pot off the stove. There were only cracked, chipped bowls to eat off. She ladled the soup into the bowls, then made us say our prayer of thanks for the food, as we did every night. I thought I would choke on the words, but I said them. None of us would ever dare disobey Mama on this issue, not because she would hit us or beat us – I only remember once that she ever even slapped my face – but because she expected us to thank God no matter what happened.

We ate our soup quickly, taking it back to our cramped room with us so that the woman with the big

mouth could use the kitchen. That night, as we slept, all
five of us in one lumpy bed we'd created on the floor, the
snores of all those others sounding around us like so
many bullfrogs in a pond, I seriously questioned whether
I could endure this. We had to wait in a queue for everything in this apartment – the kitchen, the bathroom.
There was no privacy and no dignity. And our beautiful
apartment, our security for so many years, was gone, as
if it had never existed.

I thought about running away. Some Jews already had.
They had slipped out of Budapest, claiming they were
afraid of the Allied bombings that would come now that
the Germans were here. But the real reason was to
escape the persecution by running away to a small village
in the countryside where nobody would know they were
Jewish. They could pretend to be Gentile and stay there
safely until the war ended. Alone, I could have done this,
too. Or Richie and I could have gone off into the
countryside and worked with the Underground. But I
knew, even as my heart longed for it, longed for some
kind of escape from this new prison, that I couldn't do it.
I had promised my father to stay with my mother and
help her to care for my brother and sister. Some day, I
believed, he would make his way back to us and he would
expect to find the family all together. I couldn't run off
and leave my mother to take her chances.

I moved my arm slowly and carefully, trying not to
disturb my sister as she slept beside me. My arm had
fallen asleep because she was lying on it and all I could
feel were pins and needles. I tried again to get comfortable. Who knew what new horror the morning would
bring? We would need our strength. Besides, I wanted to
walk over to Richie's house tomorrow, which was now
only a few blocks away.

By morning, the weather had turned cooler. We waited our turn to use the apartment's single bathroom as others waited impatiently right outside the door. There was no time for a bath,: we just had a fast sponge bath. And we didn't change our underwear because we knew that washing clothes was going to be difficult. I looked at myself in the bathroom mirror, scrubbing my face so that my skin shone, then brushing my hair with so many strokes that it had some shine. 'Hurry up in there,' someone shouted. I took one last look at myself, dreading the moment when I had to don my sweater with its hateful yellow star.

All four of us walked the few blocks to Richie's house, which, we found out, had been turned into a star house. The liquor distributorship beneath their large second-floor apartment had been closed and vandalized, and all the liquor looted. Richie and his parents had a couple of rooms in their former home, which they were sharing now with eight or nine families.

Richie's mother silently moved forward to hug my mother. 'I'm so glad you're all right. Did they make you leave your apartment too?' When my mother nodded, Richie's mother shook her head. 'We should have asked for you to come here, so that we could have shared.'

But none of us really had a choice about where we stayed, although we realized later that if we had made the change at that moment, no one would have been the wiser. There was no paperwork yet on where we had moved. But that realization would come with hindsight. Richie and I were just glad to be together. He had helped his parents hide whatever family valuables they could before everyone had moved in on them, but I could see the sadness and the anger in his proud father's eyes as he looked around his gracious home and saw all these other families camped there. And I was completely shocked and then overcome myself because as his parents talked quietly with my mother, they cried.

'You know, they've put people in the synagogue and even in the stalls where we kept the horses for the delivery carriages,' his mother said. 'Can you imagine? People living like animals.'

But they could do nothing, just as we could do nothing. Anyone who was sane then kept their emotions hidden from the authorities. The people who screamed and cried, who threw tantrums, were shot. So the adults consoled one another quietly, and Richie held my hand and played chess with my sister and teased my little brother. We all knew things had changed for ever and each and every one of us was scared for what tomorrow would bring.

chapter Seven

'Baby, we need to go back to our old apartment and see what's going on there, see whether your father has come back and can't find us,' my mother whispered to me on the morning of our third day in the star house.

I glanced at my brother and sister who were quietly playing chess on the small board we'd managed to bring along. 'What about them?'

My mother sighed. 'They'll be safe enough here. Mrs Szolnay will watch them for me – I've already asked her. Besides, Rose is old enough to mind Larry until we get back.'

I reached for my jacket, wincing as I saw the yellow star sewn on the front. It should be getting easier to wear this thing, I thought, but it wasn't.

We took a tram to our old apartment building, not wanting to be gone too long. As we got off the tram, members of the Arrow Cross surrounded the crowd getting off. 'Papers, please,' they said, holding their hands out. Dutifully, everyone reached for their papers. I could feel fear coiling inside my stomach. I thought I might be sick, but I knew I couldn't afford to be. I watched my mother, saw that she was calm, and tried to draw strength from it.

One of the men smiled at me, but it was a mocking smile, not the admiring kind I was used to. I blushed because I thought he was staring at my breasts, which were large for my size, but then I realized he was looking at my yellow star. A second later, I understood why. 'All Jews, line up and come with me,' he said, leading us into the courtyard of a building across the street, and then into the basement.

We sat there, fifty or sixty terrified women and children and some old men, as the soldiers guarded us.

'Give us your jewellery,' the tall, dark-haired fellow in charge ordered.

I tried to hide my hand behind my back, to save the gold ring set with three small perfect turquoise stones which had been given to each girl child in my mother's family. Beside me, my mother slowly shook her head. I could see she was terrified for me, terrified that my defiance would put me in danger. I brought my hand slowly back in front and took off the ring. Then, when the soldiers weren't looking, I threw the ring into the wood bin alongside the big, old furnace. I would rather throw the ring away than give it to these thieves.

My mother removed a ruby ring and the small gold earrings she was wearing. Luckily, she had left the rest of her jewellery with my sister at the star house. She knew we would need it later for food and other necessities. The soldiers collected all the jewellery, pulling roughly at rings that were too tight to come off easily, immune to the cries of pain from their victims.

'What do they want from us?' I managed to whisper to my mother, making sure my mouth barely moved.

'I don't know, but we need to get out of here. Your brother and sister are in the star house alone, and they won't know what's happened to us. Besides, I heard one soldier say this is the command centre for this whole district for the Arrow Cross. Nothing good is going to happen if we stay here.'

What could we do? I racked my brain. The soldiers showed no sign of letting anyone go. They could keep us here for hours or, worse, deport us. I acted almost without thinking but, miraculously, I had a plan.

'Excuse me,' I said loudly to the soldier in charge. 'We came here to report something to the Arrow Cross.'

He looked over at me, studying me as he stared, seeming to judge the truth of what I was saying.

'We have information that could be valuable,' I said, trying to sound confident. 'My mother and I travelled all the way here to tell the authorities.'

He looked at me for a minute, then shrugged. 'Follow me,' he said, leading the way up the cellar stairs. My mother walked ahead of the guard and as she slowly made her way up the stairs, probably because her legs were cramped from sitting in that damp basement, he hit her with the butt of his gun. 'Move faster,' he said.

I was right behind him and couldn't believe anyone had hit my kind, gentle mother. 'Don't hit her,' I said. 'Remember, we came here on our own, to help.' Then I went to my mother and soothed her shoulder where he had hit her. Tears were streaming down my face, but all she said was, 'It's all right, Baby. It's all right.'

He brought us into what looked like a small waiting room. 'Wait here,' he said, pointing to a couple of wooden chairs before knocking on a closed door.

'What are you doing?' my mother whispered.

'Don't worry. Just follow my lead.'

The soldier returned for us. 'This had better be good,' he said as he led us into an office with a big desk and tall leather chairs. Behind the desk was a young man who looked very self-important, almost flaunting the insignia of the dreaded Arrow Cross. I took a deep breath. Now was no time to be scared.

'What do you have to report, Jew?' he asked, so casually insulting that I wanted to hit him. But, of course, I didn't. There had already been enough violence.

'I know that people are supposed to turn in all valuables to the authorities – isn't that right?'

He nodded.

'Well, my mother and I discovered two very valuable Oriental rugs in the star house we're staying in. The people were very clever in hiding them. They wrapped them around the mattress and box spring of a large bed, then covered them with bedding.'

The young man leaned forward, a look of interest on his face. 'And this house is here, in this district?'

I let my face fall, as if I hadn't thought about that, although I had. I would never have knowingly got anyone in trouble. It was true that the rug dealer's family had hidden two rugs, but I also knew that each district had separate headquarters, and we were in the wrong one.

'No,' I mumbled. 'It's in the Eighth District.'

The man seemed to take pity on me. Perhaps he thought I was stupid, or else he wanted to encourage people to report such hidden valuables. At any rate, he turned to the soldier who had brought us in. 'Release them.' Then, turning to us, he said, 'I don't have jurisdiction over that district.' He wrote down an address on a piece of paper and handed it to us. 'You must go to the headquarters in your district to report this. Istvan here will escort you to the tram.'

My mother and I nodded, afraid to feel relief until we were safely out of the building and on the tram. The soldier even waited with us until the tram came. I thought I would die from fear, but I stayed calm. I thought I saw my mother smile faintly at me when I dared to look her way.

After what seemed like hours but could only have been minutes, the tram came and we dutifully got on it. Once the tram had gone a safe couple of blocks, I collapsed against my mother. I felt her trembling, and realized she had been as terrified as I, but she had hidden it.

'We could have been shot,' was all she said.

'But we weren't,' I said, thinking that my father would have been proud of my daring and resourcefulness. I was becoming an accomplished liar, but I didn't care, because lying had just saved our lives. If I hadn't invented a 'reason' for why we were in that building, the Arrow Cross would have kept us indefinitely. By 'reporting' the rugs in the wrong precinct, I had saved us without hurting anyone else, which I couldn't have borne.

We got off the tram at the next stop and circled back to our old apartment from the opposite direction, hoping that no more soldiers or Arrow Cross members would see us. This time, luck was with us, and we made it to our apartment without incident. In a way, I wish we hadn't.

I heard my mother gasp as soon as we entered. Our beautiful sofa, so lovingly refinished by my parents when we first arrived in Budapest, was gone. So was the rosewood chair that my mother had carefully reupholstered with a pretty velvet cushion. And the china cabinet was missing. The pieces that she and my father had gathered with such care – some art deco, some baroque – were gone, scattered; even the plants which she loved and nurtured with her amazing green fingers had vanished. I saw her eyes scanning the rooms, noting all that had been taken – more than half of what we owned, half of what we had called home.

'What do you want?' the woman who had answered the door asked sharply as we continued to stand there, looking stunned.

'This is our home,' my mother said, sounding as if she might cry, though her eyes were dry.

She snorted. 'Not any more it isn't. All of us live here now,' she said, gesturing behind her with her hand, and we could see all the families crowded into our lovely apartment.

My mother closed her eyes. 'If we could just collect the rest of our clothes.'

'There are none of your clothes here, only our things,' the woman said belligerently. Around her, others nodded. It was amazing how quickly so many people had been reduced to the animals the Nazis wished us to become.

'Perhaps I could just check my bedroom,' my mother began, and I hated to hear the tone of pleading in her voice.

The woman crossed her arms in front of her chest. 'I think you'd better go now. You don't live here any more.'

I turned to go, but my mother grabbed my arm. 'Just one more thing,' my tiny mother said, looking up at this bitter, angry woman. 'Has anyone been here looking for me or for my children? A tall, brown-haired handsome man?'

The woman laughed in her face. 'In your dreams, lady. No such man has been looking for you.'

I saw my mother's shoulders slump, but then she straightened them and held out her hand. In it was a crumpled scrap of paper with the address of our star house. 'If such a man does come here asking for Ethel Markowitz, please give him this address so that he can find us,' she said quietly, her dignity wrapped around her like a protective cloak.

I saw something like sympathy flicker briefly in the woman's eyes. She took the paper from her.

My mother mumbled her thanks and grabbed my hand. 'Let's go,' she said.

I was numb as we headed back to the star house. What more could happen? It was only early afternoon and already we had been imprisoned, our jewellery had been stolen and many of the rest of our possessions had disappeared, probably into the hands of the Gentile neighbours in our building who couldn't wait to claim them. 'We've been robbed by our neighbours. Can you imagine?' my mother said.

What else could happen, I wondered, as I saw the despair in my mother's eyes when she thought I wasn't watching her.

In the next few days, we found out. Jews, it was decreed, could no longer own businesses. All Jewish businesses were confiscated and the Jews who had owned them were forced to work for the Gentiles who had stolen the businesses from them. All radios, cars and bicycles were taken away, isolating us further from the outside world.

The synagogue, long the hub of our Jewish community, tried to help in some ways. Classes were held secretly in various apartment buildings for all the Jewish children who had been forbidden to go to school. But things became even more difficult when a curfew was imposed. Jews could only be out at certain, limited hours of the day, and never at night. All I could think of was that it was going to be even harder to see Richie.

On the fourth day after we'd been moved to the star house, a man came there looking for my mother. At first, she was terrified. 'What do you want of Ethel Markowitz?' she asked.

'I knew your husband,' he answered softly, his dark, hooded eyes looking vaguely familiar. Had this man come to our apartment before? Was he also part of the Czech Underground? We didn't ask. 'Is there somewhere we could speak privately, Mrs Markowitz?'

My mother nodded. 'Just give me a minute.' She went into the bedroom we shared with all the other families and quietly explained she needed to have a private conversation. 'Would you mind if I used this room for a few minutes?' she asked them all politely.

Luckily, the families who shared our room were fairly considerate. They all moved out, as did Larry, Rose and I, so that my mother and this mysterious stranger could talk. They were alone for about ten minutes before the man left, as quietly as he'd arrived.

'Come with me, Baby,' my mother commanded in the no-nonsense voice she used when she would tolerate no argument. 'You,' she said, pointing at my brother and sister, 'stay here until we get back. It could be a couple of hours.' She embraced my sister and whispered in her ear, 'Watch our things. Make sure no one touches them, especially Mrs Androsz who, I think, took our soap.' My sister nodded and my mother moved away, grabbing her heaviest sweater.

'Where are we going?' I asked, a little breathless from

trying to keep up with the fast pace my mother was setting.

'To see a man named Raoul Wallenberg. The man who came to the house today, who knew your father, says he will give us Swiss papers of protection that will get us into a better, safer house. All it takes is some money, and the man provided that,' she said, showing me the carefully folded bills she'd hidden in the pocket of her dress. 'They say Jews are being moved into several ghettoes, and that things will get worse there. But if you are in a house with Swedish or Swiss protection, life will be better, at least for now.'

I nodded, not fully understanding, except that once again my father's mysterious connections had reached out to help us, even if my father himself had failed to materialize.

There was a queue outside the Swedish Embassy on Vadasz Utca where that great humanitarian Raoul Wallenberg was getting as many papers of protection for the Jews of Hungary as the Nazis and his own government would allow. The Swiss and the Vatican were also issuing such papers, the only neutrals who could do so. We waited outside for an hour or so, on a cool April day, my mother glancing around nervously, hoping that this would work as smoothly as the man had said it would. Finally, we got to the waiting room, which was packed with other Jews looking for the same protection. Suddenly, someone swept out of the inner office and into the waiting room, a brown-haired man of medium height with a hooked nose. 'That's Adolf Eichmann,' I heard someone whisper as he strode through the room, his great coat open over a uniform decorated with many medals, his tall black boots gleaming in the late afternoon sunlight streaming through the windows.

None of us knew exactly why he was here, but all Jews feared him. Of course, they were right. Hitler had made it his responsibility, in the waning days of the war when the Nazis' resources were limited, to exterminate the Jews of Hungary, or at the very least, to kill as many of them as he could.

After another hour or so, we were escorted into Wallenberg's office, where he greeted us graciously and kindly, took all our information and promised us papers the very next day, if we could come back for them. Of course we could.

'Tell no one at the star house about these papers, Baby,' my mother cautioned me. Yet another secret to keep, but now I was old enough and had seen enough to realize just how important it was to keep all these secrets. I nodded, trying to look strong for my mother. Inside, I was a wreck. As soon as I could get away, I ran to Richie's. He saw, from the look on my face, that I was very upset. He led me outside the crowded apartment and we walked to the Danube. How could the river look the same when so much else had changed? I noticed that even the river had been taken over by the Nazis: its banks were lined with sandbags.

'What is wrong, *kis pofa*?'

The tears came then, so strong that I began to sob. Richie pulled me into his arms and comforted me.

'The Arrow Cross almost imprisoned us yesterday and now, today, a man came and told us about Swiss papers of protection and gave my mother some money for them. And we got these papers and we'll be moving to a safer place. At least that's what the man says.'

'So that is good news, isn't it?'

'Yes, but every day something else happens. I feel that at any moment our lives could be over. Yesterday, the

Arrow Cross guard hit my mother with the butt of his rifle. If he had aimed at her head instead of her shoulder, he could have killed her in an instant, for nothing.'

Richie held me closer, one hand caressing my hair, which had grown down my back by this time. 'Listen to me, Baby. I've told you this before but it's more important than ever now that you hear me and believe me.' And he held me away from him so that he could look into my eyes. 'You and I will survive this war. We will get married, we will go to Venice on our honeymoon. Remember how I told you about St Mark's Square? Soon, you will see it. We will recline in a gondola on a Venetian canal. I swear it. I know it here, inside my heart. Do you believe it as absolutely as I do?'

I nodded. And it was true. Looking up into his beautiful blue eyes, I could feel his strength and I could believe. 'I am sorry to be such a child, but it's been so hard living with all these people, not being able to take a bath or change my clothes. I feel dirty and ugly and . . .'

Richie placed his fingertips against my mouth. 'Never say such things about yourself, Baby. They could never be true. You are as beautiful as ever and as dear to me. The people who are dirty are the ones who are treating us like this. But their day will come, and they will pay.'

I raised myself up on my tiptoes to kiss him. No matter what happened, Richie could always make me feel safe and protected, as if no harm could come to me. I could feel the sun on my face and feel his strong arms enfold me, and I knew that whatever happened to me, I knew now the greatest love I could ever experience. In spite of everything, I was so grateful for that love that it almost made up for everything else. If only God would let our dreams come true, I could survive all this and put it behind me.

'Are you better, sweetheart?' he asked, his eyes searching mine, looking for the answer.

I gave him my best smile. 'I am always better when I am with you. I just wish it could be always.'

He laughed. 'That day will come soon enough. Perhaps today we should book the Hotel Royale, just to make sure it will be available for our wedding.'

I smiled. I knew he was trying so hard to be happy, but I had seen the shadow cross his face. Since the Germans had imposed their curfew, there were no more tea dances for Richie to play at. One of his brightest joys had been taken away from him, and I could see what that had cost him. But Richie was not someone who complained. He was a scientist, after all, a man of facts, and he knew better than to rail against the facts. On the other hand, he was a musician, an artist, and the fires of his art gave him passion and made him defy the Nazis by working for the Underground. But he wasn't taking any foolish chances. He wanted us to have our future.

He pulled me under the stairway of his building and pressed his body hard against mine as he kissed me, his hand moving up under my sweater to caress my breasts with his long, slender, musician's fingers, as if he was playing his favourite instrument. I clung to him, my hands stroking the back of his neck. 'I wish we could be alone again at the boathouse and that we would not stop our lovemaking until it was completed,' I said softly.

'Do you know how much I love you? How much I want you, Baby? But it's not safe to go to the boathouse any more and I don't want us to have to sneak away somewhere to make love. When it happens, it's going to be absolutely right, absolutely perfect, and you will be my wife in every way.'

I caressed his cheek. 'But who knows what the future

will bring? Can't we have this joy today – because, like the song says, for all we know, we may never meet again?'

He grabbed my hand tightly. 'Never say that again. We will know each other always. We will marry and have children and grow old together. I know this, Baby, and you must know it, too. Promise me that you will always believe this.'

And so I promised, holding him close, wishing with all my heart that the future was here.

'I should walk you home,' Richie said, looking at his watch. 'Your mother will be worried.'

Luckily, we had almost completed our time in the star house. If we had been there any longer, I'm sure people would have probably killed one another – that's how desperate and angry some of them had become. And sad, too. There were a couple of old people with diabetes who had to give themselves insulin injections with everyone watching, everyone waiting to use the kitchen. There was a poor woman suffering with breast cancer with no medicine for the pain, no surgery, nothing. All she had was cup after cup of very strong tea which she made by boiling it down to almost a black syrup, which acted like an opiate. Weak and sick as she was, she had to brew it for herself.

Food had become limited. You could no longer get flour or sugar. Even a piece of wood for the wood-burning stove became a commodity. If you needed a piece of wood, you had to find it yourself, sometimes walking a couple of miles to find something you could use, perhaps from a building being torn down, or extra pieces of wood in the basement of a building. You had to be resourceful. No one wanted to share because everybody felt they had to look out for themselves just to survive. It was ugly to see people behave that way. But my mother was not like that and there were others, including Gentiles, who took great risks to help us. I think that experience made me more aware of how connected each of us is to one another. Perhaps that's why years later I did so much work with Hadassah, which supports research hospitals in Israel and helps those in need.

When we got the Swiss papers of protection, we discovered that our old apartment building was now a Swiss house. As luck would have it, that's where we were sent. In fact, we were able to return to our old apartment. But, this time we had to share it with thirty other displaced Jews.

By the time we returned, a week later, there was nothing left of our furniture, clothing or household goods. We crammed into one of our old bedrooms, all four of us sleeping on the floor together, just as we'd done in the other star house.

Ten of us shared our bedroom: a mother and her children, an old man and his wife, and another mother with her three children. Our cupboards were empty; everything had been taken, so the only clothing we had was what we'd been able to carry with us to the original star house. The apartment was so crowded that people were sleeping in the bath. If we needed to use the bathroom, we had to ask those people to get out. They crawled out slowly because their muscles had become so cramped from lying in the bath – they could barely move. Actually, we were lucky to have a bath under any circumstances. The Germans turned off the water on some days, rationing the supply. We never had hot water because there were no more coal deliveries to fuel the furnaces in the apartment buildings. A cold bath after a wait on a long queue was the best we could hope for.

There was a grimness to those days, a drudgery that's hard to convey to anyone who did not live them. Every morning my mother woke at six o'clock and went out to stand in a queue to buy milk and bread. The milk was blue, it was so watered-down. After waiting for four hours, she would come home at ten and make us a quick breakfast of hot milk and bread, careful not to take too long and anger some of the residents.

By this time, the Allies had begun bombing Hungary, although they hadn't reached Budapest yet. Even so, at least once a day, sometimes more often, the siren sounded and we had to go to the basement until we heard the all-clear.

My mother still went out to cook for people. There was an elderly Jewish couple who could not cook for themselves but whose pantry was still full. She prepared meals for them which they, in turn, would share with us.

When I could, I escaped with my sister and some of the other teenagers in the building and we went up to the roof, to a vacant attic where we could look down over the city that had once been so beautiful. When he could, Richie would join us and we would talk and fantasize more about our future.

The most foolhardy fantasy was the plot a few of us hatched to throw some Molotov cocktails into the court-yard between our twin buildings, where the Germans had several tanks.

'We could destroy at least a couple, make a state-ment,' one boy said.

'At least we'd be doing something,' my friend Violet added. All the deprivation had made her restless and unhappy.

Sounding more like my mother than I ever thought I would, I said, 'They'd kill us and everyone else in the building if we even attempted such a thing.'

The others looked ready to throw me off the roof, but then I saw them thinking about what I'd said and they started nodding. They knew I was right. It had just been a fantasy, some kind of payback for all the grief that the Nazis had already caused us. But, of course, we could do nothing, at least overtly. Covertly, we could help the Underground and some people, like Richie, did.

chapter *Eight*

'They killed my father yesterday.' We were sitting in the stairwell of his apartment building and Richie was talking and crying at once.

Since the curfew had been put into place, we had agreed to meet every day at two in the afternoon. When Richie hadn't shown up the day before, I knew there had to be a reason, and that probably it was not good news.

By the next afternoon, when he still didn't appear, I turned my sweater inside out to hide the Jewish star and set out for his house, even though it would be past curfew by the time I managed to get back home. I knew when I saw his face that something awful had happened. He was pale, so pale that his skin seemed translucent and his blue eyes appeared sunken into his face.

'Come with me,' he said, his expression blank, his voice neutral. We left the apartment and huddled in the shelter of the stairwell. I was holding on to his hand so tightly that my palm hurt.

'My father was sitting there reading proofs,' Richie explained. 'His secretary said the rain was beating against the windows and she was busy typing a letter when the front door burst open and a group of soldiers appeared. They told her to get her boss. My father went out and faced them.'

Richie took a deep breath. His voice was shaking as he spoke.

'You don't have to tell me the rest,' I said softly.

Richie shook his head. 'But I do. I owe it to my father,' he said, squeezing my hand even more tightly. 'The SS came in with their guns and their flashy uniforms with the insignias that gleam like unholy symbols of some bygone pagan era. The German officer stepped forward, with a member of the Arrow Cross at his side to translate.

'He told my father he could no longer publish his political lies. You know my father, how dignified he was. My father told him *The People's Voice* was not a political newspaper, just an ordinary newspaper.' Tears were streaming down his face now, but Richie didn't even bother to brush them away. He was looking straight ahead, as if he could see the whole scene in his mind.

'His secretary said she could see that angered the SS officer. He told my father that he was the one who determined what was to be published. His secretary said my father looked puzzled. He told the officer, "I own the paper." With that, the officer told him, "Not any more," and took out his gun and shot him dead.'

Richie shuddered. 'They shot him as if he was nothing, as if he was some kind of insect. His secretary said they were all so shocked and terrified that no one did anything. His employees just stood there, praying they wouldn't be killed, too. Meanwhile, the Nazis and the

Arrow Cross destroyed all the equipment, even the presses, and then they left.'

I didn't know what to do or say as the horror of it washed over me. Mr Kovacs had always been kind, had always welcomed me into his home. I knew that Richie adored him and he, in turn, had built his entire life around his wife and son. He was a good man, an honest man. And now he was dead, as if his life meant nothing.

I held Richie to my breast and let him cry like the child we both still were, children facing horrors they should never have had to face.

'I love you, I love you, my darling,' I said over and over again. 'I am so sorry, so sorry, so sorry . . .'

After a while, he gained control of himself. By then, I was crying too, for him, for his father, for his poor mother, for myself, for all of us. 'What will you do now?' I asked.

He stared at me, absently stroking my face. I shuddered because the look I saw in his eyes now was no longer the look of a child or even of a young boy, but the look of a man, a very serious, very determined, hardened, angry man. The day they killed his father, they effectively ended his childhood. He smiled at me gently. 'I'll take care of my mother, of course. My father would expect it, and she needs me more than ever now.' Then he frowned. 'But I'm going to work harder than ever with the Underground. We have to defeat these people before they destroy us and everything we love.'

And suddenly I was very afraid, more afraid than I had ever been, that we would have no future, that there would be no wedding at the Hotel Royale, no honeymoon in Venice, no trip to Paris, no life with his mother for a few years while he finished university and then a place and a family of our own. I could see the dream dissolving before my eyes. I felt bombarded by emotions – fear, anger, sorrow. He must have seen the look on my face because he grabbed me to him. 'Don't worry, *kis pofa*. I won't let anyone or anything – not even this dirty war or those evil Nazis – keep me away from you. We are meant to be, and nothing will change that.'

I clung to him, hoping that he was right. But I was no fool. I knew that things were awful and were bound to get worse before they got better. I knew that the Germans and their Hungarian accomplices, the Arrow Cross, had only begun to torment the Jews of Hungary. The question was: would we still be alive to see it end?

I awoke in the middle of the night to the scream of air-raid sirens and leapt to my feet, throwing on my sweater, helping my mother to gather my brother and sister and head for the shelter in the basement. The bombing of Budapest had begun in the middle of April. Now, every day and on many nights, the Allied bombers would come, lighting up the night sky, dropping their deadly load all across the city. Every Hungarian faced the threat of being killed by the bombs, but only the Jews were forced to clear the rubble from the streets once the bombing had stopped. Old men, women, children, we were all made to clear the debris, including the scattered dead.

The first time we were ordered to do it, I refused. My mother grabbed my arm, rummaged in our few posses-sions for our gloves, and handed me my pair. 'Wear these and come with me. Rose, you come, too. Larry, you stay here. Small children are not forced to do this.'

We followed my mother, who calmly, methodically, and with the same focused energy she brought to every-thing she did, cleared the debris, brick by brick, stone by stone. I worked too, the rough bricks and stones cutting into my hands through the thin wool gloves, my eyes barely open as I worked my way through what looked like a scene from a nightmare. Suddenly, I screamed. My mother put her hand over my mouth. 'Watch what you do, Baby,' she hissed, looking over her shoulder at the Arrow Cross guard who was watching us, his rifle cradled in his arms.

'Mama, there's an arm here, just an arm, no head, no body, just an arm and I . . .'

My mother took me firmly by the shoulders and looked me right in the eye. 'Listen to me, Baby. We must do what they tell us and not make a scene or they will shoot us. Do you understand?'

Wordlessly, I nodded, my brain still rejecting what my eyes were seeing – this disembodied arm. My mother leaned across me and grabbed the arm and gently placed it in the almost-full wheelbarrow with the rest of the debris. We never mentioned it again. I'm ashamed to say that after the first few days, almost nothing I saw shocked me any more. I'll never forget the time I saw a child in a wheelbarrow, shot to death, his body rotting in the sun. Everyone was afraid to claim him. But that was a couple of months later and, by then, horror had piled upon horror so that we barely felt human any more.

By June, all the Jews of Budapest had been removed to several neighbourhoods that had been designated ghettoes. One of the largest was in part of the old city near the beautiful Dohany synagogue where we had worshipped on so many sabbaths and holy days. Only the Jews in the Swiss, Swedish and Vatican houses were left where they were. The synagogue itself had been gutted and vandalized, and was now used to store war materials.

The food shortages grew worse daily. Half the time,

the Germans would turn off the water for most of the day. When they turned it on, my mother would run with a bucket to stand in a queue.

One day, while she and I were queuing for water, each of us with a bucket over our arm, the woman standing in front of my mother left the queue. An hour later, she came back and wanted her place back in front of my mother.

'Then why did you leave the queue?' my mother asked her.

With that, the woman started yelling at my mother and pushing her. My mother pushed back and said, 'Stop it.'

Quicker than a heartbeat, a guard came up to them and, without asking any questions, hit my mother with his rifle butt, the power of the blow forcing her to her knees.

'Why did you hit her?' I cried. 'She didn't do anything.'

Beside me, my mother gripped my hand and pinched it. Hard. It was her message to be silent.

'Your dirty Jew of a mother was causing a disturbance in the queue. Do you want to complain about it?'

I swallowed. The anger and disgust I felt made me want to leap at him and scratch his face, punch him as he had my small, gentle mother who would not have done such a thing to a fly. But my mother pinched me again. I knew what I had to do. I had to be quiet. To keep it in. To swallow it, for her sake and for the sake of my sister and brother. Probably that duty kept me alive, because if I had had just myself to think about I would have been far more reckless.

The bombings had become relentless. There was no such thing any more as a full night's sleep. We would wait, tense, on our makeshift beds on the floor, ten of us crammed into a room, straining for the sound of the air-raid sirens and the whine of the bombs.

Potatoes had become our staple. My mother the cook, ever inventive, had come up with about a hundred recipes revolving around the potato. They were in soup, or cut up with a couple of onions to make a stew, or they could be scrambled together with the rare egg. Meat had become a delicacy for us, even with the money my mother still managed to get by selling jewellery. Budapest was a city under siege in a country that was occupied. We were told later that the Allies bombed us ferociously in an attempt to end the war quickly and save the Jews of Hungary. But obviously the Allies had under-estimated the determination of the Nazis and the Arrow Cross. They had a mission and, tragically, it was to get rid of as many of us as possible. Just as tragically, they were succeeding.

The first thing they did when they moved Jews into separate neighbourhoods was to close all the grocers' and butcher shops in those neighbourhoods, leaving the Jews without food. All they could do, within the hours when they were permitted outside at all, was to walk to other neighbourhoods in the hope of finding food for sale. Of course, since Jews were no longer allowed to work at paying jobs, most of them had no money with which to buy food anyway, unless they had managed to hide some valuables and could trade them for cash.

In that respect, we were very fortunate. We still lived in a Swiss-protected house which was relatively safe. My mother still had a few pieces of jewellery she could sell for money. She now had to sell her jewellery outright, even her wedding ring, because she couldn't go back and forth to the pawnshop and because, as she told me at the time when I questioned her, it was better to eat than to have jewellery. We had some benefactors, even at a time when most people thought only of themselves. And we had Richie. The Kovacs had managed to hide some valuables which they were slowly selling for cash. Not only that; their Gentile workers were very loyal to them and would bring them food, as would cousins who lived out on a huge farm and vineyards in the Hungarian countryside. These cousins would periodically sneak in food to them – fresh bread, even eggs, and fruit and vegetables. Whatever Richie and his mother had, they shared with us. There was not a time he came to my house that Richie did not bring some food. Once, he brought only one egg and all four of us in my family shared it. But it kept us going.

We also had Mr Kormendy, our personal guardian angel. He was an older man, already in his sixties then, a Gentile and a gentle man, with a ramrod posture and wavy grey hair. He had deep brown eyes behind thick glasses and he was very wealthy. He owned a clothing shop and factory and, when the Germans came, they quickly commandeered his business and forced him to make uniforms. In fact, he saved the lives of many Jews by giving them jobs in his factory. He offered this to my mother and to me as well, but we had to refuse, because he could offer no such protection to my sister and brother.

We'd first met Mr Kormendy years before when we'd been out for a family stroll along the streets of downtown Budapest. My father wanted to look at some things in his shop. Mr Kormendy greeted us when we walked in. He and my parents began to talk, and they became friendly after that. My father would buy some clothing there on occasion and we would visit and ask after his family.

Mr Kormendy was a family friend, but in no way did he owe us the service he so freely gave. Somehow, he knew of our difficulties and knew we were back in our old apartment. One day, he simply appeared at our door with a bag of food. After that, about once or twice a week, he would ring the doorbell when he knew we were home and then leave. When we opened the door, we would find another paper bag filled with food. He would bring us bread — a rare treat because there was virtually no flour — some fruit, perhaps a couple of apples, some peppers, even some sausage, something my mother wouldn't eat because it wasn't kosher. In fact, she wanted to give the sausage away, but I wouldn't let her.

'I'll eat the sausage,' I said. And I did, sharing it with my brother and sister and sometimes taking it with me to the Castle Hill to divide with Richie.

By then, it was expressly forbidden for Gentiles to help Jews in any way. If Mr Kormendy had been caught, he could have been shot. But that never stopped him.

The world had gone crazy. There was no routine any more. No school, no real shopping, no synagogue. All the synagogues had been closed, their Torahs and religious artefacts stolen or destroyed. Our days were a constant struggle to stay alive. One day, my brother and I were out before curfew, walking along one of the many hills of Buda, looking down into the waters of the Danube. Suddenly, the air-raid siren blared and we looked around frantically for shelter. We were too far up the hill to run for the air-raid shelter. I grabbed my brother and we crouched under a bush as the bombs fell. In a few minutes, the sky was thick with a black rain that pelted us and stuck to our clothes. I reached out a finger and let some fall on me, then tasted it. I spat it out. 'It's oil,' I said to my brother. 'They must have hit a refinery.'

We hid there for what seemed like hours but could only have been about twenty minutes, until the all-clear sounded.

There were daily searches of our house. The Arrow Cross would storm in, looking for people who were wanted, for people who might be hiding without papers. In July, things became even more macabre and terrifying. A couple of times a week, as we watched from the windows of our ground-floor apartment, the Germans or the Arrow Cross would march by with fifty or a hundred Jews marching in a line in front of them. They would stop a block and half away, at the banks of the Danube. If we craned our necks out of the windows, we could see them, although my mother tried to stop us from doing this, fearing that we would be taken, too. There would be a minute or so of silence and then we would hear the scattered staccato of machine-gun fire. And we would shudder, knowing that they had shot more of our people and simply let their bodies fall into the Danube. Some days, the river ran red with blood.

On other days, we would see long lines of Jews at the train station, and we would hear people whispering about 'forced resettlement, just like they did to the Polish Jews'. We kept hoping that the Regent wouldn't let them take us all, but things seemed to be getting worse every day.

In the midst of this, I was still a teenager in love. All I lived for, with the death and the fear and the horror and humiliation that surrounded us, was my time with Richie. I was ruthless and even devious about getting it and that would make my mother very angry with me sometimes. She tried to understand and I realize now, looking back, that she tried to give me as much freedom as she could to be with Richie, because she didn't know what the future held for any of us. For all she knew, my times with Richie would be the only love I would ever know because we could all be dead tomorrow. On the other hand, there were times when she thought it was too dangerous to go out and I went anyway. There were times when she told me to be back by curfew and I was late, very late – not always on purpose, sometimes merely because I had forgotten what time it was – but it made my mother crazy with fear for me and that made her angry.

By this time, it was the late summer of 1944 and Richie and I were struggling to be together as much as possible, which meant we were taking greater and greater chances about staying out beyond curfew. And the risks were great for both of us. I could be arrested or attacked and raped. And he was a young, able man who could be taken into forced labour if he was found out on the streets. These were the agonies that plagued my mother. She became hysterical at times. What if I were caught by the authorities? she raved. What if the Arrow Cross thugs decided to attack and rape me just for the fun of it?

One night, her worst fears almost became reality. I had sneaked out to meet Richie and we'd decided to take the risk of going to the boathouse, even though it was a long trip and it meant there was a greater chance that we would be caught. But the bright heat of summer called to us and we longed for our boat and the sense of peace we found on the river. We decided it was worth the risk.

When we arrived at the boathouse, the midday sun shone brightly off the blue-green surface of the river. It was a glorious day and, at least for the moment, we could feel as carefree as two teenagers should. I was still just fifteen and Richie was only seventeen. We looked at each other and ran for his boathouse, wasting no time in getting the boat out and launching it into the river. I shed my faded mousey dress. I had been able to hold on to Violet's outrageous swimming costume and, miraculously, my mother had never found it.

We rowed diligently up river, the breeze off the water cooling our faces as we lifted them towards the sun. When we had rowed far enough, we let the boat drift slowing back down river, the two of us lying in the bottom of the boat together, dreaming of the time when we would be free.

'Tell me again how much you love me, Baby,' Richie teased as he dipped his fingers over the side of the boat and splashed some cool drops on to my face.

'I love you enough for it to last for ever,' I told him, doing the same thing to his face.

He reached for me, pretending to be mad, but instead he kissed me, long and deeply, and then we were lost in each other as he gently slipped the top of my bikini off my shoulders and kissed my breasts until I thought I would die from the sheer pleasure of it.

I begged him that day to sleep with me, but he still refused.

'Trust me, *kis pofa*. Soon we will be together for always and I want it to be absolutely right.'

The afternoon passed as we kissed and stroked each other and tried to pretend we didn't have a single worry in this rotten world.

It was dusk by the time we started the long trip home. So many horrible things happened every day that we never knew from one day to the next when – or if – we would see each other again. In fact, the first thing we did every time we met again was thank God for this new day together. So we walked and we talked and we took the train and then I got off at my stop.

By then, it was dark and very late. The streets were virtually deserted, and I realized in that moment just how vulnerable I was, a Jewish girl out alone with her sweater turned inside out so that no one would see her ugly yellow star. I thought I heard footsteps behind me and started to walk faster, wishing I had listened to my mother. I was still a couple of blocks from home. I looked around frantically for some safe haven and, as if in answer to my prayers, I saw the light still on in the corner chemist's shop. The owner was a good and kind man, a friend to our family, even though he was a Gentile. It was so late that he must be ready to shut up shop. I thought he might be willing to walk me home.

As I entered the shop, I saw Mr Ferenc look up from behind the high counter where he was filling in a prescription, his black hair peppered with grey, his glasses slipping off his nose. He had a sharp-featured face, but it was kind.

'Betty, what are you doing out so late?' he asked, sounding frightened for me.

'Oh, Mr Ferenc, I lost track of the time and it was a long trip home and then, as I was walking down the street, I thought I heard footsteps behind me and got frightened and didn't know what to do. Then I saw your light on and I thought perhaps you'd be willing to walk me home.'

He shook his head at me, trying hard to look stern and not to smile, but finally the smile won out. 'All right, I'll do it this time if you promise me you won't stay out this late again,' he said.

Just then, the shop's bell tinkled and I looked behind me and almost died. A tall, blond and handsome Nazi soldier strolled through the door.

'Good evening, Herr Ferenc,' he said, glancing at me with a smile as he said it.

I smiled back and tried to look natural.

'Good evening, officer,' Mr Ferenc answered, trying to look calm, although I noticed he spilled a little powder he'd been pouring into a jar. It looked to me as if his hands were shaking. 'How are you?'

'Not that well, actually,' the officer said, rubbing the outside of his throat. 'I need some lozenges for a cough that does not seem to want to go away.'

Mr Ferenc practically ran round to the front of the counter. 'I have just the thing to help,' he said, reaching for a packet and handing it to the soldier. 'Please take it with my compliments.'

The officer smiled. 'How kind,' he said, making no move to go. 'And who is your pretty friend?' he asked, looking at me.

I introduced myself, using the last name of the Gentile superintendent who used to run our building. I made sure not to look down at the sweater I'd turned inside out.

'I am Lieutenant Schmidt, at your service, *fraulein*,' he said with a smile that could melt ice. 'May I ask what you are doing out so late?'

Before I could reply, Mr Ferenc answered for me. 'Her mother is ill and she sent Betty to get her some aspirin.'

I nodded, giving the lieutenant my best smile.

'Do you live far from here?' he asked.

I knew I had to find my voice or he would become suspicious. I was sure he was a man used to having women throw themselves at him. 'Not very far,' I said in what I hoped was a calm, clear voice.

'Please allow me to escort you there,' he said, with a little bow. 'It's not safe for you to be out on these streets alone so late at night.'

Mr Ferenc hurried forward. 'I was just about to do

that very thing, since Betty lives on my way home.'

Lieutenant Schmidt smiled, but I noticed his Nordic blue eyes had gone a little frosty. 'I wouldn't dream of foisting such a responsibility on to a civilian when it is the military's job to see to the safety of Budapest's citizens,' he said firmly. 'I consider it no less than my duty to walk her home.'

There was nothing else to do but to give him my hand when he offered and to pray that I could keep up the charade long enough to get safely inside my locked star house.

I chattered all the way home, giving Lieutenant Schmidt my best smile and praying that he wouldn't walk me to the door, where he might discover that I was in a star house and therefore not the Gentile he thought I was.

I said goodnight at the foot of the walkway leading up to the building. He hesitated a moment before releasing my arm and I held my breath, thinking I was caught if he insisted on coming with me. But he released my hand with a tiny squeeze. 'I'll wait until you're safely inside,' he said.

I banged on the door, knowing it was way past curfew and therefore the door was locked. We now had a Jewish superintendent who guarded the entrance. It was he who now opened the door and practically pulled me inside before shutting it firmly behind me.

'Are you crazy?' he hissed, grabbing me by the arm and shoving me against the wall so hard that my head was spinning. 'You endanger all of us by staying out after curfew and then showing up with a German officer no less. You should feel ashamed of yourself. And your mother has been frantic for hours, waiting for you, thinking you might never come home.'

I looked up at him with tears in my eyes, but I saw not a single flicker of sympathy in his. 'Do this again and I'll report you to the Nazis myself,' he said, turning away and heading for his apartment.

I climbed the short flight of stairs to our apartment with a wild sense of relief. Despite all the chances I had taken, once again I had been spared. I thanked God.

chapter *Nine*

I should have known that our luck could not last. For the past couple of months, things had grown steadily worse, as the Germans sped up their plans to eliminate the Jews of Hungary. The Regent seemed increasingly unwilling or unable to stop the Nazis and the ever-stronger Hungarian Arrow Cross.

One day my brother and I stood in the doorway of our building when suddenly we saw a man running towards us, with a box in his hands. Right behind him, several soldiers chased him with their guns raised. 'Stop,' they shouted, but the man kept on going, his face a mask of panic and desperation as he neared our doorway. The soldier in the lead got close enough to fire a shot, then two more in rapid succession. The man fell into the street practically in front of us as I dragged my brother back into the vestibule, away from the soldiers.

'Dirty, thieving Jew,' one of the soldiers muttered as

he leaned over the man and flipped him over to make sure he was dead.

'Well, that's one Jew who'll never lie and steal again. Now if we could just shoot all the rest of them as easily,' another soldier said with a laugh.

I shuddered, cowering in the doorway with my brother. The soldiers shrugged their shoulders, holstered their pistols and began to walk away. I felt my brother struggling in my grasp. 'Let me go, Baby.'

I grabbed him tighter. 'Are you crazy? If you go running out there, the soldiers could come back and shoot you too.'

Larry shrugged, still trying to remove my hand from his shoulder. 'But the box that man was carrying. It's still there, right in the gutter. I want to get it. It must be something valuable if he stole it and then ran like that with the soldiers chasing him.'

I looked down at him, my baby brother, only ten years old and yet so hardened by what he had seen that he would take a dead man's box. But I also saw the value in his idea. We had run out of practically everything. Whatever was in that box would surely help. 'All right,' I said. 'You can go and grab the box, but not until the soldiers turn the corner.'

Larry waited impatiently, then darted out from under my grasp as soon as the soldiers were gone from view. He ran to the box, and not a moment too soon. Several others had seen the entire incident and were after the box as well. But Larry was quick and got there first, clutching the box to his chest and running back to the doorway with it. We waited until we were safely inside the downstairs hall before we looked inside. There, stacked neatly, were several bars of soap. My hands began to shake as I looked at the white bars. A man had just been killed for a few bars of soap. And no one had done anything. No one had cared.

'We can use these, Baby,' Larry said, examining the finely milled bars. 'We can trade these for food and even keep some for ourselves.'

I didn't have the heart to share these thoughts with him. He was only ten. Let him enjoy the soap.

In the midst of this madness, my mother remained calm most of the time and still tried to do charitable works through the rabbi and his wife. She would meet secretly with the rabbi's wife and help tend to those Jews who were too old or too sick to tend themselves, although this became increasingly dangerous to do.

And she still tried to have Friday night dinner. She would save up a couple of potatoes (what else?), an onion or two, and maybe a pepper, and she would make a goulash. Many Friday nights, Richie would come over and he would bring a coveted loaf of bread, some precious eggs or a couple of crisp apples.

After dinner, he would play chess with my brother or sister or me. He was a very good chess player. Nobody ever beat him.

Once, as we were playing, he told me a story about a poor man who had taught an ancient king of Egypt to play chess. And, he explained, the king said to the poor man, 'I would like to reward you for teaching me this game. Here, take this bag of gold.'

But the poor man declined the bag of gold. 'I don't want gold,' he explained to the king. 'All I want is just one grain of wheat for each square of the chess board, multiplied by two for the second square, by two again for the third, and so on for each succeeding square.' By the time he was done with the sixty-four squares, there wasn't enough grain in Egypt left to pay him with. The moral, Richie said, was that if you wanted to save money, you had to save it one grain at a time, always making sure it gained interest.

In a sense, he brought the world to us on those nights when we sat with him. He was very smart and very well educated. He had already started university then, though once the Germans came he could no longer attend. He taught all of us so much.

The air raids came every day now. Some days were filled with the almost-constant thunder of the big heavy planes and their deadly cargo of bombs. But as much as we feared being killed by the bombs and as much as we hated cleaning up the debris after each strike, we prayed for those raids because we knew that each bomb brought Germany's defeat closer. But the question still remained: would the victory come in time to save us?

In the meantime, my mother used her dwindling resources to keep us fed. She insisted we eat potato peels, telling us that she had read they were rich in potassium and so provided nourishment. We didn't like it, but we ate them. One day, she was looking out of the window studying the large sacks that were being used to sandbag the Danube. Suddenly, I saw her smile. 'I'll be back in a little while,' she said as she strode out of the door. Half an hour later, she returned, lugging one of those heavy sacks with her.

'What in the world are you doing, Mother?' I asked.

'Read the printing on the sack,' she said, triumph in her voice.

I looked at the stencilled black lettering. 'MILLET', it said.

'We can eat this,' my mother said with excitement. 'We can cook it up into a porridge, and we can bake it and eat it like a snack. And look how much there is in just this one sack. We can share it with everyone here. And there are so many more of these sacks on the banks of the river.'

I simply nodded my head, not sure whether to laugh or to cry. But once again, my mother was right and once again she had helped us to survive a little bit longer.

Unfortunately, nothing could keep us safe from the violence and chaos all around us. Our life was more difficult by the day, with daily air raids, with nights spent in the cellar seeking safety from the bombs and cleaning up the rubble. There were still daily searches of our house. The Hungarian Nazis were relentless in their search for men who could be used in forced labour and for people without papers. And there were some of them in our building, people who were hiding in relatives' apartments, hoping to survive. The problem with that was that every person who was hiding somewhere in the building put us all at risk. When, as often happened, someone was found, not only was that person shot or arrested, but so were the people hiding him.

During one search, a young man came running into our apartment, begging us to hide him. He was someone I had gone to school with and I felt terrible for him. I knew they would shoot him if they found him. But I was terrified. I was at home alone with my sister and brother, but there were others in our apartment and someone might tell the authorities. 'Hide in the chimney on the roof,' I whispered in his ear, then, stepping back, I said loudly, 'Get out of here now.' He ran for it and managed to wedge himself down the chimney, hidden from the search party. He met me in the hallway later that afternoon, as I ran out to meet Richie. 'Thank you for what you did earlier,' he said, giving me a quick hug.

'It's all right,' I answered, looking over my shoulder to

make sure no one was spying on us. 'But you have to leave here tonight. I'm sorry, but it's too dangerous for us and for you.'

He sighed wearily. 'I know. I have been running and hiding for weeks, in between helping the Underground. Maybe now it's time I took a holiday in the country.' He gave me a jaunty little salute before slipping out of the back door. I took a deep breath, and said a small prayer for his safety. Then I ran all the way to the Castle Hill. I needed to feel the warmth and security of Richie's arms around me more than ever.

One day in mid-September, I heard the pounding of boots on the stone balconies. This time, the Arrow Cross wasn't just conducting a search.

'Everyone outside in the courtyard,' the leader barked, banging on doors as he went from one floor to another, his troops following self-importantly behind him. We were terrified. But my mother never lost her self-control. 'Take your pillowcases, each of you,' she said quietly, but I could see fear in her eyes.

Ever since we'd been taken to the first star house, my mother had made us keep a pillowcase packed with our necessities so that if we were ever taken again, we would have at least enough to survive. Now each of us grabbed our pillowcase and followed her out into the courtyard. The Arrow Cross guards stood watching impatiently, waiting for everyone to assemble, their rifles at their shoulders. Once we were all there, the leader said, 'All those with Swiss protection papers, form a line to the right.' Dutifully, all of us with Swiss protection papers went to the right. 'All of those with Vatican protection papers, form a line to the left.' Those with Vatican papers went to the left.

'Now, the rest of you return to your apartments.' The

leader surveyed our two groups for a minute, then said: 'Fine. All of you with Swiss and Vatican papers, follow me.'

They marched us to St Istvan Park about two blocks away. It was mid-morning, warm for September. We were crowded into the park with hundreds of other Jews who had been gathered from neighbouring buildings. We stood there, in this pretty little park across a wide boulevard from the Danube. Luxury apartment buildings ringed the park, and people watched from their windows, but nobody did or said anything. We stood there, my mother holding our hands, saying over and over again, 'Stay together. Stay together. We will be all right if we just stay together.'

In her pillowcase, she had brought some stale pieces of bread, but we had nothing else – no food or water. The sun was hot and we just stood there for hours, with nothing to eat and nowhere to go to the bathroom. It was horrible.

Then we heard the sound of marching behind us and, out of the corner of our eyes, we saw a long line of Jews being taken to the banks of the Danube, the Arrow Cross guards at their backs. I saw my mother's body stiffen at what was to come. We heard the rapid fire of machine guns and the thud of bodies falling into the river. Beside me, my mother shuddered, but she said nothing; she just gripped our hands more firmly, as if her grip could save us if these Arrow Cross guards decided to shoot us.

'I can't stand up any more, Mama,' my little brother Larry said. My mother lifted him up into her arms, handing me her pillowcase to hold.

'It will be all right, little one,' she told him softly. My brother was small for his age, and frail. At ten, his body had taken the brunt of the malnutrition from the wartime food shortages. He looked as if he was seven, and he had very little stamina. My sister Rose still tended to be sickly too, and stress would really get to her. I was the one who had to be strong, to help my mother and my family. Just as Papa had said.

Eventually, at about four o'clock, the guards ordered us to start marching. By this time, we were exhausted and hungry, but we had no choice. We marched through the streets of Budapest, hundreds of Jews, our heads down, our feet dragging, our arms hugging our pillowcases to us. And the people of Budapest watched us go by, saying nothing, doing nothing, the silence punctuated by an occasional shout of, 'You're finally getting what's coming to you, you dirty Jews,' or 'Death to the Jews.' At least we had been marched away from the river, away from the machine-gun fire and certain death.

The walk seemed endless. My mother had to carry Larry for at least half the way. Finally, after a couple of hours, we arrived at our destination, Sip Utca 12, a building that had been used for Jewish education, set in the heart of what had become the ghetto. Now, it was whispered, it was Eichmann's headquarters.

The courtyard of that building was a scene from a nightmare. There were people lying everywhere, sick and dying, some of them already dead. Others stood huddled in groups. We were hustled up into a third-floor waiting room so crowded that we had to stand upright just to fit.

My mother asked to talk to someone about our Swiss protection papers, but it seemed that there was no one to talk to that night, and she would have to wait until the next morning. We stood there, crowded together. There was a single bathroom down the hall for all of us to use, if we had the stamina to squeeze through the crowd to get there. We were hot, hungry and tired. We were also scared. What would happen to us now?

The bombs came that night. One came right through the roof of the building we were in, causing a few minor injuries. An explosion near by killed some people and injured many others. The guards asked for volunteers to help tend them. Here we were in the middle of the ghetto in a state of constant blackout, trying to save even the smallest bit of candle, and now we needed to tend the wounded. I raised my hand, because I wanted to do something, to make a little bit of difference. That was the night I found out that I could never be a doctor. There was so much blood and, much as I wanted to be brave and strong, I could not stand the sight of so much carnage. Eventually, I became physically ill and had to come back inside.

It took two days for my mother to find the right person who could look at our Swiss papers of protection and allow us to go back to our 'protected' house which right now didn't feel like much protection. Somehow, we lost a few of our possessions along the way. With each move, we had less and less. Our supplies were pitiful but still absolutely priceless to us, and necessary for our survival.

Richie was frantic about us. He was pacing up and down in front of our building when we came back. I gasped when I saw him and ran to him, my arms flying around his neck even though it was broad daylight and we were in the middle of the street and my mother was watching. He held me so tightly I thought I would faint from the pressure. 'Baby, Baby, I thought you were gone. I thought they had taken you away. No one could tell me anything. Thank God, thank God you're here, you're still all right.'

I don't know how, but I managed to smile at him.

'Don't you remember that I have to be all right, other-wise what about our honeymoon in Venice?'

He couldn't answer me, and I saw tears in his eyes as he just hugged me close again.

He followed us up to our apartment and wanted to know all that had happened to us. We tried to work out a way we could let each other know when something had happened to one of us, but in the end, we came to the sad conclusion that there was no way to get messages to one another. If we were both free, we could leave notes in the crack in the wall at the Castle Hill, as we had done often. But if one of us was in custody, there was no way to let the other know. And somehow, that realization was more terrifying than anything that had come before.

My mother's faith in God remained steadfast. Even with my father gone, our home taken from us, the daily bombings, the lack of food, my mother was certain that God was in His heaven. I was not so sure. I looked around at my friends and my family and saw us as pretty and handsome people caught up in a nightmare, the kind in which a bath was a luxury and our very survival hung by a thread. I knew we did not deserve this fate, and I could not understand why God had done this to us, sup-posedly His Chosen People. It was a topic my mother refused to discuss. God's will was not to be questioned by mere mortals like us.

My friend Violet felt as rebellious as I did. She was a very lively, passionate girl, and astonishingly beautiful as she was, being a confirmed flirt who liked nothing more than to have men following her was just part of her zest for life, a zest her equally handsome brother and pretty sister shared. Her parents still had enough money hidden away to provide some food, even in a star-house envi-ronment, and she kept waiting for the day when the war

would end and she could enter the Miss Hungary
Pageant, a contest often won by the beautiful women in
her family.

My mother liked Violet but felt she might be a bad
influence on me. As for Violet, as Richie and I became
closer and closer, she became even more resentful of
what she saw as our exclusive relationship. She didn't
like it when I wouldn't let her come with me to meet
with Richie, but I lived with this because we just wanted
to be alone. Then, suddenly, in early autumn, Violet had
a beau of her own. He was one my mother would never
have approved of, so I didn't dream of telling her about
him. Violet's boyfriend was in the Underground, a former teacher, and married, though he claimed he was
unhappily so. He was also an 'old man' of thirty. But
Violet swore she loved him and when I saw them
together I saw a happiness in her eyes, a contentment I
had never seen there before.

They came for us again, two weeks later, the Arrow
Cross thugs with their guns and their heavy boots that
sounded like thunder in the stone hallways.

'Everyone outside *now*,' they shouted, ringing a bell
from floor to floor, their footsteps reverberating through
the hallways like hell-sent cannon fire. My mother and I
looked at each other, and I saw her lips moving in a silent
prayer as she signed for me to get the pillowcases. My
sister began to cry, but my mother immediately told her
to be quiet. Larry looked lost, as he so often did these
days.

We went out into the hallway. Next door, the Arrow
Cross were banging on the door, demanding that everyone come out immediately. A young man, the son of the
people who had been the original owners and still lived

there, came to the door and begged the guards to leave his parents alone. Without a word, without a thought, the guard shot him in the face at point-blank range, turning his face into a mangled mass of blood and tissue. When his parents came out a few minutes later, they stepped right over him without recognizing him, because he had no face left.

Once again, we were marched to St Istvan Park and made to stand there for hours on end. Once again, hundreds of other Jews were also brought there. They were the lucky ones. The unlucky ones took a walk to the river and were shot there, landing like so much flotsam on the gently flowing Danube. How could the river absorb so many bodies, so much blood, I thought desperately as I listened to the awful sounds of mass murder. I wanted to look but made sure I didn't turn round. Once again, my mother held our hands. 'You will see, it will be all right,' she said over and over again.

Late in the day, they forced us to march to the same ghetto again. The ghetto was even worse than before. The bomb damage was devastating and the buildings were riddled with bullet holes. The entire ghetto was like a giant shooting gallery, with Jews the target. Outside the venerable Dohany synagogue, the bodies of dead Jews were piled up like garbage. Other Jews were forced to dig mass graves in the synagogue's beautiful courtyard, then drag the corpses to them and sprinkle lye over them so that they would disintegrate and still more bodies could be put there. Could hell be any worse?

My mother kept reassuring us and once again we were shepherded to Eichmann's headquarters. We walked through the same courtyard, past the dead and dying, and into the crowded waiting room, but I didn't find any comfort in her words. My mother was all that was good, but how would that save us when we were surrounded by evil?

We stayed there for another two days, the sound and smells of the sick and dying all around us. How could such a beautiful building, a place that had once been dedicated to learning about religion, have become such a bleak, awful place? But I knew the answer even as I tried to stretch my cramped muscles before getting up to reach the bathroom: the Nazis – German and Hungarian – had created their vision of hell on earth and we were living it.

The bathroom was down the hall and obviously had not been cleaned for weeks. The sink was black with grime and the toilet was filthy. I closed my eyes. We had no choice, at least not while we were here. Once we were back in our own apartment, at least there would be a clean bathroom, even if we still had to wait in a queue to use it. I used the filthy, reeking toilet. When I tried to wash my hands afterwards, ready to rub them dry against my already-dirty skirt because there were no towels and only a small, soiled bar of soap, I discovered that the water had been turned off. That explained why the toilet would not flush. I tried not to think about it. I tried to imagine that I was floating down the river with Richie, the soft breeze on the Danube ruffling my hair. I made my way back to my mother, through the congested, suffering mass of humanity that was also huddled in one room.

As it turned out, we spent another night sleeping among these strangers before our Swiss papers once again won our release and we were permitted to return to our apartment. That day, the Germans had not turned off the water, so we had some in the bathroom. I didn't care that the water was ice-cold. I took my threadbare towel and one of the bars of soap we had kept from the man who had died stealing them and made my way to the bathroom. Politely, I asked the three men living in there – one of them in the bath – to leave while I washed. I removed all my clothing, even my underwear, which my mother only allowed us to change once a week since doing washing was so difficult. Then, using one end of the towel, I sponged my body with soap and water, trying to scrub it clean of all the dirt, the smells, the filth, the death, the fear of where we had just been. I knelt beside the bath and washed my hair in the stream of cold water, soaping it once, then again, and taking a long time to let the water get all the soap out. By then, someone was banging on the bathroom door. 'This is not a hotel, miss,' Mr Karpinsky, a cranky old man who lived among us, shouted. 'Others need to use the toilet.'

Hurriedly, I dried myself, then wrapped the already damp towel around my head before slipping into clean underwear and a faded blue flowered skirt and a white embroidered blouse. I felt like a gypsy, but at least I was clean. I would be able to brush my hair dry in the sunshine on the roof. Then I would be ready to go and meet Richie. I needed to feel his arms around me. How many more times would we be taken away, only to be allowed to return? And what would happen when we were taken and not allowed to return? I shuddered and ordered myself to stop thinking this way. I must be strong in my belief that we – me and my family and Richie and his mother – would survive this, that our lives would once again be normal.

chapter *Ten*

*W*hen would the horror end? And would we survive it? Each day things got worse. By October, Horthy had been removed as Regent and placed under house arrest. Szalazy, the man who replaced him, was a rabid Nazi and founder of the Hungarian Arrow Cross. Now his unholy organization felt free to attack us at will. So many times we were taken from our apartments and made to stand in the courtyard for hours while those thugs went through our belongings, taking anything they wanted. And we could say nothing, do nothing. We had Christian friends, like Mr Kormendy and others, who were shocked by the way other Hungarians were treating us, but they were as helpless as we were to do anything openly. If they had tried to help us and were caught, they would have met the same fate as the Jews they were trying to protect.

We heard so many rumours of Jews being taken away and we saw them, every day, taken out on trains. Some said they were being sent to Germany to work in the factories. But why would they take women and children to do this work? No one knew, and everyone was afraid of what the answers might mean.

Some days, I felt there was very little hope, and even my mother would remain silent in the face of more troubling news. Every day, news came that people were being rounded up out of the star houses and taken away. In the meantime, the Underground organizations grew and I desperately wanted to join one, as Richie had, but my mother forbade it. A couple of times I did deliver messages for Richie and even let him use my brother as a courier, although I knew that if my mother found out she would be outraged.

The daily air raids continued and, with them, our work of clearing the debris. It was such hard, horrifying work. We had to pick up the broken, jagged bricks, pull bodies out from under pieces of broken glass, and haul everything to the waiting wheelbarrows. Our hands were always bloody and we braced ourselves for the day when we would haul out of the rubble the body of some-one we knew and loved. So far, that had not happened. When we went out, my sister would push the wheelbar-row, although she could barely do it, and my brother picked up smaller pieces of rubble. Because he was only ten, he was excused from this horrendous work, but my mother made him come along because she felt it was safer if we all stayed together. My mother and I picked up bigger pieces of rubble and she kept an eye on all of us.

We were forced to clear the rubble no matter what time of day or night the air raid occurred. And when we had finished, we dragged ourselves back to our crowded apartment, so exhausted that we fell asleep in our soiled, dirty clothing. We didn't even wash our hands, which were rubbed raw. The Germans were trying to reduce us to the level of animals and day by day, it seemed, we were getting closer.

The feeling of helplessness was driving me mad, but there wasn't much I could do. There was hardly any food, and we thought we would starve to death if we couldn't find a supply soon. One man in our building did die of starvation, and that saddened and terrified the rest of us. How could we possibly survive much longer? It was worse in the ghetto, where they had closed all the butchers' shops and grocers'. There, people had to go miles to other neighbourhoods to try to buy food, and they had to be careful to return before curfew began at four o'clock every afternoon. From four until ten the next morning, Jews were not allowed out on the streets.

I became afraid to go to sleep at night. As a child, I had been a wonderful sleeper, falling asleep almost at once and getting a full night's rest. But now, even when I was starving and exhausted, my sleep was fitful. The only thing that helped me was my love for Richie and the meetings we still managed to grab during the chaos and horror of our days.

It was already beginning to get cold and there had been a fair amount of rain, but nothing, not even our increasing hunger, could keep me from meeting Richie every day. His eyes were solemn now, rarely the laughing eyes of the young boy I had known. He was doing many things for the Underground, such as delivering arms to people around the city, and helping to blow up train tracks so that supplies couldn't get through to the Germans.

Even though Szalazy, Horthy's replacement as Regent, had unleashed a new reign of terror against all the Jews, especially in the ghetto, where hundreds were killed, miraculously we had still been spared. Even Richie, who could so easily have been taken away or shot because he was an able-bodied Jewish male who had not yet been sacrificed to slave labour, had managed to survive and even have a relative degree of freedom. It had taken some quick thinking on his part and the help of some false papers, which showed his age as only sixteen, and helped keep him safe. We hoped liberation would come soon, and that it would be the Americans or the British, not the dreaded Russians, who would free us. We feared that the Russians might do to us whatever horrible things the Germans had not thought to do.

The autumn days sped by, as swift and constant as our beloved Danube. It was mid-October and the cold set in for good, with brisk, crisp days and icy rain. But each day, I gladly faced that cold and my fears of being outside, potentially at the mercy of some Arrow Cross officer, to see Richie.

'We must hold on to our dignity, *kis pofa*, no matter what comes,' Richie told me one day as we sat in our private bend in the serpentine wall that surrounded the Regent's Castle on Castle Hill. He had spread his coat out on the ground for us so that we wouldn't freeze, even though a strong wind was blowing, and there was a hint of frost in the air.

I shook my head. 'You sound just like my mother. She is always telling me to hold my head high to show them that we are not giving up, that the more they hurt us, the more we will bounce back.' I threw an acorn at a scampering squirrel. 'But I don't want to bounce any more. In fact, I would like to give in.'

'No,' Richie said fiercely, cupping my chin in his hand and forcing me to look at him. 'You must follow the rules so that they will have no reason to target you, no reason to shoot you. Don't you understand, Baby? You are my everything. You have to survive.' He took my two hands in his, caressing my small, cold fingers with his long, slender, warm ones, stroking them as if they were the keys of his beloved piano. 'We are young and we will fight the system on our terms, but our terms are not to defy them to their faces. Right now, they have the guns and the bullets, but they are losing the war, we know that.' He looked as if he might say more; then I could see by the expression on his face that he'd decided not to. 'Just promise me you will not take unnecessary risks.'

I nodded my head and looked up at him. There was such a look of love on his face, strong and fierce, like some handsome warrior in a fairytale. But this was no fairytale. He had turned away from me, and was doing something to the wall, scraping at it I thought, but he wouldn't let me see.

'Richie, let me look,' I said, trying to peer over his shoulder to get a glimpse.

'You'll see it, but not until it's done, *kis pofa*. You must be patient. In the meantime, have you brought me any tempting delicacies to eat? Where is this fabulous cook who made lesco for me only the other day?'

I blushed, remembering my poor attempt at the Hungarian dish. Of course, we barely had the ingredients and I knew virtually nothing about cooking, but Richie had gallantly eaten it all. I suppose there are some advantages to always being hungry. But today I had brought him a treat. I had had a hard-boiled egg and I had mashed it with onion to make a kind of egg salad and used the last bit of yesterday's bread to make it into a sandwich for us.

'I'll give you the sandwich when you let me see what you are doing,' I bargained.

'You are a tough woman, *kis pofa*.' But he still wouldn't let me see. After another few minutes, he moved away from the wall and grabbed my hand. 'Now look.'

There, on the wall, in the place where we had spent so many hours holding each other and talking about the future, Richie had painstakingly carved a heart into the stone. Inside it, he had written, 'Richie and Baby for ever.'

I could feel tears sliding down my cheeks. Gently, he brushed them away. 'There, you see, our love will live for all time,' he said softly.

I ran my finger over the heart and the words within it. Please God, I prayed, make this true.

The sound of the air-raid siren split the cool afternoon air, shattering our peace and our hopes with a single piercing blast. Richie and I jumped up. It was almost cur-few now and it was becoming more dangerous to be out after it was in force. There was always the chance that the punishing bombings would take out one of the bridges between Buda and Pest and then we would be stuck and unable to get back home in time. Richie grabbed me to him for a quick, desperate kiss. 'I love you, Baby.'

'And I love you, with all my heart,' I said, placing both hands over my heart, giving him my best smile before I turned and started running down the winding hill to the bridge below. He was running, too, now, to the bridge further north on the Danube which linked Buda to his section of Pest. I turned one last time and, as if he sensed I was looking at him, he turned, too, and we both waved. The sun was behind him and he was illuminated for a moment, as handsome as a film star or some mythical god. 'See you tomorrow,' I yelled before turning to run the rest of the way to the bridge.

Suddenly, I noticed that there was a crowd of people streaming down the Castle Hill. Most, like us, had been looking for privacy so that they could kiss or make love. But now we were all running for our lives as the Allied planes appeared overhead, flying so low that we could see the bombs drop. Through the steady, deadly whine and thump of the falling bombs, we ran across the bridge spanning the river, people jostling each other for position as they ran. We were all scared. But by the time we reached the end of the delicate suspension bridge, the air raid was over and the all-clear was sounding. Still I ran, because sometimes there was more than one wave of bombers and I wanted to run the fifteen blocks home so that I would be safe if the planes came again.

I could feel the wind beating at my face and the breath pounding in my chest as I raced along the river. All I could think about, even through my fear, was how much Richie loved me and how much I loved him. He was my everything, and I hoped with all my heart that none of those bombs had found him as a target; that he, too, was safe, as I was safe.

I could see my building now, just a short half-block away. But what was wrong? Why was my mother standing outside and why were other tenants from the building milling around as well? I didn't know whether to slow down or speed up, but the look of panic on my mother's face told me I had to run. My mother, who was always calm, even in the face of unspeakable events, looked terrified.

'Oh, thank God,' my mother said, grabbing me by both arms. 'Where were you? It's past the time I told you to be home and then there was an air raid and I was so worried about you.'

I pulled away from her grasp. I hated it when she was like this. I knew my responsibilities, but I needed my freedom too. 'I'm here and that's what counts,' I told her.

'And look, I got here without the Germans finding out I was not here.'

I noticed that there were German soldiers and a full battery of Arrow Cross around the building as well, but suddenly I didn't care. I'd had enough of what these people could do to me. Besides, Richie and I were destined to survive this. He'd told me so millions of times. 'Don't get so worried,' I said.

My mother, who never lashed out at me, yelled at me now. 'What is the matter with you? Don't you understand what is happening? They're making us leave the building again, and this time they're waving their guns as if they mean it.'

'I don't care,' I shouted back, and at that moment, I meant it. I felt as if my heart was breaking. Here I was, so in love, and, in the next moment almost, I was being ordered to pack up the few things still scattered around and leave this apartment behind for God knew what. Everywhere, there was confusion, as hundreds of people streamed out of the building, some of them screaming and crying. My mother rushed me upstairs, where we crammed into our pillowcases as much as the two of us could carry. Our suitcases were long gone and, in any event, would have been too heavy for us to carry at this point. Rose and Larry were too small and frail to haul anything very heavy, so Rose carried a smaller pillowcase filled with some food and some spoons to eat it with, and my brother carried the small pillow he had become attached to.

I watched my poor mother packing once again. By now we had so little left that it was not difficult to determine what must go and what could stay. That was just as well, since we only had half an hour to assemble outside in the courtyard between our twin buildings. Just as we were about to walk out of the door, my mother grabbed the heavy woollen blanket we had used as both our mattress and our comforter in our 'bed' on the floor. She draped it over her shoulder and guided us downstairs, her arm once again around us, as if such a fragile barrier could protect us from the evil that had us in its grasp.

Outside, a light, cold rain had begun to fall. Even the sky was weeping at our predicament, I thought, feeling my own tears stuck in my throat in a tight ball that felt as if, at any moment, it would choke me. As we waited in that courtyard, we heard the sounds of murder coming from inside. There were people in our building who were too old or too sick to move, people who could not walk, mothers with newborn babies. The guards just shot them there in their apartments, as if they were nothing, some nuisances who had got in their way. Standing in the courtyard, I could almost feel each bullet as we listened to the staccato bursts of machine-gun fire. I looked at my mother. Her lips were moving, but no sound was coming out. I knew immediately what she was doing. She was praying. I tried to do the same, but I was so angry at our plight, at these murderers running free while innocents were being slaughtered, that I could not even say God's name. I know now I was mad at Him for everything. I wanted to be so much older, to be a man, so that I could stand up to those murderers. But I was only a young girl struggling to help keep herself and her family alive.

The Arrow Cross guards took us out on to the street and made us walk along the Danube to St Istvan Park once again, where we stood in the rain until dusk, with no idea of where we might be going. They lined us up, my mother holding on to us tighter than she had ever held on to us before. I was crying, for the very first time outside, in front of everyone. My mother hugged me against her.

'Baby, don't cry,' she said. 'We are together and that is all that I can ask for now. But God will help us, you'll see.'

I could not look at her, because I did not believe, as she did, that God wanted to test us and that we had to endure. I just kept on crying. My mother stood there, straight and strong, refusing to give in to the sorrow.

There were many more Jews gathered in the park, people who had been taken from other neighbouring buildings, including my friend Violet and her sister, Amy, who managed to find us.

'Where are your parents and your brother?' I asked her, my teeth chattering from the damp cold I could feel even through the wool of my shabby winter coat. My feet, protected only by flimsy leather shoes instead of the more sensible boots I had had no time to think of taking, had begun to ache and feel numb.

Violet's vivid, almost-purple eyes looked wild. 'They were out shopping – not that there is much to be had,' she told me. 'They will go crazy when they find us gone. I have to get back home so they won't worry.'

My mother smiled at her kindly. 'You know that sooner or later they always let us go back home. Just be patient, Violet.'

Violet looked a little calmer, but I wasn't fooled. I had seen the flash of uncertainty, even fear, in my mother's eyes. I wasn't so sure that this time we would ever go home again. And that thought made me more frightened than I had been by anything that had come before. How would Richie find me now?

As night fell over the city and the temperature dipped even lower, they marched us across the Danube at the Arpad bridge into Buda and made us walk another four miles to an abandoned brick factory. It was to become our filthy, muddy prison for almost three weeks.

chapter Eleven

Even in the dark, the brick factory looked daunting, its stark, brooding buildings looming in the rain and the mist. It was a big, sprawling complex, a couple of city blocks square, surrounded by yards of open, muddy ground stained the colour of terracotta bricks. Surrounding it was a high wrought-iron fence. There were stacks of bricks all over the place, and a couple of stone ovens in which to bake the bricks. The factory was in a heavily industrial part of Buda that I had never seen before. It was off the busy, bustling Vienna Road, a two-lane highway that ran clear across Hungary into Austria. A combination of homes and businesses lined both sides of it.

The rain had begun again and the ground in and around the factory yard was pure mud. But what was most horrifying about this place was that there were thousands of other Jews already crowded there, most of them in far worse shape than we were.

I saw my mother rapidly assessing the situation as the rain streamed down and the guards shouted at us to find a place within the gates. All the areas that afforded any shelter from the elements were taken, including a spot protected by a wide overhang that was already clogged with people. My mother pushed and prodded her way through the crowd, trying to find us the best spot, holding our hands tightly so that we wouldn't get separated in the pushing, shoving throng. Violet and her sister Amy came along with us. In the absence of their parents, I could see that my mother felt responsible for them.

The deep, smelly mud sucked at our shoes and oozed up over our ankles as if it were going to consume us at any moment, like some huge slimy mouth. All around us, we could hear the cries and moans of the sick and the dying, or the merely weak. At the sight of such massive human suffering, some people in our group became hysterical, screaming and crying, struggling to get away somehow, although the walls of the sprawling factory yard were high and the guards had their guns trained on us.

'Shut up,' the guards shouted.

Quite near us, a woman continued to shriek, pulling at her hair as if she had lost her mind, which, at least for the moment, she probably had – how could any rational person absorb such a nightmare? A guard shot her, and she fell face down into the mud. Very few screamed loudly after that.

Wordlessly, my mother gathered us around her, making a space for Violet and Amy. She spread the blanket on that filthy, dirty ground, in the midst of all that mud, and told us to sit down.

I felt numb, too tired and too terrified even to think straight. The only certainty that remained right now in a world suddenly gone even madder than usual was the calm sound of my mother's voice telling us to sit down. I sat down, along with my sister and brother. My mother glanced around furtively at the miserable mass of humanity packed in around us, then reached into her pillowcase for some food.

'Eat slowly, and chew every bite,' she told us. 'From the look of things, the food we've brought will have to last until we get out of here.' We shared what we had with Violet and Amy, and all of us ate the hard bread and small pieces of cheese as if they were gourmet delicacies. Out of the corner of my eye, I could see some of the others watching us, their mouths moving as if they were chewing along with us, although their hands held no food. Would that be us in a few days, when my mother's carefully packed and hoarded supplies ran out? For the first time, I actually felt that I might not survive this awful war.

When we'd finished our meagre supper, my mother led us in our evening prayers, even through the din of the crying and muttering all around us. I moved my mouth, but my heart wasn't in it. No God I could conceive of would have brought us here, to this.

I heard a man calling for his maid to bring him tea. I looked over, incredulous that anyone had been allowed to bring servants to such a place. But when I looked his way, I saw that he was frail and elderly and obviously delirious, possibly dying. Slowly, an older woman in a wet, shabby coat, her head wrapped in a soaked cotton print handkerchief, lifted herself laboriously from the mud and made her way over to the man. She crouched down next to him and gently lifted his head out of the gooey mess, cradling it in her hand. With her other hand, she lifted a tin cup filled with some kind of warm liquid to his lips and held him up as he drank.

'God bless you,' I heard him say to her and I could swear that his eyes had cleared for a moment and he had known exactly what was happening – that someone had acted out of kindness, even in a nightmare such as this. I felt humbled by that woman and what she had done. I closed my eyes and tried to pray again, this time with more conviction. I needed to believe that there was still goodness and mercy in the world. I had seen enough of evil.

My mother sang us all to sleep with the lullaby she had crooned to us in our childhood. I was sure I would not be able to sleep here, that I would not be able to survive here, in a place where even getting to the filthy latrines was such a trial that some people could not and had to sit in their own filth in the rain and the mud. But slowly I felt my eyelids drifting shut to the soothing sound of my mother's voice. The next thing I knew, it was morning.

For centuries, philosophers have debated which is stronger, the human body or the human spirit. I have lived through hell and I still do not know the answer to that question. All I know is that my mother's spirit willed us all to keep going even when the conditions were so vile that all I wanted to do was curl up and die.

My mother wouldn't allow it. That first morning, she made us stand up and move around to exercise our stiff, sore muscles and keep up what little strength we had. She managed our food ruthlessly, refusing to allow us even an extra bite beyond the rations she had allocated to us. Sadly, we had to guard all our food and our possessions from others who were far less fortunate and totally desperate.

One day faded into another. We were still in the mud, still in the rain which seemed as if it would never stop. Each day, more people arrived, crowding into the already impossibly crowded space. Each day, more people died from starvation or exposure or illness or simply loss of will. The guards threw their bodies on to a large pile. Every couple of days, they'd make some of us bury them in huge pits; then they would sprinkle the bodies with lime so that they would disintegrate. Each day, I would ask myself: how much longer can this horror go on?

We could still hear the thunder of the daily bombings and I found myself praying that the bombs would hit the brick factory. At least that would be a release of sorts. I had never been so filthy in all my life. There was virtually no water to wash with, and what good would washing do when we were living in mud? Had it not been for the meagre protection of the wool blanket my mother had brought along, we would have been wallowing in the mud like pigs on a farm. As young girls, my sister, Violet, Amy and I rebelled at what we had been reduced to. We had all been pretty girls and had taken great pride in our appearance. Now we had mud on our faces, mud caking our hands and embedded under our fingernails. Our hair hung limp and stringy, and our clothes had become a filthy, sodden mass of torn, dirty fabric.

The only food dispensed by the guards was a thin 'soup' stirred by some of the inmates. We got two small bowls a day and sometimes a crust of stale bread. It was perhaps 300 calories a day, not enough to live on for long, which is why so many people were dying.

Fortunately, I had set myself a daily mission that kept me from total despair. From the first day we were there, I pushed my way through the crowd of what grew to be about 5,000 people, searching for Richie. I didn't find him. I would ask anyone I could find, especially young men and women, 'Are you from the Eighth District?'

But no one was, and no one had seen Richie.

The days were not only miserable; they were monot-onous and boring. There was nothing to do. Sometimes we would try to play jacks, using stones for jacks. My mother tried to keep us clean, and tried to wash our underwear, but there was nowhere to hang things to dry. Besides, if we left our possessions for even a minute, our things would be stolen. Some people had been arrested on the streets, and were brought to the brick factory with nothing. Those people were desperate and every-body's things were fair game. We were all Jews together and you could say we should have all helped each other, but in situations so desperate many people think only of themselves. My mother was strong enough to show us how to survive, although she also showed us how to be kind when we could. We held the hands of many who were sick and dying and prayed for their souls, which I believed then that God had forgotten.

As the days turned into a week and then two weeks and we were still stuck there, living in our own filth in that godforsaken brick factory, I think even my mother knew we would not be going back to our old apartment. With each day that passed, I felt more and more of a sense of doom. I felt I would never see Budapest again, would never have my life back again and, most impor-tantly, I would not have my Richie. I could not share with anyone, even my mother, how strong my feelings were for him. She knew we were serious, but she had always told me I should date more boys before making such a serious life decision. I was still not yet sixteen. She might have relied on me as she would an adult because she had no other option, but in many ways she still saw me as a child. And in many ways I suppose I was, although most of my childhood had vanished at the start of the war and

I felt the rest had left with the Occupation. My mother's dreams for me were different from mine. She saw me finishing secondary school and even attending university once the war was over. But all I wanted was to be Richie's wife.

Sitting in the mud, I had to laugh. Neither of our dreams for my future were likely now. We could easily die in this brick factory, as so many were doing every day. The Germans were frantic now, pushed back on both fronts by the Allies, with equipment in short supply and a central government that was descending into chaos around its evil, crazy leader. The easiest solution to the Hungarian Jewish 'problem' would be for us to die here and now.

Some days, I was ready to do just that. But still my mother wouldn't let us. Every day, she got up and she moved and she pushed us and told us we had to survive. We had to show them, she said, that no matter what they did to us, we could take it.

'They cannot break us unless we let them,' she told us over and over again as we sat clutching our stomachs, which were always growling now, starved of enough food to sustain us. By the second week, we no longer had any of our own provisions. We were totally at the mercy of the thin slop that passed for soup and the stale bread that didn't even appear on most days.

Every night, Violet and Amy would cry silently for their parents and their brother, wondering what had become of them, wondering if they would ever see them again. And I would cry for Richie, who was my every-thing, and for my father, who had disappeared, and for my family, which was fading away before my eyes. But even through my tears, I would hear my mother's voice singing her lullaby, trying to tell us, day after day, that everything would be all right; that she would stay strong and God would protect us. My head no longer believed her, but my heart refused to give up. I would fall asleep on that blanket which was our last vestige of home, comforted by the sound of my mother's voice.

The days faded into each other, but my mother told us it was important to keep track of what day it was. We were into our third week in the brick factory and October had given way to November. Beyond those high gates, as incongruous as it seemed, life continued on the Vienna Road. The leaves fell off the trees, leaving the limbs bare, cars and trucks passed by, and the good citizens of Hungary went about their business, somehow managing to ignore the torture of their fellow Hungarians, clearly visible through the wrought-iron fence.

Sometimes, at night, I would dream of being rescued. Mostly it was Richie, with some of his friends from the Underground, who rescued us, killing all the dreaded guards and breaking down the gate to set us free so that we could run into the surrounding countryside or hide somewhere in Budapest. Other times, it was my father, somehow dressed in his old Czech army uniform, who would appear leading a band of his old 'friends'. He would smile at me and say, 'Did you doubt that I would come back to take care of all of you?' And I would hug him fiercely until my sister, who so adored him, pushed me away so that he could take her up in his arms. I could see my mother's face, her eyes shining with tears as she looked at him, their hands touching with such love and longing. And then my father would laugh and lift Larry high on his shoulders and say, 'Follow me. I have a plan.'

But, of course, nothing like that happened. No one came to rescue us. No one even tried. If we were going to survive this, it was clear we would have to help ourselves. At least, that's what I believed. My mother thought it was all in God's hands, and I must say, looking back, even now, that that belief gave her a certain serenity and strength, enough to share with all of us, no matter how much we lost hope.

Every day, as I still desperately searched for Richie or at least some word of him, I listened for the sound of approaching tanks. Surely, the Allies must be close to winning. By that third week, even the prospect of being liberated by the dreaded Russians was beginning to seem better than staying here to die in the mud like animals. But no tanks came. The bombing continued, but it was not near enough to either help us or obliterate us.

The only things that changed were our physical condition and the weather. Both deteriorated. We were all weaker than we had ever been, our bodies so thin that every vertebra in our backs was clearly visible through the thin layer of skin and fat that remained. Our eyes looked sunken, and the filth had set in with such a vengeance that it was hard for us to tolerate ourselves. To our undying shame, we, who had been so scrupulously clean and meticulously groomed, now had lice, and we could do nothing about it but scratch miserably like the poor wretches our tormentors wanted us to become.

How could life get any worse, I wondered one morning during the third week of our captivity. I knew as soon as my brain formed the question that I should not ask it, even silently, lest the gods show me just how bad things could get. But, as if my question had conjured it, a new trial began that very morning, by dawn's early light, and it was one that would decimate our group of 5,000.

chapter *Twelve*

'Get up, get up, we're moving out,' the guards shouted, using megaphones along the perimeter of the crowd. We were barely awake in the cold November dawn. There had been frost overnight and the mud had frozen into a hard, solid mass. I felt my stomach clutch. Where were they taking us now, and how? There were no trucks, there was no train station. Then I realized, as my mother gathered up the last of our possessions and gently shoved me forward towards the heavy iron gate, that wherever we were going, we would have to march there.

My legs were stiff from sitting and sleeping on the ground, but I moved along after my mother, who was already carrying my brother, our heavy woollen blanket slung over her shoulder. Rose held on to my hand for dear life and Violet held on to her hand, her older sister Amy holding on to her. I still could not understand how my short, thin mother could physically carry such a burden as my brother and that heavy blanket. She was barely five feet tall, but when she walked, with her back straight, she had the bearing of a queen – a tall queen. That's how she looked that awful day in the dull grey rain and sleet.

As usual, we had no choice but to walk briskly behind her. In this, my mother turned out to be right, as she had been about so much else. The very old, the very young, the sick, the dying – all those who could not rise and follow – were shot dead where they sat in that foul mud in the abandoned brickyard, their blood staining the terracotta mess a deeper shade of red. The soldiers shot them with complete indifference – fewer Jews for them to worry about, wherever they were taking us. I stumbled as I heard the machine-gun bursts, but my mother gripped my hand tighter, pulling me along. 'We can do nothing,' she whispered fiercely, her lips barely moving, her eyes looking straight ahead. 'All we can do is stay alive ourselves.'

I straightened my shoulders as tears streamed down my cheeks. Someone should cry for those poor souls whose only sin had been to be born Jewish. I cried for them but I kept moving.

When we were all assembled on the Vienna Road, it was like a mighty sea of suffering humanity. We were somewhere in the middle of the line of march and we could see neither the beginning nor the end of the line – that's how vast it was, 5,000 people being herded like a bunch of cattle, and not very valuable cattle, at that. We were in the middle of the line by design. My mother had determined that the best place to go unnoticed and therefore, she hoped, unpunished, was in the centre of this huge group.

There was major confusion as the guards shouted for

everyone to form rows that spanned the entire two-lane road. People were pushing and shoving, women were crying, babies were screaming. It was a scene from hell.

I tried to look calm, but inside I was terrified. I realized that once we were on the road to Vienna we would never come back to Budapest again, at least not until the war ended, whenever that might be, and maybe not even then. This time, my insides were a mass of anxiety. Every feeling within me told me this was to be our end, this crazy march across Hungary in wintertime. I didn't tell my mother what I was feeling – I didn't dare, for she would have chastised me for sounding as if I was giving up. I couldn't tell my sister because she would surely tell my mother, and Larry, at ten, was too young to have such ominous information.

So I told Violet all my fears as we waited there in the rain. She looked as frightened and as desperate as I felt, but she grasped my hand and said, 'We will just have to make the best of it, Baby.'

That first day was worse than anything I could have imagined. They made us march thirty-two kilometres in driving rain and sleet, with only a small bowl of soup in our bellies. On the way, people would sit down to rest, only to find they couldn't get up later. The soldiers simply shot them where they sat, leaving their bodies there like animals killed by traffic.

There was a young woman who was heavily pregnant. She walked for about four hours and then I noticed she was doubled up in pain. I wasn't that much of a child. In our cramped quarters during the Occupation I had seen more than one woman give birth. I could tell that this woman was about to do so. Surely these soldiers – these fellow Hungarians – would let her stop to have the baby? But no one even seemed to notice her pain, and a tight squeeze of my hand by my mother let me know that I was not to say anything. 'Bring no attention to yourself or to our family, Baby,' she whispered. I knew she was right. I hated it, but I said nothing.

A mile or so later, the young woman collapsed on the road, her body writhing from the force of the birth contractions. The baby almost delivered itself, a small miracle in the midst of so much despair. But just as I felt a bit of joy, the air was shattered by a blast of machine-gun fire and I saw the mother and the baby torn apart by a hail of bullets. For a moment, I just stared at the horror of it. Then I felt as if I was going to throw up and actually started heaving – not that there was anything there to come up. My mother pulled on my hand, but I could feel her hand shaking against mine and when I looked up, I saw tears streaming down her face and her lips moving silently in prayer. I felt no desire to join her in that. Apparently, I thought bitterly, God had once again forgotten His Chosen People.

The Vienna Road is the main road across Hungary into Austria. Houses, farms, shops, factories, businesses, even vineyards line its route, depending on what town or city you pass through. All that day, our raggle-taggle, stumbling, sick and dying, dirty band marched down that road, while all along both sides the shopkeepers, tradesmen, farmers and villagers watched us go by. I could see horror and pity on the faces of some, but I also heard jeering from others. The rest looked totally blank, as if they thought that if they registered no emotion, they would feel nothing for our suffering. For us, it was the final punishment and humiliation – to have our own countrymen and women literally stand idly by as we were driven from our country, starving, beaten, terrified, but obviously never to be helped because we were dirty rotten Jews.

By the end of that first endless, icy day, every bone in my body hurt. The soldiers said that we could have a fire if we could find the wood. My mother urged my sister and me and Violet and Amy forward. 'Find some wood — we need the warmth of a fire.'

Barely able to take another step, we looked along the side of the road where there was a row of trees, looking for any fallen branches or pieces we could use. The cold wood hurt our already aching hands, but we managed to find enough to ensure a fire for at least a little while, certainly long enough for our daily bowl of soup to heat. The thin gruel was only one more punishment in a day that had been filled with them.

I couldn't sleep that night. It was too cold and too wet, and I was too tired even to be able to relax enough to drift off. Violet felt the same way, restless, as if we could not afford to sleep. So we talked softly to one another.

'Why are they doing this to us, Baby?' she asked me. 'We didn't hurt anyone, we didn't do anything wrong. And all those things the Germans blame on the Jews, they're not true.'

I nodded. 'I know, Violet. Life could have been kinder to us. We certainly don't deserve this, for our lives to end here on this awful march.'

We had taken great care to speak quietly so as not to wake the others, but my mother, with her uncanny sense of what was needed, had heard everything we'd said.

'Please don't try to settle the problems of the world, Baby,' she said calmly. 'Come over here where I can cover you and keep you warm and sleep, my child.'

Without a word, I scooted over and Violet came with me, tucked under the same small blanket. We hugged each other. 'Maybe tomorrow will be a nicer day. Maybe they will even let us go home,' I said, knowing I was dreaming, that this would never happen, but needing to say it anyway, needing to have hope, even if it came to nothing.

Violet gave me her beautiful smile and closed her eyes. We fell asleep in each other's arms, my friend and I, safe at least for a few more hours.

The next morning, they woke us while it was still dark.

'Line up for breakfast. We begin marching again in twenty minutes,' the guards bellowed.

I got up slowly, my bones still so sore I could barely move.

'Stretch your body, Baby, everyone, like this,' my mother said, demonstrating a stretch upwards and then downwards and from side to side. 'It will make you feel at least a little better.'

My mother was a marvel. How could this woman, at forty, have more energy than we did as teenagers? How could she have such strength of will in the face of so much going wrong? She had lost my father, she had not heard from her family in Zeteny for months and must have feared the worst for them, and now the rest of us were being marched across Hungary, yet here she was telling us matter-of-factly to do stretching exercises.

We did as she told us, and she was right. We did feel a little bit less stiff. Looking around, I realized that we must feel a lot better than many other marchers who couldn't seem to stand up at all. I saw pain flash across my mother's face as she watched them. She helped one old man standing close beside us, lifting him up by putting her hands under his shoulders and pulling with all her might. He staggered upright. 'You can do it,' my mother told him softly. He smiled at her and nodded. 'Thank you,' he said simply.

I helped an old woman on the other side of me. She was swaying on her feet, but she was up and, as I moved away from her, she blew me a kiss.

When we'd lined up, they gave us soup with some kind of turnips in it, and a piece of bread. My mother took charge of the bread so that we wouldn't eat it all at once. That way, we would have something to eat later when we became hungry.

'My mother is holding our bread for us so we don't eat it all at once,' I said to Violet. 'Do you want her to hold yours too?'

Violet tossed her head. 'I can hold my own bread, but your mother's right. I'll make sure not to eat it all at once.'

I looked at Violet and smiled. I knew her so well, and I knew without a doubt that if she had the bread she'd eat it all right away. She had had a lifetime of getting whatever she wanted or needed, and she still had no patience for waiting, but all I said was, 'Are you sure you'll be able to do it?'

I saw how angry that made her. 'You think you know everything, Baby. Why do you assume I will just go ahead and eat it all?'

I tried again, aiming for my mother's calmness and reason. 'It's not a sin to want to eat all your bread, but you need to think about how it will feel later when you're hungry and you have no more bread left to eat.'

Violet just gave me that smile of hers and grabbed her piece of bread. I noticed that she ate the whole thing, then looked around at me guiltily, wondering if I'd seen. I pretended to look away. I didn't need any more fights, and I knew that she and Amy were edgy and anxious because in the midst of all this they were without their parents, who had always taken such good care of them. I knew how awful it would feel to be without my mother's guidance. And they had no way of knowing whether their parents were still safely in the ghetto or whether they'd been taken somewhere else. When I did look over at her, I smiled and offered her my hand.

We linked arms and walked together, talking along the way, trying to pretend we were normal teenagers. At least today it wasn't raining. On the other hand, the temperature was so cold that if something did begin to fall, it would probably be snow. Looking up, I saw that the sky was darkening, and there wasn't a hint of the sun. Sighing, I forced myself to move at the strenuous pace the soldiers had set — a pace so fast that they took rest breaks, riding in a truck that travelled alongside us, while their compatriots took a shift of walking. But there was no riding for the rest of us.

We walked and we talked about boys. I told Violet how much I missed Richie and she told me how much she missed the married, older dentist she had been seeing. Her sister's boyfriend was high up in the Jewish Underground and I knew Amy kept hoping that somehow they would rescue us.

'I just can't believe this is happening to us,' Amy said. I could see she was beginning to limp and that her shoes were falling apart, as mine were.

All around us, people were crying and saying they couldn't walk any more. We urged them to keep walking.

'It will be easier tomorrow,' I said, knowing that I was lying but hoping that the lie would help them go on at least for another day. Some of them drew on whatever reserves of strength they had left and kept walking. But others just couldn't, so they sat down. They were shot where they sat.

In the meantime, Violet gave me something else to

worry about. As she walked along, she flirted with the men at the side of the road as if she was on her way to a picnic.

'Don't do that, Violet. Someone will notice and you'll get into trouble.'

But she shrugged off my comments.

I tried again, a while later, when I saw her wink and smile at yet another young man at the side of the road. 'Just let it be, Violet.'

She turned on me. 'You're just jealous because they're all looking at me.'

I was stunned. 'You know I love Richie. What need would I have to flirt with other boys, especially boys who do nothing when they see us suffering?'

But Violet just tossed her head and continued to smile at anyone she thought was attractive. I tried to be understanding, because I knew she felt that perhaps one of these men would rescue her. I thought it was a foolish notion, but if the fantasy helped her cope with the march, who was I to tell her not to? Besides, I didn't have the energy to fight and walk.

On the second day there were several pregnant women in our group and one guard took pity on them and let them ride in a small cart for a few miles. I could see the relief on their faces at the thought that now, at least, they wouldn't have to walk. But their respite didn't last long. Another guard, surveying the line of marchers, demanded to know why those dirty rotten Jews were riding instead of walking.

The guard who had helped them mumbled, 'They're pregnant and can't walk so far.'

'Is that so?' the guard asked, smiling nastily. 'Stop that cart and get them out,' he ordered the soldier who had helped them.

'Don't worry, ladies, you will have no more problems,' he said as he lined them up on the side of the road. Then he opened fire with his machine gun and shot them. My mother stumbled when that happened, but she caught herself and caught my brother to keep him from falling, and we walked on, as if nothing had happened. And once again, from the side of the road, people watched us and did nothing. Of course, what could they do? Still, we noticed a couple of marchers slip through the line of people watching us and escape into the countryside. If their luck held, people in the line were silent and they would get away. Sometimes, though, a fellow marcher or someone on the side of the road would shout to the guards and the person would be shot.

Oh, how I longed to run away. But I couldn't leave my mother and my sister and my brother. So I walked.

On that second day, they began to give us rest breaks.

'Don't sit down,' my mother warned, 'you may not be able to get up.' Instead, she had us all do stretching movements with our legs.

Even wet and dirty, Violet was still a strikingly beautiful young woman, so it wasn't surprising that one of the young guards in a Hungarian Nazi uniform with the Arrow Cross band on his arm started eyeing her up.

I'd noticed him looking at her a couple of times on the first day of the march, but decided to say nothing. But on the second day it was even more obvious.

'That boy is looking at you,' I whispered to her as we walked along.

'So what?' she said. 'He wouldn't dare talk to me. Don't you recognize him? He's that awful Istvan Menosz who followed us home from school that day a few months ago, when we could still go to school.'

Then I remembered. He was a tough guy from a poor

neighbourhood, in a social class way below Violet's. But that had been in a saner world than the one we inhabited now. 'Stay away from him. He's trouble.'

Violet just nodded, but that night she told me he had come over to her on one of the rest breaks and talked to her.

'What could he possibly have to say to you?'

She smiled, as if she was planning something, but I couldn't imagine what. 'Oh, nothing special,' she answered. 'But he did say never sit down on a rest break – death awaits you if you do. So please promise me, Baby, that no matter how tired you get, you won't sit down.'

'I promise, but I want you to promise to stay away from that Nazi.'

But she didn't answer, and I began to worry. I knew how stubborn Violet was and it occurred to me that she thought she could get some special treatment by being friendly to this guy. But I knew his type. He was no Jew's friend, no matter what he said to Violet. Quietly, I went over and talked to her sister Amy, asking her to talk to Violet.

Amy came up to me at a break the next day, shaking her head. 'My sister just won't listen to me,' she said, pushing her soaked hair off her face, her teeth chattering from the ice-cold rain and wind. The weather was so miserable that it was very difficult to walk. When we reached a town in mid-afternoon, they settled us in for the night in a big open space – what could have been, in normal times, the town marketplace. They served some soup, which looked and tasted more like slop for pigs than food for humans, but we were so hungry we pushed each other in a queue to get to it.

'What did Violet say to you?' I asked her, as I handed over my tin bowl to be filled.

'She has some crazy plan that if she sleeps with him –
which is what he wants, by the way – he will let us go,
let us just slip through the crowd at the side of the road
and disappear.'

I stopped eating, the spoon midway to my mouth.
'That's crazy. Why would she trust him or believe him?'

Amy sighed. 'I told her all that, but she's desperate to
get away. She says she'll die if she has to march much
longer.'

'She'll die if she trusts that Istvan,' I said firmly.

Amy sighed again. 'You know how Violet is when she's
made up her mind.'

I finished my soup and then walked over to my
mother, telling her what Amy had just told me. I could
see fear and concern in my mother's eyes.

'She mustn't do that.'

'I know, Mama, but she won't listen to me or to Amy.
Maybe she'll listen to you.'

My mother nodded and walked over to where Violet
and Amy were eating their soup. I could see her talking
calmly, earnestly, to Violet and I could see Violet shaking
her head. Ten minutes later, my mother walked back to
me. 'She just won't listen. She thinks this man will do
anything for her and she is willing to do anything to gain
her freedom. I told her that he is an evil man and that
she will regret this for ever, but she will not listen to
me.'

I tried one more time, but Violet just hugged me and
told me not to worry so much. 'You'll see, it will work
out for me,' she said.

Later, when it was time for bed, my mother gathered
us around her, but this time Violet and Amy settled at a
distance away from us instead of drawing close. My
mother shook her head as she told us to lie down on the

big woollen blanket with which she also covered us, singing us her favourite lullaby.

The next day it was raining so hard that it was difficult even to start walking. We had what passed for breakfast, a piece of bread and something that was called coffee but tasted like black water. My shoes had shredded into nothing and I was desperately trying to keep what was left of them on my feet by tying pieces of string around them to hold them in place. My feet felt so bruised from walking virtually barefoot on the pavement.

My legs were tired and sore, but I could not allow my mother to see how much it cost me to go on. I thought of a rhythm and walked to it, as if I was back in the marching corps that Richie and I had belonged to in a time that now seemed so long ago. In my mind, I could not imagine a more cruel way of treating Jews than this, but I was to find out later that this was merely the beginning of the horrors.

We were not dressed for this kind of cold weather. As I marched along, freezing, every bone hurting, I thought about the holidays which were coming soon, and about our Chanukkah celebrations before the Germans came. The candles for Chanukkah, the Jewish festival of lights, would be lit in the living room and there would be a bright, merry fire in the fireplace. Each of us would get a gift, my mother would lead us in Chanukkah songs and we would play with the dreidel, a little spinning top. How well I remembered our fireplace, a large green ceramic Dutch stove that normally we lit only when there was no heat in the apartment. How I wished I could be back in that apartment now, or better still, in the tiny boathouse with Richie, where he could hold me tightly and keep me safe. If only I could go back to those care-free days on the Danube, when Richie and I were free and there was only our love for each other to think about.

I could feel a lump forming in my throat as I realized that those days were gone for ever. In their place was this horrible march with the rest of these unfortunate Jews. I had the additional agony of watching my poor, dedicated mother carry my little brother — and I still can't imagine where she got the strength to do this. I held on to my sister's hand, just as I used to on those long-ago Saturdays when we'd go for a walk as a family, but this walk is not like those walks at all. We had no idea what was waiting for us at the end of this walk. There was no news, there was no one who had a radio, and we dared not ask the villagers on the side of the road what they knew of the war's progress.

I hoped some of the Hungarians watching our march would do something to help us — give us some food or offer us some water. But they did nothing, said nothing. They merely watched as the Jewish population was exterminated, silent as the softly falling snow that had now begun to cover us in a blanket.

Several days passed, days of twelve-hour walks and short nights of sleep in miserable weather. We were losing people every day. Some died on the road from illness or exhaustion. Others were shot by the guards because they couldn't get up or they couldn't walk quickly enough. There were families like ours with mothers who simply couldn't walk any more. Children had to leave their mother behind or be shot themselves. It was very sad to see children leave their mothers behind. On the other hand, being with a family was in some ways a liability, because you could only be as fast and as strong as your weakest link. Fortunately for our family, my mother continued to walk and to carry my brother. So far, none of us had been left behind.

Violet continued to flirt, especially with Istvan. When I talked to her about it, she threatened to walk ahead of us so that she wouldn't have to listen to me any longer. I remember thinking that the march had got to her in some way; it had changed her, making her more reckless and defiant. She was not the same Violet I had known. She had never been as abrupt with me before, but I blamed it on her being separated from her parents and being worried about them on top of everything else. She would be all right once the march was over.

chapter Thirteen

The days were colder now, but even snow had not slowed down the march. We were always cold, so cold that we thought we would never be warm again. The cold was a deadly presence on the march, enveloping us as we slept on the frozen ground, biting at us as we walked through snow and fog, chilling our bones, making us ache as if the frigid hand of death was upon us, as indeed it was, for some of us.

As we walked, I saw everyone around me becoming piteously thin, losing the will to live. But not my mother. She had her faith, and because she believed in God, everything was acceptable. We were going through this for a reason, she said; God has a reason. She always went back to God. Whenever we were in some kind of trouble she always said that God would help us. I could not argue with my mother because she believed and I did not. I had not had the same Chasidic upbringing that my grandfather had given her, in which she had been taught to see

God's will, terrible as it might be, as some kind of lesson.

But even her God couldn't protect Violet from her own folly. Day by day, we watched as she encouraged Istvan, who clearly lusted after her.

'Don't do this,' my mother pleaded with her. 'He wouldn't be in the Nazi party if he were the kind of guy to let a Jewish girl go. He's just looking for the satisfaction of the moment.'

Violet would smile and nod at my mother, but the next day she would be flirting with him again, talking to him.

'I know he will let me and Amy go if I sleep with him,' she told me one morning as we tried to stretch our legs in a biting wind. 'Once we slip through the line of people along the road, I am sure we will be able to persuade someone to hide us, perhaps find the Underground or even the Allies – who knows? Anything is better than this, being led to slaughter and doing nothing.'

I felt tears in my eyes. 'But what if you give yourself to him and he doesn't let you go?' I asked. 'You would have to live with that all your life.'

Violet just tossed her head. 'At least I would still be alive and I would have tried to save myself and my sister.'

Later that day, as we ate our poor excuse for soup, we saw Istvan approach Violet and tell her he'd be back for her later.

My mother tried to dissuade her one last time. 'Don't do this, Violet. Think about what your parents would say and don't do it.'

Violet looked my mother right in the eye. 'My parents would want me to survive,' she said.

It was already dark and my mother spread the blanket for us and sang us to sleep with her favourite lullaby. I closed my eyes, but sleep would not come, because I was so worried about Violet. After a while, I heard a slight sound, and opening my eyes, saw Istvan leading Violet away down the road, into the trees. I shuddered at the thought of what would happen.

The next morning, they woke us before dawn, as they always did. As we were stretching our frozen muscles, I saw Violet slip back into the camp. I went up to her, but she refused to meet my eyes.

'Are you all right?' I asked.

'Why wouldn't I be?' she answered, her voice sharp, but close up I could see that her lower lip was bruised and she was shaking slightly.

'Was it that awful?' I asked her quietly.

She nodded, still not able to face me. 'It was brutal,' she said, her voice sounding as if it would break. Then she drew herself up. 'But now it's over and he has promised he will let us go today.'

The march began and I could see Violet watching for Istvan and for the signal he was supposed to give her to run for it. But we never saw him the entire day, and I could see anger and disappointment etched in Violet's face. She had sacrificed herself, her virginity, to a man who wasn't fit to lick her shoes, and now he had disappeared. That night, as we talked before falling asleep, I could tell she was distraught.

'Just stay away from him now,' I said, hugging her close. 'As for the rest, what's done is done.'

The next day, we marched at dawn again, another cold, bleak day of hell. About midday, I saw Istvan coming down the line. Violet tried wildly to get his attention, the attention he had so freely given her for days before they'd slept together, but he pretended he didn't hear her. I saw rage erupt on Violet's face. No man had ever used her and moved on.

'When are you going to let us go?' she asked him loudly.

'Shut up, you dirty Jew, and get back into line,' he yelled.

Violet was screaming now. 'You promised to let me go if I slept with you. You promised,' she yelled, running at him and pummelling him with her fists.

Istvan reared back and raised his gun as Violet jumped towards him again. He shot her at point-blank range as her sister, screaming, ran to shelter her, to comfort her. Istvan shot Amy too, leaving them both dead, lying in their own blood on the side of the road. And we had to watch, unable to do anything. I tried to move forward but my mother held my hand in a deathly grip and hissed, 'Don't. You cannot help her now. We must keep walking.'

That was the most horrible moment of the march for me, watching my best friend die like an animal, left in a drainage ditch at the side of the Vienna Road.

I looked back after a while and could see nothing but hundreds of tired, dragging feet walking in the road where my friend was shot. Nobody had said a word – there was no more fight for life left in any of us, including me – and that hurt more than anything.

Late that night, as I lay weeping on the blanket, my mother tried to comfort me.

'We will find him after the war and we will bring him to justice, Baby, you will see. God will help us.'

But there was no God for me that night. I could not believe in a deity who had taken two such beautiful young beings as Violet and Amy and allowed them to be killed by the scum of the earth.

After ten days of walking, we were moving like zombies. The only thing that kept us going was the knowledge that if we didn't keep walking, we would freeze to death. Perhaps wherever we were going, there was shelter. At least, that's what we hoped for, because now winter itself was our enemy and we knew we could not survive it living out in the open. It was a walk without end, it seemed, without let-up, and every day we lost more people.

We lost our friend Mrs Cohen and some of our neighbours one day when they decided they could not walk any more. They just went to sleep in the ditches and were shot there as they slept. Just to make sure all those who had stopped in the ditches were dead, a second group of soldiers followed the first and shot them all over again. And still we watched and said nothing and marched on.

Each night my mother, who must have been exhausted and heartbroken herself, would try to comfort us. She would tell us fairy tales which she made up. All of them ended happily ever after, so different from our reality. She still sang quietly to us at night and she still made us say our prayers. I didn't feel like praying but, after so many years of practice, the prayers just came to me automatically. My mother demanded that each of us say them loudly enough so that she could hear them.

Because we ate and drank so little, we needed to relieve ourselves less and less, which should have made us feel better, in an odd sense, since we had felt so shamed and humiliated to have to relieve ourselves at the side of the road with no privacy. But by this time, we had no more shame, no more energy for humiliation. We no longer even cared what the Germans were going to do to us next. We were just existing without any emotions. We were the walking dead who somehow managed to continue putting one foot in front of the other.

We were the last Jewish transport out of Hungary and Adolf Eichmann himself was in charge of it. He came by many times in his car, watching as we marched along in misery. We all knew what he looked like because we had seen him often in the streets of Budapest and especially in the ghettoes, where he had sent so many Jews to their deaths over the past eight months.

The Nazis were being pushed back in the west and the Russians were pushing them back in the east, but here, as we walked across Hungary, the German Reich still ruled. So we marched.

At one point, a Swiss truck came by and members of the International Red Cross asked for people who had Swiss papers of protection to stand aside. We still had our Swiss papers, so my mother said, 'We have them. We have them.' I remember asking her, 'What do you think is going to happen now?' And she answered, 'I don't know, but I'm sure it's going to be better.'

As the Red Cross truck drove down the line, the Hungarian soldiers followed after it, gathering our Swiss papers as they went, pulling them out of people's hands. Then they destroyed them in front of us. By the time the Swiss truck with the Red Cross volunteers came back, no one had protection papers any more, so the Red Cross couldn't protect us. That was a terrible day for us. If we had been allowed to keep those papers, the Swiss would have been able to take us somewhere safe for the rest of the war, probably back to the Swiss house in Budapest. But that was all lost now.

That night, we cried, my sister, my brother and I. But not my mother. Instead she sang to us softly in Yiddish, her favourite lullaby: '*Shluss meine faigle. Mach der zi dein eigeleh. Shluss mein taeir ziss kind.*' The familiar words washed over us: 'Please my little bird, close your eyes. Sleep my little bird, sleep, my darling precious child.' And after a while, we slept.

My sister and brother and I cried a lot during the march, but my mother rarely did, at least not when we could see her. When I did catch her crying, she would always make excuses for why she was sad, saying that her feet hurt or her bones ached. She would never say that she was crying for us, for our desperate situation.

I didn't understand then what she was going through, watching us suffer on the march. But years later, when my grandson Derek was dying from a brain tumour, when I cried over him and prayed for God to take him so he wouldn't suffer any more, I realized how my mother must have felt as she watched other children dying all around her, wondering if hers would be next, unable to do anything to stop it.

We had been walking for about three weeks now. It was hard to say exactly how long because we had lost all sense of what day it was or what the date was. We were still in the middle of the line, but so many had died or been killed along the way that now we could see the front and the back of the line. We were filthy, and so riddled with lice that not even daily combing of our hair could begin to make a dent in the problem. Worse, I had finally lost my shoes. The soles went first, then they fell apart totally, the material just disintegrated. I bundled my feet in some rags I was able to gather from litter bins in the towns we passed through and tried to walk like that. By the end of the first day of walking that way, my feet were rubbed raw, with ugly scabs forming on them, and I was afraid that they would become infected and that then I would no longer be able to walk at all.

My mother tried to bundle my feet by tearing up an undershirt and wrapping it carefully around them. But nothing helped. On the days when it didn't rain or snow,

I simply walked barefoot. Because the days were cold, my bare feet froze and infection set in.

One day soon after this, when I was in constant agony with my feet, I saw a woman's body lying on the ground. All I saw was her shoes. She was already dead, I thought, and didn't need her shoes any more, and I wanted to take her shoes and wear them. But I couldn't stop long enough to get the shoes off her frozen, stiff feet, so I had to leave them there and continue to suffer the agony. The bottoms of my feet were on fire. I had no padding left on the soles of my feet and who knew how much longer we would have to walk? Inside, I knew I wouldn't be able to walk much longer.

By the next day, I had a cold and was running a fever, but I didn't tell my mother. I didn't want her to worry. I should have known better. My mother could see how sick I was. She made me take the last of the aspirin she had with her and forced me to drink the horrible soup they fed us, to keep up my strength, she said. That night, I tossed and turned, with feverish nightmares, sweating so much that my clothes were soaked by morning. My mother was so worried about me that she gave me her morning coffee, fearing that the fever would totally dehydrate me.

That night, I felt so much worse that I wanted to die. I closed my eyes and wished that God would take me, because I couldn't go on any longer. But my mother held my head in her lap and stroked my hair and whispered prayers for me not to die. I guess my mother's prayers worked, because by the next morning I had no fever and felt well enough to go on.

A couple of days after that, we came to the Austrian border, where the Germans packed us on to a train in cattle trucks with eighty to a hundred people jammed into each car. We were shoved together like sardines with no room and no air to breathe, but luckily the trip was not a long one. When the train stopped, we peered out of a tiny hole in the side of one of the doors. We thought we were in fairyland — that's how beautiful the countryside was. We looked up and saw the name Gunzkirchen on a gate on the other side of the railway siding, but thought nothing of it. We still did not know about concentration camps, or that Gunzkirchen was one of them. All we could see were the mountains and rolling hills of the countryside just outside Linz, a picture-postcard landscape covered in pure white snow, and some healthy and prosperous-looking Austrians peering at the train, walking around it, and looking at the cattle trucks that carried the remains of the Hungarian Jews.

They kept us in those trucks for a day and a half. During that time, some people died, but that didn't make the Germans let out the rest of us. They merely shouted to us to throw the dead bodies out of the doors and carted them away like garbage.

It was early evening of the second day before we arrived at the gates of Gunzkirchen. We were made to stand there long enough to feel frozen to the spot before we were roughly ordered to move quickly into the barracks that lined both sides of the open yard. All I could think of was that at least we had a roof over our heads and we wouldn't be so cold. It was now mid-December and full winter had come to Middle Europe.

They told us to find an empty bed and claim it. We were able to get beds next to each other before they locked us into the barracks for the night. It was dark and we were hungry. We had not eaten anything for three days, so we were beyond hungry: we were starving. But we slept that night. It was the first time we had done so in a covered area, like human beings, since we had been taken from our homes almost two months before.

The next day, they woke us up at five o'clock in the morning and made us stand outside. Sick, starving and exhausted, we stood there shivering as they yelled at us, 'Who is a cook? Who is an electrician? Who wants to be an orderly in a hospital?'

It was clear that the Germans were putting as many of us pitiful specimens to work as they could. No one in my family volunteered. I was too weak, my sister was too frail and my brother was too young. My mother didn't want to leave us to go and cook for others. Luckily, plenty of others volunteered in our place. Gunzkirchen was a death camp, but at least there was a roof over our heads.

I was still feverish, and I was allowed to stay in bed after going to the camp doctor and being given some quinine. I still prayed for death, but every time I told myself I couldn't take it any more, I would think of Richie and how much he loved me, and how I would let him down if I gave up. So I didn't give up.

I don't know how long we had been there – it must have been a few days – before the Nazis made us get out of the barracks. Once again, they led us out of the camp like cattle, hoping that some or most of us would die on the way to wherever we were going now.

We walked to Mauthausen, a quaint little town with winding tree-lined streets, guest houses and restaurants, and pretty, neat little homes. It was a perfectly normal, charming town. Although it looked as if it had been bombed a couple of times, there wasn't the kind of major damage there had been in Budapest. The town looked virtually untouched by the war.

But Mauthausen was hiding an ugly secret. Out of the

town and high up at the top of a winding mountain, there was Mauthausen the concentration camp, a place where Jews and gypsies, dissident Austrians, rebellious Poles and Hungarians, and other 'enemies' of the Reich, were sent to suffer and die. But at the time I knew nothing about it, except that it was our destination after yet another impossible walk.

I'll never forget the seemingly endless trek up that steep, winding hill, my painfully thin mother holding Larry in her arms, looking as if, at any moment, she would have to stop walking because she just couldn't go any further. I was terrified for her and for us. I had never seen her so weak, so frail and so defeated. But then all of us were in terrible shape, the walking dead, freezing in the cold December wind.

Somehow, we made it to the top of the hill, and there was nothing beautiful about what we saw — but then there is never anything beautiful about human suffering. Mauthausen was a place devoted to it.

chapter Fourteen

The first thing we saw as we neared the top of the hill was a stone quarry, where men were bent double from the weight of heavy stones they were carrying up a steep flight of steps. It looked as if there were about two hundred stone steps set into one side of the quarry wall. Guards with vicious Alsatian dogs patrolled the quarry, shouting at the men, and threatening them when they faltered.

It had been cold down in the valley at Gunzkirchen, but here it was frigid, with a wind that felt as if it had come right out of the Arctic. It assaulted us as we stood there, whipping us back and forth, stinging our eyes, forcing us to bow before it.

As we continued up the hill, I held on tightly to my sister's hand. At that point, I didn't know who was helping whom. I only knew that I felt as if any minute I would sink to the ground and never get up. My sister must have felt that, because she kept telling me to please hold on, we would be there soon. We were walking as a group but I hardly heard any voices, which I suppose wasn't surprising. I hardly had any voice left myself. The Germans were killing us, bit by bit.

Moving slowly, we arrived at a clearing at the top of the hill and looked down at the view, part of which was obscured by trees. My eyes rested on a house not too far down the hill from the camp. It was a pretty little alpine house with smoke curling out of its chimney. I wondered if, if only I could run down that hill and knock on the door, they would let me in. Would they feed me? Did they have children? Were the people who lived there kind or mean? It seemed so cruel that so much happiness and serenity could exist so close to our misery.

I turned sharply because I heard my sister sobbing.

'What is wrong, Rose?' I croaked, barely able to get the words out, the wind drawing them away, lacerating my chapped lips.

My sister was shivering. 'Look over there, Baby. That is a pile of naked dead bodies.'

I saw what she meant. It was yet another horror. To our right, on the side of the hill, was a field of tents flapping in the wind. Between the regular tents and what I learned later was the sick bay was a pile of corpses, all the more nauseating because they were naked, as if even in death they could be given no respect, only humiliation.

'That is what they are going to do to us, Baby,' Rose said quietly.

I looked around. My mother was ahead of us, struggling to keep climbing and still hold on to Larry. I answered Rose like the good big sister I was supposed to be. 'Don't be afraid, little sister, they won't kill us. So long as we keep going and we stay together, we will survive.'

Rose hugged me, and I hugged her back with as much strength as I could muster. I had said the comforting words, but I didn't for a minute believe them. I stared at what was left of the 5,000 of us who had been gathered in the brick factory. There were barely 500 of us now, and surely we were more dead than alive.

The German soldiers herded us up past the tents and the quarry to a cobblestoned courtyard, at the end of which was a huge wooden door into a massive stone structure that looked like a fort or a prison. They took us through the door, yelling when we didn't move fast enough to suit them. They made us stand in a queue for hours in that courtyard, exhausted, starving, freezing. My sickness was back with a vengeance and the high fever made me sway on my feet. My mother held on to me tightly and tried to shield my brother from the wind by pulling his face tight against her chest. She made my sister put her face against her arm, also to shield her.

The courtyard was lined on both sides with buildings. Some, on the left, were barracks. Others, on the right, we were to learn later, had more sinister uses.

Finally, when we thought we could not stand a moment longer, they assigned us to one of the tents on the ice-cold, windy hill. The tents were large but hardly adequate for the 200 people they housed in each one. There were no beds — just some wooden pallets on the floor covered in straw, and not enough of those to go around. Luckily, Rose and I were able to get a straw-covered pallet to share between us. They assigned my mother to the kitchens as a cook. Once she got all of us settled in the tent, she had to leave for the kitchens straight away. My sister and brother were in a terribly weakened condition, too, but at that point they had no fever. They were dehydrated, though, and were so weak they had no appetite. I could barely make it to lie down on the pallet, and all around us people were grumbling about how sick I was, saying that maybe I had something contagious and they didn't want to catch it.

I must have fallen into a fevered sleep, because the next thing I knew my mother was shaking me awake. She had been told that I would have to be moved to the sick-bay tent. I cried then because I didn't want to be separated from my mother, sick as I was, and I was terrified that if I were sent there, I would soon become part of the pile of naked corpses. I could see that fear mirrored in my sister's eyes as she begged my mother not to make me go there. But my mother had no choice, so she held me and soothed me, promising to visit me all the time. A wagon, pulled by men, not horses, picked me up from our tent, stopping at a few other tents for more 'patients' before depositing us all in the hospital tent. The conditions there were awful. Four or five sick people were shoved into a single bed. When one of them died, that person was often left there for hours or even half a day until somebody moved the body out. The doctor who came to see me did not make me feel any better. A Jew himself, Dr Katz had, I suppose, seen so much suffering that it had destroyed his capacity to feel anything. He was totally cold and emotionless when he told me that I had typhoid fever and that I had better eat anything I could get my hands on, because otherwise I had virtually no chance of surviving. The only help he could give me was some quinine, the only drug available in the camp for treating any illness. I would survive or I would die, and of course I knew the Germans would prefer that I die. One less Jew.

Even Dr Katz could not care less.

I have no clear remembrance of the next two weeks. I

know now that I faded in and out of consciousness as the typhoid raged through my body. My mother came to visit every day and brought me food which she somehow got me to eat. It must have been terribly difficult, because not only was I barely conscious but I could hardly chew because my gums were bleeding due to our vitamin-deficient diet. But my mother would never allow such trifling obstacles to stand in her way. She fed me their vile soup and raw potato peelings which she smuggled out of the kitchen every day. She had read somewhere that sailors on long sea voyages often ate them to prevent scurvy, which she thought was the cause of my bleeding gums. And she found some stale pieces of bread which she somehow got me to chew and swallow. Once again, my mother simply refused to let me die.

'If you give up, what will happen to the rest of us?' she would ask me, as if that question was enough to keep me alive for one more day.

After the first two weeks, as typhoid continued to ravage my body, I cried a lot, thinking about Richie, wondering whether he was still alive. I lived only for him. Every time I thought I was losing my fight for life, I would think of him. Most of my dreams were nightmares, filled with images of all the terror we had lived through. But once in a while, I would dream I was back in Budapest, walking along the Danube with Richie, talking about our future, feeling how soft and gentle his lips were when he kissed me, comforted by his arms around me. In those dreams, I would feel good, and the woman next to me would tell me that I had been talking in a gentle, dreamy voice, instead of screaming, the way I did when I had nightmares.

I slept as much as I could, praying for the good dreams. It was hard to wake me from those, and I remember people shaking me insistently to rouse me. How could the grim reality compare with my memories of Richie?

Eventually, I began to feel a little better. My fever broke and I was able to sit up and become aware of my surroundings, a decidedly mixed blessing. The hospital mattress was better than sleeping on the bare floor, but it was filthy and filled with lice.

When I tried to get up, I was so weak that I swayed on my feet and the room began to swirl around me. I had to sit down as I took in all the pitiful, suffering, dead and dying people around me: people with broken minds and skinny bodies, who looked more like skeletons, their faces blank, devoid of expression.

One day, about six weeks after I'd been put in the hospital, my mother came to visit and told me she had found out what day it was. Time had been taken from us on that long march and we had only a vague sense of what month it was, and no idea what day it was. But that day was 27 February 1945, two days before my sixteenth birthday. When she told me what day it was, I became very emotional. I started to cry and told her that I had a date with my only love. We had always planned to be engaged on my sixteenth birthday.

'How long have I been here in this infirmary?' I asked her, tears streaming down my face.

She pushed my damp, limp hair back off my forehead. 'About six weeks, my darling Baby.'

I was shocked. To me, it had seemed like a lifetime, lying there somewhere between life and death. But now, somehow, I felt a new determination to survive.

'When can I move back into our tent?' I asked my mother.

The next day, Dr Katz, without a smile or a nod, released me from the infirmary.

We celebrated my birthday very quietly, but I realized how much I had to be thankful for. In the midst of so much death and suffering, my mother, my brother and my sister and I were still alive, and I was getting better all the time. Now, I thought, if only I could find Richie, who was everything to me, I could truly withstand even this misery.

During this second part of my convalescence my sister really helped me. Every day, she watched over me, taking me outside to the toilet when I was too weak to make it on my own, sitting by my side and talking to me, feeding me when I was too weak to do it myself. Slowly, day by day, I felt some strength returning. I could stand up by myself and get to the toilet – although I didn't have much to expel. Soon after that, I began walking a little bit further each day.

We didn't trust many of the other people in our tent. It was freezing, even with the combined body heat of 200 other lost souls crammed inside. We were all from different countries – Czechs, Poles, Hungarians – and everyone was out for themselves, always watching to see if someone got a bigger piece of bread or a larger portion of soup than they did. Still, being together with my family made a big difference to me. I was happier spending the days with my sister and brother, waiting for my mother to return from her job in the kitchens. The tent we were in was for women and children only, and in that respect was an improvement on the dreaded infirmary.

Once I had regained some of my strength, my sister and brother and I were asked to keep the tent clean and take care of each other while my mother worked from early morning until dark in the kitchens.

I was able then to see more of the camp, and was allowed to walk through the tent area and look over the barbed wire at the wooden barracks beyond the stone walls and some of the other buildings. I made my way slowly through the prisoners, looking, as always, for Richie or for some word of him. But as I wandered through that camp, I felt as if I had been plunged into the lowest depths of hell, and I discovered some things I wish I had never learned.

Death has a smell. It is a combination of mustiness and decay, terror and despair, overlaid with ashes. I will never forget that smell, which seemed to cling to everything at Mauthausen – the walls, our clothes, our hair, the barracks, the very air we breathed, which was thick and acrid. We did not find out why the air was so thick and why the smell of ashes was so prominent until later.

A place of death has a weight. The atmosphere is close and oppressive, filled with the fluttering wings of the souls of those who died so horribly and painfully there. Mauthausen had that weight, and it was strong enough to crush you if you let it. But my mother would not allow us to dwell in despair. We were all still alive, she would tell us, even as she watched my brother grow weaker every day. God would provide, as He had so far.

In the meantime, my mother was not above helping Him. Every day, she would sneak food out of the kitchens for us, something she would have been killed for if it had been discovered. But she was careful. Who would care about potato peelings? Stale bread? Who would miss it? And so on. She would sneak the food into our tent, then bring us outside to eat it in secret, far from the prying eyes of our fellow inmates and the vicious guards and their vicious Alsatians. We could never talk about the extra food we got, because we would be killed as well, so we told no one. It was just another secret piled on top of all the rest we had kept from the time we were children.

We were filthy and living in rags. And we were still full
of lice. We had thought that once we were at least inside
a tent the lice would die. What we discovered was that
the lice multiplied there, nurtured by the warmth. My
mother tried to keep us as clean as possible, even though
we had no means of washing ourselves. And she killed
lice on all of us every day, brushing our hair every night
with arms that seemed too weary to move.

In one way, I believe my mother was relieved that my
sister and I were so dirty and so tiny that we could pass
for much younger. Older girls — or those who looked
older — were raped by the guards. My mother never
mentioned this to us, but we knew it, and I think she did
her best to keep us looking like children, not women. In
this, she was aided by nature. Whether it was the
unhealthy diet, something they slipped into the food or
just exhaustion, neither one of us ever got our periods
until after we got out of Mauthausen. Many have said,
and I myself believe, that the Nazis put something in the
food to kill people's sex drive and make the men more
docile so that they wouldn't revolt or try to escape.
Others have said they put something in the food to keep
women from having their periods because they didn't
want to deal with the mess.

The days were a bizarre mix of monotony and horror
that only former prisoners of war and concentration
camp survivors can fully comprehend. I would look for
Richie, with no luck. I never even met anyone who knew
him or his family. Or we would watch the men digging
in the quarry, a task that could turn from backbreaking
to fatal in an instant. The 186 steep steps into the stone
quarry were called 'death steps'. The guards delighted in
pushing a man who had reached the top of the steps and
watching the domino effect as all those behind him went

down with him, falling to their deaths in the unforgiving quarry below. This was done for fun and, of course, as an efficient way of killing still more Jews and other undesirables, among them Poles, Greeks, Russians, Yugoslavians, Spaniards, Frenchmen, Italians, gypsies, Austrian dissidents and even American pilots who had been shot down over Germany. One day, a group of 400 Dutch Jews, newly arrived, died on the steps of the quarry when the Nazis pushed the person at the top and they all collapsed against each other and fell to their deaths. The inmates of the camp, kept in these miserable conditions, had built most of the camp with stones lugged so laboriously from the quarry, stones that had taken the lifeblood of so many people.

The Alsatians there were kept hungry and were trained to be vicious. If anyone attempted to escape, they were used to track them and tear them apart as the guards looked on, laughing. My sister saw this happen once, to a young boy who was not quite right in the head and worked in the kitchens. He tried to escape, but the dogs caught and killed him in full view of everyone in the courtyard.

Every day, someone died in the tent. Before anyone was notified of the death, the body was searched for food and any usable article of clothing. When we thought about it, when we had enough energy to think beyond the next moment of survival, we were disgusted by our own behaviour. Yet when one is reduced to the level of an animal, the worst instincts come into play.

Once the guards were notified, a cart would come to take the dead person away, putting all the corpses, naked, on one of the many rotting piles that were maintained all over the camp.

We learned to dread the sound of music, because at

Mauthausen it was only played on days when there were executions, presumably to muffle the sound of the shots and the screams of the victims. The Nazis added a macabre element to their executions by having a small band playing at the front of the open carriage in which the condemned men rode. The men were asked to name their favourite classical piece, and this was played while they were shot. But some of these men were so brave that, as they were being carted to their deaths, they sang. Perhaps the music announced their entrance into heaven. I hope so.

On days when nothing evil happened, we were merely bored, if we could summon enough energy even for that. My mother would still sing to us and encourage us to play jacks, using small stones for the jacks, or she would tell stories, which would keep our minds occupied and off the suffering all around us.

Others were not so lucky. Some of those who worked in the quarry under those inhuman conditions couldn't take it any more, and they would jump to their deaths as their only escape. Others would risk burning to a cinder by trying to climb over the electrified fences. We would hear the impact and then the lights would dim around the camp and we would know that another person had made such a desperate attempt. Then other inmates were made to drag the body away to the corpse pile. My mother had told me over and over again not to go near those fences, but in my constant search for Richie I would sometimes find myself near them.

On one such day, I heard the Nazi guards shouting, 'Hurry up, Jew. Make it fast, you dirty, rotten Jew.' Then a man ran past me, straight into the fence, screaming as the electricity stiffened him and arched his body up and off the fence. What had once been a living, human being became in a matter of seconds a pile of limp rags. And that's exactly how he was treated. Some women working out there in the snow were told to move his body to a pile. And even then, the Nazi guards were yelling, screaming, 'Hurry up, you dirty Jews.' Sometimes I thought I would scream myself if I heard those words shouted at me one more time, but of course I never did because I knew that that scream would be my last protest on earth. So I kept quiet. But inside, I was screaming.

The days passed, one exactly like the other, beginning at dawn in the cold as we were ordered outside to line up and say 'Present'. We got out there no matter what, because people who didn't would disappear. Even when my sister got typhoid and could barely stand, my mother forced her outside and made her line up.

Every night, before we fell into an exhausted sleep, my mother would pray to God for a miracle. Dutifully, we would echo her prayers, but we never believed He would answer them.

There were others who were more optimistic. In fact, one group of women in the camp began collecting scraps of material which they painstakingly sewed into a quilt designed to look like the American flag. I would look at those bright stars and stripes, and the country they represented seemed as remote as the moon.

'The Americans will come, you'll see,' one of these women said to me as I stood looking on as they worked. 'The rumours are everywhere that this can't last much longer.'

I would nod politely, thinking to myself that she was mad. The women were careful to hide their work. They knew they would have paid with their lives if the guards had found this symbol of their perfidy.

Somewhere out there, beyond those grim barbed wire

fences, spring was beginning to come to Austria. But inside the camp's boundaries, there was only the winter of death and despair.

chapter *F*ifteen

I woke up slowly, my body aching from lying on the flimsy straw-covered pallet. The fever was back, making me feel too weak to move. It was spring, but the nights were still cool enough to chill our bones, making them stiff, as we slept in the unheated tent on the hillside. As my eyes adjusted to the light, I tensed. Something was terribly wrong. For one thing, it was bright inside the tent, much too bright to be dawn, yet we were always awakened at dawn. And there was silence. There were no guards shouting, 'Hurry up, you dirty Jew.' There were no vicious dogs barking. There weren't even the sounds of workers in the quarry. There was just silence.

My sister and brother were still sleeping, their frail bodies so thin that they looked more like skeletons than flesh-and-blood children. There were no mirrors, so I couldn't see how I looked, but I suspected I looked as bad. I looked around for my mother and saw her mur-

muring quietly with several of the other women at the
far side of the tent.

I lifted myself up off the pallet and painfully made my
way over to them. 'What's wrong?' I asked my mother,
dreading her answer. What new calamity had befallen us,
I wondered.

'We're not sure, Baby, but look over there – there's a
German uniform lying on the floor.'

I looked and saw it, too. 'What does it mean? Was
some Jew actually able to kill a German and take his uniform?' But I knew as soon as I'd asked that question that
it was dumb. The Jew would have put on the uniform and
tried to escape in it. He wouldn't have left it lying on the
floor.

As I was ill, I was too weak to go out and look around.
But some of the other women made their way outside
the tent. That's when we heard the screams. It took a
while for my ears to assimilate the sound, because those
screams were not like all the other screams we had heard
those last months. They were not screams of pain: they
were screams of joy.

A woman came running back into the tent, her thin,
lined face radiant. 'The Americans are here,' she shouted.
'They've come to save us. The Germans are gone –
they've run away. We're free, we're free.'

My sister and brother awake now, we struggled, fighting back tears, trying to take it all in. My mother came
over to me and wrapped her arm around my shoulders.
'I told you we would survive this horror.'

I closed my eyes, swaying on my feet. Thank God, I
thought, and then, simultaneously, what will happen to
us now?

We peered through the flap at the arriving Americans.
They looked so young, so healthy – and so horrified,

their eyes scanning the piles of naked corpses, and the living skeletons who were well enough to go out and greet them. I saw tears streaming down their faces, and I was glad that they could cry for all of us, those who had survived and those many, many thousands who had not.

The women in our tent proudly presented them with the American flag quilt they had so lovingly made. The officer in charge hugged the woman who handed it to him, but he did so gingerly, as if she would break from his touch, and I have to admit she looked fragile enough to do so.

They ordered us to remain in our barracks while they searched the camp for any remaining SS officers who might be hiding there. They found a few hiding in the forest not far from the campsite. The soldiers brought them back into the camp, their hands up, their heads down in shame and defeat. The soldiers made them face us, the inmates, the people they had tortured and abused for so many years.

We were all very quiet during this encounter, still afraid, I suppose, that these horrible, hateful men would somehow escape and punish us if we cheered. But a few of the men among the inmates gathered the emotional and physical strength to spit in their faces. Some of them even wanted to attack them, to even the score right there. But the Americans would not allow it, and they took the German soldiers away.

Eventually, in the afternoon, they allowed us to walk freely around Mauthausen, although we were not allowed to leave the camp. The soldiers explained that they wanted to have an accurate head count of all who had survived, and have as much information about us as possible, so that they could reunite families that had been split up. My first thought was of Richie, and then of my father. Now that this horrible war was over, would we see them again?

In the meantime, the Americans had begun to take care of us. They were handing out candy bars and sharing their rations; they were sending their doctors through the camp to examine the sick and give them medicine; and they had rounded up Austrian civilians from Mauthausen and other towns to bury the dead. Many of the Austrians said they had not known what horror was taking place here. But the GIs were unmoved. They were outraged and angry and wanted someone to pay, and the witnesses who had done nothing to stop it were the closest they could get to retribution.

As I lay on my pallet, still too weak to move around freely, I thought of the irony of that day, which we learned was 5 May 1945. We had been confined in a Nazi ghetto and then in a concentration camp for more than a year, and now, when the world had been given back to us, a lot of us were not able to move. A few people even died from the shock of being liberated, which seemed the ultimate terrible irony in the months of inhumanity we had been subjected to. Others were still so terrified that they followed the troops around, as if only by staying close to them would they be spared any more horror.

In the afternoon, two young soldiers carried me out of the tent on a stretcher. It was a beautiful spring day and there were celebrations going on all around me, but I was too weak to enjoy them. My brother Larry was so weak that he was lying down beside me.

As we watched the festivities, the soldiers interviewed us.

'We need to gather as much information as possible,' an earnest young lieutenant explained through an interpreter. 'Every statistic is important. We need to know what country you came from, how many of you were deported at the same time, how many of those are still alive.' He paused, pulling out a pack of chewing gum and offering it around to us. No one took any. 'We need to know about the dead, too. Who they were, where they were from – as much as you can tell us.'

At first, all I could do was stare at his mouth, this healthy, wholesome-looking young man with blond hair, blue eyes and rosy cheeks. His mouth was a wonder, and indeed those of many of the other Americans. They had very white, perfect teeth. We had not been able to brush our teeth for nine months. They were yellow and gritty, and our gums were bleeding because of malnutrition. And here was this young man with a mouth that looked as if he was a millionaire. I was mesmerized. Finally, for the first time, I smiled.

He smiled back, practically dazzling me, before turning to my mother. When he asked us about relatives, she told him about her two sisters in the United States. Her father had sent them there just before the First World War in 1914. As they talked to us, the soldiers were so kind and compassionate that I wanted to weep. They were so different from the Nazis, and even from our own Hungarian soldiers, who had treated us like animals. They treated us like human beings, very special human beings, especially my brother, who was one of the youngest survivors they'd encountered.

They offered us food constantly, but my mother wouldn't let us eat too much at once, because we had been starving for so long. In this, as in everything else, my mother turned out to be right. Some people died from eating too much too quickly – their systems simply couldn't handle it. Others became violently ill. But, thanks to my mother, we were gradually introduced to real food without any major problems.

We learned one shocking detail that first day.

'You don't know how lucky you are,' the lieutenant told us. I wish I could remember his name, but I was still so ill and it was so long ago that I cannot. 'We had information that the Germans planned to kill all of you before the camps were liberated, so that there would be no witnesses to what they had done here. If we'd arrived a day or two later, you all would have been dead.'

I remember beginning to shake then, realizing just how close we had come to death. Even the day before liberation, the music had played as others were marched to be shot or hanged. But we still had no idea about Mauthausen's ultimate horror. It wasn't until we were liberated that we were told about the gassing of so many Jews and their incineration in the crematorium. In time, we learned that Mauthausen was the central camp for all Austria and that between its beginning in 1938 until Liberation Day in 1945, 195,000 people of both sexes were imprisoned there. By Liberation Day, there were less than 80,000 left. The rest had all died or been murdered. I had thought that nothing else could ever shock me, but that mass murdering, in such a clinical, ghastly way made me violently ill, even weaker than I had been before with just the fever to contend with.

I think the lieutenant must have seen the desolation on my face, because he smiled at me before saying gently, 'In a few weeks, your lives will be back to normal and, if you want to, you can go back home. You'll see.'

Sadly, that wasn't true, but none of us could have known it at the time.

A lot of the soldiers were very sympathetic to us, probably because we had survived almost intact as a family. Only my father was missing. Because I was still ill, they put us into heated barracks where the SS had lived. They gave us blankets and food and, most importantly, hope, although my mother despaired of ever finding her father and her other sisters alive.

They also de-loused us, spraying us all with DDT. Given that it is now known to have dangerous side effects, I have often wondered, since then, what cancers and other ailments suffered by survivors were caused by this wholesale spraying of DDT.

Now that we were safe, my mother allowed herself to be sick. Starved, exhausted, dehydrated, she also came down with typhoid, but this time there was medicine to treat it, and compassion instead of punishment.

Within a couple of weeks we had learned that all the Jews of my grandfather's village of Zeteny had been taken away and sent to death camps. We all cried at the thought of our loving grandfather and aunts and uncles destroyed for nothing except that they were Jewish. We heard that Budapest had been liberated by the Russians on 5 January 1945. But that had been a mixed blessing. The Russians were as brutal in their own way as the Germans had been. When they reached Budapest, they looted and stole virtually everything the Germans hadn't, and they raped a lot of women. The Russians didn't discriminate either. They raped nuns as happily as they raped Jewish girls. They took everything of value and had no respect for anyone, young, old or in between. We were glad we had been liberated by the Americans and, at the same time, we became even more worried about those who had remained behind in Budapest. The day I heard that the Russians had taken any young men they could find off the streets and sent them to prison camps in Siberia, I wept bitterly. Had my darling Richie survived the Nazis only to be imprisoned and possibly killed by the Russians?

I wrote a letter to him, but I never received an answer. My depression, which had been growing even in the face of our new good fortune, deepened. What would any of this mean without Richie?

The soldiers had said life would be normal again, but they had no way of knowing the damage that had been done to us. I relived all the horrors in my nightmares, which would last for years and still occasionally haunt me to this day. I would see Violet and her sister lying on the side of the road in their own blood; my father as he waved and walked out of our lives; my grandfather marching with what I was sure had been great dignity to his death, the beloved patriarch unable to do anything to save his family. Many nights, I wept bitter tears into my pillow. Our lives had been taken from us. Could we now rebuild them into something worthwhile? I thought I could, if only I could find Richie.

Meanwhile, life in our liberated camp turned into days of questioning and documentation.

After a few weeks, I was able to walk, and that made me very happy because I didn't want to be a burden to anyone. The soldiers had been so compassionate during my convalescence, bringing me medicine, milk and bread – all things we had not seen for so many long months. We were slowly getting our strength back and I went walking with my mother to build up that strength. I was impatient to be totally well again, but this clearly was not something we could rush. After all that we had been through, our strength came back slowly, and Larry was still so small for his age and so thin that my mother worried that permanent damage had been done to him by the exhaustion, the exposure and the starvation we had endured.

I walked around with my sister and brother and we looked down the road and remembered how, not many months ago, I had to hold Rose's hand to make it up that hill.

'You don't know how much I wanted to kiss you for how you helped me that day, how you held me up,' I told her. 'Because you pulled me up and encouraged me when I would have stopped, I survived.'

Rose's eyes filled with tears as she hugged me.

'Papa would have been so proud of you,' I whispered in her ear as we held each other close.

In fact, we were always hugging each other, saying how we couldn't believe that we were alive and free. We had gone through so much together, and had survived, but only by a hair's breadth.

'You know, I don't remember much from my days in the hospital,' I told her one day as we walked around the camp. 'I only really know what Mama told me, and she didn't tell me much.'

Rose nodded, taking my hand. 'She didn't want to scare you by telling you just how sick you were, Baby. She would come back to our tent and tell me how high your fever was, and how you had almost constant diarrhoea and how it was so hard to get you to eat anything. And she said the infection on the bottoms of your feet was so bad she thought you might die from that alone.'

I shuddered and pressed my sister's hand, tears brimming in my eyes.

'You're so lucky to be alive,' my sister said softly.

And most days I felt that way, until I remembered Richie, and then I knew that without the thought of seeing him again, I would have given up many times over. Now I needed to find out whether he was still alive.

Some of the Turkish and Yugoslavian former inmates

were very angry and very daring. Against all the rules, they went into town, demanding food, clothing and alcohol from Austrian families. At the time the Austrians had no choice but to give them what they asked for, but they complained to the Americans. Other male inmates were so angry that they went into town and beat up anyone who even looked at them in an odd way. The Americans made an announcement that anyone who did such things again would be punished severely.

Finally, when they had documented all our lives, the army was ready to move us out. The new camp, called Kleinmunchen, was a fair distance away, but that was no longer a problem because the Americans had no thought of making us march there. Instead, they transported us by truck to the railway station and put us in open carriages for the trip. I'll never forget that ride. It was a magnificent spring day – it was warm and the sun was shining and my sister and I were able to sit at the side of the carriage with our feet dangling out, feeling the gentle breeze caress our feet and legs. Some people were singing and the fields were a study in vibrant colour, bright red poppies swaying against rich blue cornflowers and white daisies.

'Look,' I said to my mother, pointing to the field of flowers, 'aren't they beautiful?'

My mother nodded, smiling. 'Those red, white and blue flowers are celebrating our freedom from the Germans with all the colours in the American flag. We must thank the Americans, but we must also thank God for allowing us to live to celebrate this freedom.'

I wasn't sure that I was quite ready to thank God since, in my view, He had put us in this perilous situation in the first place, but I did love those Americans. We all did. Their generosity and kindness, especially after so much cruelty, was like a balm to our wounds. Their food sustained us and restored us. Luckily, I didn't have access to a mirror for a few weeks, so I couldn't see how awful I looked after months of sickness and starvation. My brother told me I looked as much like a skeleton as he did, and I'm sure that was true. Once I was feeling better, I was determined to be pretty again, and to have my good figure back. With this in mind, I tried to eat everything the Americans gave us. I even drank the thick, condensed milk that came in cans, thinking that it would put weight on me quickly. But it gave me stomach cramps, so I had to stop drinking it.

Kleinmunchen was a camp of about 500 tents. For us, it was truly the beginning of a better life. For one thing, there were only ten of us to a tent, instead of hundreds. The sheer luxury of this relative privacy after months of living on top of others was exhilarating. And, for the first time since before the Occupation, we were sleeping on beds – or at least on cots – instead of on the hard ground. The army gave us pillows and blankets, but my mother refused to give up the blanket she had carried across Hungary and into Austria.

'But it has lice all over it,' an army sergeant protested.

'I don't care,' my mother said stubbornly. 'This blanket protected us and kept us safe. Lice can be removed.'

The sergeant sighed, but he was no match for my mother. Finally, they took the blanket from her, put DDT all over it and put it outside the tent to air. Once that was done, my mother took it down to the river and washed it, then sprinkled it with DDT again.

The blanket wasn't the only thing we wouldn't part with, and in this way, all the survivors were the same. We had lived so long with nothing and with not knowing where the next meal was coming from that we collected and hoarded everything – pencil stubs, pieces of paper, cigarette butts, scraps of fabric that someone had discarded, bread, chocolate bars, apples. Our pockets were full of treasures. And we were so fearful that somehow we still might be sent back to a concentration camp that we hid everything, just in case we needed it. We had no real reason to do this, but psychologically we were so afraid that someone was going to take this accumulated junk away from us that we did it anyway.

My mother had a whole new agenda for us now that the war was over.

'We have to have a plan for the rest of our lives,' she told us all as we were settling in. 'We need to decide where we will live and what we will do. All of you need to finish school so that you can make something of yourselves out in the world.' She sighed and clasped her hands in her lap. 'And we have to find out whether anyone in our family is still alive, besides my sisters in America.'

'I have to find Richie,' I said, as I always did when we talked of the future.

My mother smiled and nodded. I began trying right there in Kleinmunchen, going from tent to tent, looking for him and asking all the people I met whether they knew him and knew what had happened to him and his mother. But no one did.

There was an outdoor kitchen in Kleinmunchen, used to feed the whole camp, and my mother went there immediately to volunteer to cook. The Americans had official army cooks, so they didn't need her to work full-time, but they were happy to have her as a helper.

The kindness and help from the Americans were almost too much, overwhelming to people who had been treated like animals for so long. There were plenty of doctors to treat any ailments we might have. Red Cross volunteers were there to help us. The army gave us food and some of their rations. There was no indoor plumbing, but at least there were clean portable toilets where one could once more have privacy, dignity and cleanliness. There were no baths or showers, either, so we had to divide the tent into a sleeping area and a washing area where, using basins, we gave ourselves sponge baths, a luxury after so many months of filth and dirt. We were still ridding ourselves of the lice, which seemed to have become so attached to us that they refused to leave.

We realized that our clothes would have to go, because they had become a breeding ground for the creatures. We had an official burning ceremony for those clothes, which were a constant reminder of our imprisonment. The new clothes we received were nothing special, I suppose, but to us they were wonderful. They were clean and they were ours, and no one was going to take them from us. The clothes, which arrived in huge bundles that looked more like bales of hay than clothing, were used clothes collected in America and shipped to Germany for all the refugees. We were supposed to wait our turn for the clothes, but I had a good contact through which I was able to make sure my family was first in the queue.

I loved the outfit I found – a grey plaid woollen flared skirt that just hit my knees, a soft cream-coloured blouse and a grey cardigan. My feet were still a problem – they were so sore that I had to keep them wrapped in padding. But I managed to find a pair of low-heeled shoes two sizes larger than my usual size and I wore those with ankle socks. When I eventually saw myself in a mirror, I cried. For the first time for a long time, I looked like a pretty girl again, my shoulder-length hair shiny and clean, my face glowing. If only Richie were here to see me now, I thought, as I twirled in front of the mirror, to see the skirt billow out from my legs. Soon, I promised myself, soon we will find each other.

I found myself depressed about Richie yet at the same time greedy for life, for all the things that I had missed and longed for.

There was a Hungarian American soldier who became friendly with our family, although at first my mother was suspicious of his intentions.

'Remember what happened to Violet when she befriended that soldier,' she'd whisper to me when she found me talking to him.

But that was then, and this was now. He was an open, friendly American boy who was far from home and was trying to be kind. He gave us extra chocolate and other rations, and he taught me English. I had always been good at languages and, living as I did in Middle Europe, with a Czech father and a Hungarian mother, I knew those languages, as well as German, which was still an 'official' language in Hungary, a leftover from the days of the Austro-Hungarian Empire. But English was the language of the future, I felt certain, and I wanted to learn it.

'Don't speak to me in anything but English,' I begged the young soldier, and he was kind enough to agree, although it must have been annoying for him to try to communicate with someone who understood only a few words. Still, I'd learned some English in school and spoke enough to do the daily U.S. Army announcement detailing camp events in Hungarian, translated from the English, and I was a fast learner.

He wrote a letter to Aunt Rose in America for us, and this touched my mother greatly.

'Here he is, of Hungarian background and a Gentile, and he is helping us, even though we are Jews,' she said to me one night right before prayers. 'I will thank God for bringing him to us, and for showing me that not all Hungarians are haters.'

I volunteered to do anything for extras. I wanted a blanket of my own, so I washed the soldiers' socks. I'd sampled canned fruit juice for the first time and, although grapefruit juice was bitter, I knew it was good for me, and I demanded more, just as I demanded peanut butter and cookies. The soldiers liked me and gave me what I wanted. Now, after all those years of going hungry, we had more food than we could eat, and we thought we were blessed simply because we weren't hungry any more. To this day, I can't throw away food. Even when a piece of bread falls on the floor I 'kiss it up to God', as my mother used to tell us to do, and eat it. I cannot bear to throw away what was once so precious to us. I will never forget the feeling of being desperately hungry.

But my mother was right. We needed to plan for our future. The Americans asked us if we wanted to go back to Hungary and my mother immediately said no. Reports from the east made things sound too chaotic. Besides, our memories of our fellow Hungarians were not good ones. The Arrow Cross had terrorized us as much as the Germans, even though they were our own countrymen. I wanted to go back for just a little while, to look for Richie and for my father, and even for my grandfather and aunts in case they had perhaps survived the concentration camp. But my mother insisted it was too risky. Europe was still in chaos, and she did not trust the Russians, who were occupying Hungary.

'If we go back, we may never be able to get out again,' my mother said. 'Besides, we can probably go to America because Aunt Rose and Aunt Lina are already there, and I'm sure they will help us. In Hungary, we have no one, unless we can find our family.'

I felt desperate about looking for Richie back in Budapest. 'What if just I go?' I asked, but I knew the answer before I asked. There was no way my mother would allow her sixteen-year-old daughter, whose trim figure was coming back, to travel alone through Europe and into the hands of the Russians.

'We have to move on, Baby,' she said gently. 'In the meantime, you can look for Richie through the Red Cross.'

I nodded, but I had to turn away quickly so that she wouldn't see the tears that filled my eyes. Would I ever see my love again?

Only time would tell.

chapter *S*ixteen

*W*e were being moved again. After a couple of weeks in the temporary camp at Kleinmunchen, it was time to go to a more permanent camp until we knew where we would be living for the rest of our lives.

We had about three days' notice before the move. We learned we were being sent to Wetzlar in Germany. We'd never heard of it, but someone in our group told us it was a town known for being the headquarters for Leica cameras. We had made some firm friends among the other refugees and now we were being separated from many of them, as each group was assigned to different permanent camps. We wished each other good health and happiness and said we'd write once we had our new address. We had no idea that, with the war just ending, the postal system was in chaos and letters could take weeks to be delivered.

It was 1 July 1945, two months after we'd been liberated. Once again, we found ourselves in cattle trucks, but once again the Americans were kind and thoughtful enough to leave the doors open. There was a lot of apprehension about where we were going. Once again, the army had told us we could go back to Budapest if we preferred, but my mother wouldn't hear of it. The train moved slowly, stopping at every station along the way. The Germans looked at us with curiosity and we stared back at them with hatred. Some people even yelled at them, 'Why are you staring? Haven't you seen enough yet?' I suppose it was fortunate that the Germans did not understand the languages in which they were being yelled at.

It took two days and three nights to get to Wetzlar, located in western Germany, near Frankfurt. We had to walk from the train station to the camp, a fairly long distance. I had already walked more than I would ever wish to in my life, but I made it. Wetzlar turned out to be a former German army barracks. The space assigned to us was a room on the third floor, which we shared with twelve people. The room was divided into thirds. My family got the third near the entrance, the second third went to four men, and the final third went to a husband and wife and her two sisters. Each partitioned 'room' was equipped with four small folding beds, each with its own blanket and pillow, and one box for storage. It wasn't exactly home, but at least we were no longer sleeping in a tent.

The camp itself was large, with its own kitchen, bakery, mess hall and even a post office.

Luckily, we all got jobs as soon as we arrived. We'd become so bored even in Kleinmunchen with nothing to do that the days had seemed endless. Now we had work, and a purpose. My sister got a job in the post office and I was chosen to work for Major Daniel, the provost

marshal of that sector of Germany, and one of the kindest people I've ever met. He and his wife adopted our
entire family. They could not have been nicer or more
generous to us. I worked as Major Daniel's translator,
going from camp to camp with him as he spoke to
refugees. This was a godsend for me, because it meant I
could check at each camp for any word of Richie. The
records were sketchy at best. There were millions of us
adrift in Europe without papers or identification of any
kind. There were no computers then, not even electric
typewriters, so the records were in the form of either
typed lists or handwritten notations on small file cards.
At each camp, I had to go through all the lists and cards
searching for Richie's name.

I went with Major Daniel to the nearby camps of Fulda
and Wurzburg, but had no luck finding Richie. There
were a lot of young men who had survived. I only hoped
that Richie was somewhere among them.

After I came home from one of these trips, I went into
the room and cried myself to sleep. My mother knew
why by now, and she no longer asked me for the reason.
She had been through much the same thing, losing my
father the way she had, but she was a much stronger person than I. I got very emotional whenever I thought of
the good times with Richie. Part of my problem was that
every free moment I was reliving in my mind my best
memories of Richie. I was glad no one could see into my
brain because it was my secret world, my link to the past,
and it was where I lived most of the time. I ate, I slept, I
worked, but I had very little interest in other people. I
found gossip awful and just a waste of time. I didn't really
want to go to youth meetings or dances. I wanted to be
left alone.

About six months into the process of searching for

Richie, I finally found his name, at a camp called Kassel. It listed him there, plain as day, Richie Kovacs, aged twenty, and I thought I would die. It said he was dead. I remember seeing his name and the word 'dead,' then swaying on my feet. The next thing I knew, I was sitting on a soft, upholstered chair in an office. When I opened my eyes, Major Daniel was watching me, a worried frown on his face.

'Are you all right, Baby?' he asked.

I blinked, trying to remember what had happened. Then I saw Richie's name and the word 'dead'. I closed my eyes again. 'I must have fainted,' I said.

Major Daniel looked concerned. 'Did you find Richie on that list?'

I nodded, chewing on my lower lip to keep from crying.

The Major looked puzzled. 'Then that's good news, isn't it? That you've found him?'

I shook my head. 'The list says he's dead,' I said in a voice I didn't even recognize as my own.

The Major was quiet for a while, studying me. 'That could be true, or it could be another Richie Kovacs. It's not all that unusual a name. I wouldn't give up on him yet, Baby, but I wouldn't have false hope either.'

I tried to smile, because I knew he was trying to be kind, but all I could see was a vision of my handsome, good, kind love, lying dead somewhere, in a pool of blood, or maybe in a pile of naked corpses. I shuddered and willed my mind to stop it. I thought I might truly go insane from that thought, and I wouldn't allow myself to do that. The Major was right. It could all be a mistake or a coincidence. Against all odds, I had survived the war. He could have, too. I would not give up, not yet. I would keep on searching.

But after that day, I felt as if I was just going through the motions. I would go to young people's gatherings when my mother told me to and I made a few friends, including a funny, charming young man named Fery, who had a sister in a nearby camp, but inside I felt numb. My life was without laughter.

Life at Wetzlar had settled into a routine. We still couldn't take a bath or shower in privacy, but there were great sponge baths and we were getting used to being truly clean again. My sister and brother were gaining weight, and I was, too, although we still looked like concentration camp survivors. My mother was very skinny but she was the strongest among us. We were sleeping in clean beds, even if we only had one set of bedding, because it was summer and the sheets dried quickly in the sun, hanging from a line strung out the third-floor window with our clothes, which my mother washed for us. I thought we would be in the United States by the winter.

The Americans came to realize how traumatized we had been by what we had gone through and what we had witnessed. To their undying credit, there in the displaced persons' camps, they began group therapy and counselling for the survivors, trying to help us find our way out of the nightmare that had consumed our lives for the last few years. In therapy, we all told heartbreaking stories. We realized, as we heard from survivors about their loss of everyone in their families, how lucky we four were. We kept hoping that any day my father would find us.

We met one family whose story made us laugh as well as cry. They were Romanians, a father, a mother, a grandmother and a couple of children, who had been rounded up by the Nazis for deportation. This family found itself in a railway carriage with a travelling troupe of people of restricted growth, then known as dwarves, who just happened to be caught in the round-up as well. The family and the dwarves became friendly as the train made its way from Romania into Poland and the concentration camp at Auschwitz. When they were told to get out of the packed carriage, the grandmother had trouble getting up and one of the dwarves went to help her, saying, 'I've got you, Baba,' using the Polish word for grandmother.

It just so happened that the diabolic Nazi doctor, Joseph Mengele, was standing there when this happened, and he turned to stare at the sight of a dwarf helping a perfectly normal old woman out of the cattle car. 'Are you all related?' he asked.

The father of the group answered quickly. 'Yes, we're all one family,' although later he confessed that he didn't have any idea why he'd said that.

Mengele raised an eyebrow. 'I have never seen a family where some are normal and some are dwarves. What kind of genetic game is this?' he asked.

Of course, no one answered him. He motioned to the guards to take the 'family' away to a special building, where they remained for the rest of the war, well fed and taken care of, and safe, as the Nazis took endless blood samples from them in an attempt to understand the magic of their genes. It was so rare that we heard a story where anyone had outwitted the Nazis in order to survive.

The months passed. I turned seventeen. It was the spring of 1946 and my friend Fery had been sent to another camp in Weilheim, Germany. Because his sister was still in a nearby camp, Fery came back to visit us even after he moved. Although he, too, had suffered during the war, he retained his sense of humour and he had a spirit that refused to give up. I looked forward to his visits. The summer came and went, and my English got better, although it has never become perfect. I learned the GI slang and became quite a favourite with the soldiers. But I barely noticed. I was still looking for Richie, hoping that the name on that one list had been another Richie Kovacs, and not my own true love. I knew that I was lucky to have my life, but how could I live without my 'everything'?

My mother was worried about me. She said it wasn't natural for a young person to look only backwards and not forwards.

'You should be ashamed of yourself, Baby,' she said to me one day as we made up the bed. 'You should be enjoying yourself and you should be thankful you have survived.'

My eyes flashed at her. 'And are you enjoying yourself?' I asked.

My mother looked at me for a minute before replying calmly. 'Yes, I am. I am enjoying being with my children and being safe from harm. Besides, whatever God wants to happen, that's what happens in life, so we have to accept it, to take life as it is.'

I nodded, but inside I rebelled. I could not accept a life without Richie, or a God who could test His Chosen People so much.

My friend Fery tried to help me in another way. He thought that if I met somebody new I would forget Richie. One day in late summer he sent me a letter and told me about a young man he'd met in Weilheim who was always telling jokes and had a great sense of humour, even though he had lost his entire family at Auschwitz. He asked me to come to visit him at Weilheim so that I could meet this young fellow, whose name was Otto Schimmel. He also asked me for a picture of myself that he could show to Otto, because he had told him about me. I sent Fery the picture, then forgot about the whole thing.

It took a couple of months for my aunts in New York to answer our letter, and when they did they wanted to know what had happened to my grandfather and the rest of their siblings, but we couldn't tell them. Then they wrote to us, telling us that my mother's youngest sister, Sari, who had been with my grandfather, was alive and recuperating in Sweden, and had contacted them through the Red Cross. The two sisters had arranged for Sari to go to them in America, and my mother wrote to her there. Sari wrote a long letter back, describing in horrible and agonizing detail what had happened to my grandfather and the rest of the family. My mother cried so bitterly that I thought that she might finally curse God for what He had done to her family. But she did not. After reading the letter over and over again, she even said her prayers.

I could not put the letter down, feeling searing, tearing pain of grief and rage course through me as I read Sari's words.

They had gathered all the Jews together in the tiny village of Zeteny and marched them down the main street, past their Gentile neighbours who had known them for generations but who did nothing to stop the soldiers. They made them march into the next town, where there was a railway station, and stuffed them, along with the Jews from neighbouring villages, into a closed cattle truck. One of my aunts was eight months' pregnant. Her husband had been taken away to a forced labour camp months before, so she had stayed at my grandfather's house. Another of my aunts was older and still single, and then there was Sari, who was only eighteen.

Sari explained that my pregnant aunt was very thirsty and uncomfortable. When the train stopped somewhere, the Germans had opened the doors of the cattle truck and someone had handed in some water. My aunt asked for more, because she was so very thirsty. She was ignored, and they closed the doors on her pleas. She was crying loudly now, begging for some water. A German guard opened the door and yelled at her to be quiet, but she wouldn't. The German soldier pulled out his bayonet and stabbed my aunt in the stomach, killing her and her unborn child instantly. Then he closed the door, leaving my aunt's dead body in the middle of that cramped cattle truck, with my grandfather saying the prayer for the dead over her as he cried out his grief. At the same time, he tried to comfort my two other aunts, who were devastated. They rode on for hours in the hot cattle truck, the body of my aunt decomposing along the way and giving off such a tremendous stench that people in the truck were gagging. And hers was not the only dead body festering in the heat. Finally, at one of the stations, the guards removed the dead bodies.

When they arrived at Auschwitz, there was a wrenching moment for the family as my older aunt stayed with my grandfather and was sent to the left, and my Aunt Sari was sent to the right. Sari wanted to stay with her father and sister, but she had no choice but to follow the Nazis' orders or be shot on the spot. She learned later, in her barracks, that my grandfather and aunt had been murdered in the gas chambers. Her will to live was gone, but apparently God did not see fit to take her, because she survived being transported to yet another concentration camp, Bergen-Belsen, where she was liberated by the

Allies. By that time, she was very sick and underweight. The Red Cross sent her to Sweden to recover. After she emigrated to New York, she learned a trade and learned English, married and had two children. But her life had been ruined all those years ago at the age of eighteen and, in all the years I've known her, I have never seen her smile.

That night, after I read Sari's letter, I admit I cursed the God of Abraham, the one my grandfather had so revered. How had God repaid him? He had deserted him. Sometime in the middle of the night it occurred to me that my grandfather would not want me to lose my faith, and I tried to believe as simply and fully as my mother did, but I did not achieve it. At least, not then.

In that same month, December 1946, my mother discovered that her older brother, Ignatz, was alive and living with a German family in Augsburg. She wept tears of joy when she heard he was alive, and told me I must visit him. This was an uncle I had never met because he was living in Czechoslovakia when we fled to Hungary in 1938. Sadly, my mother wrote and told him what had happened to their father and his sisters. But she also told him how glad she was that he had survived.

Poor Uncle Ignatz was not so sure he was glad he had survived, because he had lost his wife and children in the camps. When I heard that, I decided to go and visit him straight away. At least I was family. I could not replace those he had lost, but perhaps he would not feel so alone if I went to see him.

It was very cold when I boarded the train in the second week of December. Since Augsburg was on the way to Weilheim, I wrote to Fery, saying that I would take a train there after visiting my uncle and asked him to meet me at the train station.

The visit to my Uncle Ignatz was touching and painful. He was a slight, thin man whose narrow face bore the marks of much suffering. I understood why after he told me what had happened to him and to his family during the war.

They, too, had fled Czechoslovakia for Hungary when the Nazis invaded and tried to wait out the war in a small village. But the Nazis found them eventually and took them into a ghetto in a neighbouring city. There they were rounded up again and put on cattle trucks to be taken to Auschwitz. That was in June 1944. They were separated at Auschwitz. Uncle Ignatz was sent to the right; his wife and daughters were sent to the left, and put to death that same day in the gas chambers, but Uncle Ignatz didn't know that. All the time he was in Auschwitz, he searched for them, but never found them or anyone who knew of them. He was moved from Auschwitz to Dachau, where his life was a living hell. He was beaten all the time because he was a small man and could not work as hard as others building a railway track. The work was killing him. One day when a German officer was looking for a barber, Uncle Ignatz raised his hand, even though he had never cut hair in his life. He was so nervous that his hands were shaking as he worked the scissors and combs. The officer's hair was a mess when he was finished, and he had Uncle Ignatz beaten for it. When he could walk again, they sent him back to building the railway. He was sure he would have died there if the Allies hadn't liberated the camp soon afterwards.

While he told me his story, I took his hand, squeezing it in mine when I saw tears fill his eyes as he spoke of his wife and his daughters. So much pain and loss. I felt it washing over me. How my family had suffered, and how many of them had died.

I hadn't known Uncle Ignatz before the war, but we became very close during my visit, as we shared our tears over what had happened to our family. Amazingly, he was able to get along well with the Germans whose house he slept in, although he ate all his meals at the hotel in town where the other survivors had been housed by the US army. I stayed at the hotel, but he showed me the house he lived in – a real Bavarian-style German house, complete with a crucifix on the wall. I tried not to shudder as I thought about what the Germans had done to the Jews of Europe, but it was hard. Yet somehow my poor uncle, who had lost so much more than I had, had found the grace to forgive the German people, and even God. Perhaps I could, too.

After two days, my uncle walked me to the train station, and we hugged each other and cried when I had to leave. When I got to Weilheim, no one was at the train station to meet me. After waiting for an hour, I walked into town to the Brauwastl Hotel where the survivors were staying. When I got there, I asked for Fery, but he wasn't there. Then I asked for his friend Otto, but he wasn't there either.

I was exhausted, because my uncle and I had stayed up all night the night before talking about the family, so I asked if I could wait for my friends in Otto's room.

'Could I lie down and rest while I wait for them?' I asked their friends.

'Of course,' said George, a nice young man whose family had all been killed by the Nazis. 'Make yourself comfortable.'

I made myself so comfortable that I changed into my pyjamas and fell sound asleep. And that's how Otto found me when he walked in half an hour later. He told me he saw a young woman in his bed, looked at the picture of me that he'd pinned to the lapel of his jacket and then back at me again. By this time, I was awake, aware that someone was staring at me. He was tall and handsome, with blond hair and twinkling blue eyes.

'You are even more beautiful in person,' he said to me, holding out his hand. 'I am Otto Schimmel and of course you are Baby.'

'How do you know me and where did you get my picture?' I asked.

He laughed then. 'Don't you remember? You sent the picture to Fery last spring.'

I nodded, my eyes beginning to close again, as I was so tired. 'Would you mind if I slept for a couple of hours?' I asked him.

He smiled again, an infectious, warm smile. 'I don't mind. Get some sleep,' he said.

I slept as if someone had hit me on the head. When I woke up a few hours later, I wandered into the bathroom next door, drawn by the luxuriously large bath there. I couldn't resist it. It had been so long since I had had a real bath. I ran back into the room, got some clothing and filled the tub. This was truly heaven, I thought. Not since before the Occupation of Budapest had I had the luxury of a long soak in a hot tub.

I didn't even think to lock the bathroom door, and so someone opened the door to see if anyone was using the bathroom. While the door was briefly open I saw Otto walking by outside and called to him that I was taking a bath but would be out in a minute.

He waved at me. 'Take your time. I'll be waiting back in my room.'

He was very kind and even came to the bathroom door to ask me if I was all right, because I was taking so long.

'I'm fine,' I called out, washing my hair for the umpteenth time, luxuriating in the feeling of being able to use so much water on my hair again.

'Would you like me to bring you a cup of tea in there?' he asked.

'No, not now,' I answered quickly, looking down at my naked body only partially hidden by the soapy water.

I knew that he was only trying to be a good host, but his solicitude was irritating me. I just wanted to enjoy this first bath in peace. But he is only trying to please you, to be a good host, I told myself. It didn't help much.

When I finally came back out into the room, I was fully dressed, with a big towel wrapped around my head. When I took it off and shook out my hair to comb it in front of the mirror, even I marvelled at how shiny it was. My hair hadn't been this clean since before the Occupation.

I could see Otto watching me intently in the mirror.

'We must stay in until your hair dries,' he said with a smile. 'I don't want you to catch a cold out there. After all, it is December.'

We talked for the rest of the afternoon, and Otto mentioned there was a dance that night that we could go to. In a way, I felt that I should go dancing and try to bring some gaiety back into my life. On the other hand, I still thought of Richie and didn't really want to dance with anyone else. But I remembered what my mother had said. I did have to get on with things, at least a little. I had brought a pretty dress with me, another find in the bundles of clothing from America; it would be nice to be able to show it off. And I could see from the look in his eyes how much Otto wanted me on his arm that night.

'All right, let's go,' I said, giving Otto a big smile and

seeing how affected he was by it. He smiled right back at me.

We ate dinner in the main dining room of the hotel, where I met the rest of Otto's friends. They all came over to ask him, 'Who is this young lady?'

Otto looked very proud to be with me. 'I just met her today,' he said, explaining that I was one of the 'lucky ones' whose immediate family had survived.

At the dance, which was held in a big hall in town, I could see young men looking at me with longing. Very few young women of my age had survived and still looked like pretty young girls. I realized all over again how lucky I had been, in spite of everything that had happened.

I had a nice time at the dance. I felt like a star there, and it was good for my ego, although my heart was not engaged.

Snow was falling as we walked back to the hotel, arm in arm. Otto told me to look up at the snowflakes, and when I did, he kissed each of my cheeks.

'Don't ever do that again,' I said sharply. 'I'm engaged to a boy.'

I saw his face fall, and I felt bad for a moment, but I didn't want to give this young man false hope. He had already had enough awful things happen to him, and he needed a woman who was free to love him. I was not that woman, because my heart already belonged to someone else.

The next afternoon, he insisted on going on the train with me back to my uncle's, even though I said I would be perfectly all right by myself. He bought me some dinner and handed me a note he had scrawled on the back of a paper bag when we parted at my uncle's door. 'Someday I will marry you,' the note said.

I didn't laugh in his face; it wouldn't have been polite. But as soon as I was alone with my uncle, I showed him the note and we both had a good laugh together.

'There is no way I will marry him,' I said, still smiling. Then, abruptly, I felt all the sadness again. 'I only want to be Richie's wife.

chapter *Seventeen*

On the train back to Wetzlar, I thought about Otto. He was the opposite of Richie, with light blond hair, tall and skinny. He was good-looking, even though he still had the telltale signs of a concentration camp survivor about him — too thin, too pale, his eyes too blank.

But Otto was a charmer. Even when he saw that I wanted to laugh at his note about marrying me, he was trying to persuade me.

'Just wait and see,' he'd said with a smile, as if he held the secret to getting me to say yes.

He was always joking, but I realized almost immediately that that was to cover up his sadness. He had a lot to be sad about, I thought, looking out at the snow-covered countryside as the train rumbled on. He had grown up in a close, loving extended family of aunts and uncles and cousins. He adored his dashing older brother and his gentle older sister, and he worshipped his mother, whom he described as an angel. His father had died a couple of years before the Occupation and in a way that was a blessing, because a parent should never outlive his children.

Otto had grown up in New Pest, a town that was part of the urban sprawl of Budapest. He had been an apprentice in the leather goods trade and was loving his work when the Occupation began. A month later, he and his mother, sister and grandmother were rounded up in the ghetto and deported. They were packed into a cattle truck and taken to Auschwitz. His grandmother could barely move because her legs became numb on the long, cramped ride. The Germans had no patience or pity for those who could not move. They would simply throw an elderly person into a truck and you could hear their bones break on impact. When they reached for his grandmother, his mother and sister moved forward to support her so that she would not be thrown. All three of them climbed on to the truck and it rumbled away. The guards would not let Otto get on that truck.

Later that night, in the cold, cramped barracks, Otto was frantic. 'What has happened to my mother and my sister and my grandmother?'

Another inmate turned sad eyes towards him. 'Look out of that window. See the smoke coming out of the chimney? That's all that's left of your family.'

And that's how Otto found out that his family had been murdered practically right in front of him, and he had been able to do nothing, even though he was a strong young man of seventeen. Even so, he had found within himself the strength to survive. His best friend from kindergarten, Paul, and his father were there with him, and they helped him to survive. In fact, Paul's father

Clockwise from top left:
I am six months old in this
photograph found in my aunt's
album. (Courtesy of the author)

This picture was taken in
Budapest, 1942. My father had
taken me to get my first
grownup haircut and permanent
and I was devastated by the
results. (Courtesy of the author)

I am seventeen years old in this
photograph. (Courtesy of the
author)

My dear mother,
Ethel Markowitz, in 1924.
(Courtesy of the author)

Jacob Schwarz Markowitz, my father, about 1936. He moved his wife and three children from small villages in Czechoslovakia to Budapest, Hungary, in 1938, to escape the Nazis.
(Courtesy of the author)

Dohany synagogue in Budapest.
(Courtesy of the author)

Richie and I often used to join the
families strolling along the promenade
by the Danube in Budapest.
(Hulton Getty)

The sight of the notorious 'death steps' filled us with horror on our arrival at Mauthausen concentration camp. (The Wiener Library)

The Displaced Persons camp in Wetzlar, Germany, where we lived from 1945 to 1949. (Courtesy of the author)

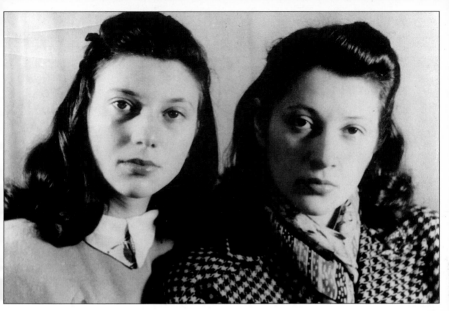

My sister Rose and I in Wetzlar, Germany, 1946.
(Courtesy of the author)

My family, just before leaving for the United States in 1949. Left to right: Betty, Larry, Ethel and Rose. (Courtesy of the author)

A photograph of Otto and I taken in March, 1947, just before our marriage. A friend of Otto's cut it in half because he didn't believe I treated Otto well. (Courtesy of the author)

My firstborn, Robert, and I in New York City in March, 1950. (Courtesy of the author)

The Schimmel family at Jeffrey's bar mitzvah in June, 1970.
Left to right: Bobby, Sandy, Jeffrey, Betty and Otto.
(Courtesy of the author)

Otto and I soon after our move to Arizona in August, 1973.
(Courtesy of the author)

In this photograph I am standing in front of the wall where Richie once carved our names. Budapest, 1999.
(© M Bouquet / *Woman's Journal* / IPC SYNDICATION)

The author today. (Courtesy of the author)

often gave his crust of bread to Paul or Otto. He died in Otto's arms, from starvation and exhaustion.

When Otto and Paul were liberated, Otto immediately contacted his cousins in Budapest. 'Where is my brother?' he asked. He learned that his brother, who had worked for the Underground, had been killed because, even though he was wearing an Arrow Cross armband to disguise his identity, he was recognized as a Jew and shot dead on the day after Christmas, a week before the Russians liberated Budapest. Otto's entire immediate family was gone.

But instead of crying he laughed. I could admire that, even though I have never been much of a one for jokes.

When I got back to Wetzlar, I told my mother about Otto.

'He's handsome and tall and funny, and I feel so sorry for him because he lost his whole family in the war. But he's also a little pushy and I don't like that. Still,' I said, smiling now, 'he is kind and gentle, and was considerate enough to take me back to Uncle Ignatz's house.'

My mother smiled at me. 'Are you interested in him, Baby?'

The question was like having cold water thrown in my face. 'I've told you, Mama, I still love Richie. I don't want anyone else.'

But I hadn't counted on Otto's persistence. Before long, he arrived in Wetzlar without an invitation. He had put on a few pounds and his body looked strong and powerful, but I still felt annoyed that he'd just shown up like that.

'What are you doing here?' I asked him.

He flashed me a jaunty smile, like a born salesman. 'I could not get you out of my mind, Baby. I couldn't eat, I couldn't sleep, all because I was thinking about you.'

I was appalled. 'Get over it,' I said. 'I'm in love with another boy.'

But Otto paid no attention to what I said. He kept on smiling and talking and joking. When my mother came into the room, he immediately began to charm her, and I could tell he was drawn to her, my gentle, strong mother. He sat and told her about how his family had died, how his last picture of his mother and sister was of helping his poor, sick grandmother on to that truck. My mother listened, and when he had finished his story, she put her arms around him and hugged him.

'I'll adopt you,' she said to him, rocking him back and forth. 'That way you'll have a family again.' And then both of them cried.

I could tell they had formed a new mutual admiration society. My mother made dinner and invited Otto to stay. I made a point of letting him know that I didn't care whether he was there or not. I was not interested in his advances. He was a nice young man, but he was not for me.

Otto stayed for about a week, and my mother took care of his every need. She fed him regularly, telling him she wanted to fatten him up. He was constantly with me when I was at home. When he said he wanted to go into town, I told him to go ahead, but he wouldn't go without me. I was annoyed that he stuck so close to me, but my mother told me to leave him alone.

'Don't insult him, Baby. It's not nice and it's not like you,' she said one day after I'd told Otto to go away.

I did try to be nice, but Otto wanted more, and he was always pushing.

I was glad when Otto went home. It was easy to breathe again. I no longer felt suffocated by Otto's constant presence, pressure and confessions of love. I lived my life just as everyone else in the camp did. I had a small job, I went to a study hour, I saw the doctor for the weekly examination each of us in camp received. In every bit of free time I had, I went to nearby camps looking for Richie, or at least for word of him. I couldn't bring myself to believe that he was really, truly dead, even though his name had appeared on that list at Kassel camp. I could not accept his death. I always hoped I would find him, and I never gave up.

As the weeks passed, our life in camp became more normal, if living in a displaced persons' camp with people recovering from the unspeakable could ever be termed 'normal'. More used clothing arrived, from the Joint Committee for Refugees which provided international relief for displaced persons, and we were thrilled to go through the clothing. I still had a good contact and was one of the first to go through the clothes, and my mother, sister and I found some very special things – dresses and skirts and shoes. It is hard to describe the feeling of having a real wardrobe again after a couple of years of living in rags. I was looking better and feeling better, except for the ache in my heart which only Richie could ease.

Otto came back again. This time, he had travelled all night to get to us. I wanted to run away when I saw him, but my mother said I shouldn't make something out of nothing. She said that he was just coming to visit us as a family member. Against my better judgment and what my own instincts told me, I chose to believe her. I think my mother had already begun to think of him as a son, and I know she had great compassion for what Otto had gone through.

Otto had gained some weight and some muscle. He said he'd been exercising, and it showed. He also had got some new clothing that was in better condition and more stylish. He certainly looked more like a civilized man and less like a former inmate of a concentration camp.

He still pursued me, and I was able to brush him off because I had begun to handle him better. When he visited, he slept on the floor in the middle room with the four men. I was impressed at how organized and clean he was. He kept all his things neatly and, in a situation where there was not a bathroom, he found a way to keep clean.

Otto was very spiritual, a deep thinker, and he talked about his ideas and beliefs. Sometimes his constant talk drove me crazy. He told me about his trade of making leather goods. He wanted me to know everything about him, and I wanted to scream, 'I don't care.' I still didn't want to have anything to do with him. Poor boy. He was trying so hard to impress me. I told him over and over again that he should leave, and maybe go back to Hungary and find an old girlfriend who was still alive.

'I don't have any old girlfriends,' he told me earnestly. 'I only have school friends. I'm not interested in anyone but you.'

Otto was determined to be my friend and more, but I had such a strong feeling that if I let him get close to me I wouldn't be able to get away that I did my best to avoid him. I told him again to leave, but he lingered for another few days and then went away without saying goodbye. I was happy to see him go, but his absence didn't last long. In about two weeks' time he was back, and he looked terrible, like a concentration camp survivor once again.

My mother was very concerned about him. She went over to him and put her arm around his shoulder. 'What is wrong, Otto?'

He kept his head down, as if he was ashamed of his

strong feelings. 'I'm in love with Baby and I haven't been able to eat or sleep since I left here.'

My mother was very gentle with him. 'Baby needs time before she loves anyone else again. She's still in love with Richie.'

'But I would give her up if Richie ever came back,' Otto said.

My mother just shook her head. 'I know you well enough to know you would not give her up once you were committed to her. You need to go back to your camp and live the life that God gave you back. You are a good person and you deserve love, and you shouldn't be running after someone who keeps rejecting you. She is not rejecting you as a person, it's just that she's still in love with someone else.'

Otto thought about what she'd said, and then he left again. He grabbed his rucksack, carefully packed his neatly folded belongings into it and said goodbye to all of us. He looked so sad at that moment that I felt something in my heart for him. I even felt sorry that I had asked him to go. But I was relieved when he left.

I was working long hours for Major Daniel, travelling with him to other camps. I still hoped I would find Richie.

A month later, Otto came back for a visit. He looked really good. He was eating well, he was exercising and, he told us, he was going to box in Munich, representing the camp at Weilheim. He wasn't pushy. I was happy about that because I thought it meant he had found a girl-friend and would leave me alone. But I found out later he was only playing a game, pretending to be just a friend. After that visit, I walked him to the train station, wished him luck with his fight and even let him kiss me goodbye.

As I waved to him as the train drew out of the station,

I felt I was finally free. Otto had found something else to occupy him, and I could go on living my life as I had to. He wrote to my mother, and he also sent regards to me. That was fine – much better than having him visit. A month went by and one morning the camp newspaper ran a story about a boxing match that had taken place in a camp in Munich. The picture with the story was of Otto, lying unconscious on the mat, his arm wrapped around his neck. The story said he'd been knocked out in the first minute of the first round. I started laughing as I looked at the picture, and couldn't resist writing him a note, enclosing the article. He never answered my note, I suppose because he was embarrassed by his ignominious defeat. I wrote to him again, this time an ironic note asking him whether he was now in training to fight Max Schmeling, a famous German boxer of the time. Once again, I got no answer.

Spring came, and with it, my birthday. Otto arrived at our camp, this time with some milk he had carried all the way from Weilheim. It had got so shaken up on the train that it was more like yoghurt than milk by the time he arrived. He also brought me chocolate and salami, both still hard-to-get delicacies in post-war Germany.

He smiled down at me. 'I would have brought you flowers, but I couldn't find any,' he said, 'and none were growing yet in the fields.'

I smiled back. 'That's all right, Otto.'

He took my hand. 'I wish you all the happiness in the world . . . with me,' he added slyly, his eyes twinkling.

I pulled my hand away, laughing. 'I'm sure you'll find your happiness and I'll find mine. You can leave now. I don't want to see you again,' I said, half teasing.

To my amazement, Otto grabbed his rucksack and walked out without looking back.

'Now you've done it, Baby,' my mother said sadly. 'You just let the most wonderful boy walk away. He loves you and he has no one. He came for your birthday and to celebrate life, and you threw him out. You had no right to do that. You could have been nicer.'

I just stood there, listening to my mother. Her voice was shaking, and she actually started to cry. 'I'm ashamed of how callous you are, Baby.'

I was devastated. My mother had never spoken to me that way, and she'd never told me how much she loved Otto. Without thinking, I ran out of the building, through the camp and across the fields, my high heels sinking into the dirt as I ran to the station. I felt I had to reach Otto before he left; had to tell him I was sorry. I ran faster, panting, jumping over some bushes that were in my way. I felt terrible. This man had said he'd loved me from the first day we met, had told me over and over again how he wanted to marry me and take care of me, and I had treated him badly. My mother was right. I had been mean to him, and now he was walking out of my life for ever. I had hurt my mother terribly by my behaviour too. And how could I have done that when my mother had sacrificed everything to save us during the war?

I knew what I had to do to make things right. All I had to do to make everyone happy was to marry Otto. I ran faster. The train would be coming any minute and I knew how fast Otto walked. He must be at the station by now. As I neared the bridge, I could see him. He was almost at the station.

I started yelling, calling him Karcsi, my pet nickname for him, which was short for Karl, his middle name and one I preferred to Otto . . . 'Karcsi, please, don't go. I love you. I will marry you.'

I saw him stop dead in his tracks. Then he turned and

ran towards me. When he reached me, his arms opened wide and I ran into them. We hugged and he kissed me. I had turned eighteen that day, and Otto was almost twenty.

We walked slowly back to the camp, his arm around my shoulders hugging me closely to him. Inside, I felt numb, in shock at the decision I had made so quickly. And I knew I had lied to Otto. Oh yes, I would marry him, for I had promised and I would not break his heart after it had been broken so many times before. But I did not love him. I loved Richie, and now, it seemed, I had ruined my chances of finding him for ever, even if he were alive.

'There is one thing, Karcsi,' I said as we walked back. 'If I find Richie before we are married, I will not marry you. And, even after we are married, if I find Richie, I might leave.'

He stood absolutely still, his body rigid beside mine in the moonlight, his arm still around me. I looked up at his face and I saw that he was staring out into the distance. I thought maybe there were tears in his eyes, but after a moment he nodded his head. We kept on walking and I felt his arm tighten around my shoulders. 'Never forget how much I love you, Baby,' he whispered down at me.

By the time we got back to the camp, my mother was frantic. She thought I had run out in anger and she was frightened that something had happened to me. When she saw me with Otto, she started to smile.

'You were right, Mama, I had to run after Otto and apologize and thank him for his lovely gifts,' I said, holding Otto's hand in mine.

Mama laughed. 'I am glad you children have made up. Now we can have the fine dinner and a beautiful cake I've made for your birthday, Baby.'

I hesitated, and I knew she saw from the look on my

face that there was something I wanted to say to her.

'What is it, daughter?'

'I've told Otto I will marry him,' I said. 'I know it's been your wish and now it will be so.'

'No,' my mother cried. 'I never said that you should get married, and certainly not now. If you want to get married after we get to the United States, we will talk about it then.'

But Otto was having none of that. I knew he was afraid that if I had too much time I might change my mind altogether. 'We are getting married here, and as soon as possible,' Otto said firmly.

'Please reconsider,' my mother begged. But Otto was adamant, so in the end we consulted the rabbi, who said we had to get married by 17 April or wait for six weeks after Passover. It was now 1 March.

'We'll get married on 15 April,' Otto said without hesitation.

I said nothing. Inside, I felt numb, as if all of this was happening to someone else, some other girl who perhaps really loved Otto, as I did not. But if Otto noticed my emotional distance, he never said anything about it. Then again, I had never been very cordial to him in the three months I'd known him, so he probably didn't expect more from me, even now that we were engaged. Besides, he was happy enough for both of us.

The weeks passed by in a haze. The only thing I remember clearly is visiting two more camps, hoping that I would find Richie there. But I didn't. Major Daniel and his wife took charge of the wedding. We had nothing – no money, no extra clothes – so the Major managed to find, somewhere in Germany, a beautiful white silk charmeuse street-length dress to serve as my wedding gown. He found fresh flowers for a bouquet and even managed to find a couple of barrels of salt herring for the celebration dinner.

Before I knew it, my wedding day had arrived. As if the gods were mocking me, it was a beautiful day – clear and sunny, warm enough to be May instead of April. Some-how, the Major had contrived to build a chupa for the ceremony and found a glass for us to break, as was the Jewish ritual, and the rabbi had handwritten the catuba, the Jewish marriage contract. I looked beautiful and Otto looked handsome in his borrowed suit. My sister stood beside me as my maid of honour as the rabbi led us through the ceremony. When the time came for the wed-ding ring, Otto produced the gold band proudly, even though we had had to borrow the money for it from a friend. I didn't care whether I had a ring or not, but Otto was determined that I should wear one. Evenutally the ceremony was over and the rabbi told Otto to kiss the bride. I raised my face up to his, closed my eyes, and imagined he was Richie.

The entire camp had turned out for the wedding, which was held outside. There were several thousand people there, many of them still suffering from what we had all been through. They sent up a great cheer of pure joy when Otto kissed me, as if this one life-affirming act could erase all the horror they had witnessed. We were the first to be married in camp, so I think we symbolized a new beginning for everyone.

How I wished I could have shared their hope and joy, but inside I was still numb. A part of me was angry at Otto for pursuing me so, and angry at myself for giving in. It had only been five months since I'd first met Otto and I felt as if I had been consumed by a whirlwind. Otto had suddenly become an integral part of the family, so close to my mother that he could have been her son. But

I felt like two people, the real Betty who still loved Richie and who would never deceive her husband by telling him she loved him when she didn't, and the Betty who had married Otto, who kissed without responding with any real feeling, who had to close her eyes and think of someone else to kiss at all.

But I hid all my turmoil behind a façade of fierce gaiety. It was my wedding day, and I would try to enjoy it. We ate and drank and danced, and we sang all the old Hungarian and gypsy songs, and I tried to make my heart feel light after so many years of pain. And I tried not to think of my coming honeymoon.

I needn't have worried, at least not right away. We were all very, very ill from the herring. It took about a week for us to feel human again. I was throwing up and had severe stomach camps, as if I had dysentery. Otto wasn't much better. We spent our wedding night on opposite sides of the sheet dividing my family's part of the room from the men's part of the room. He held my hand through the sheet and kissed my mouth through the sheet. We were too sick to do anything else.

It was two weeks before we consummated our marriage, and to do it in privacy we had to leave the camp and climb to the top of the mountain that towered over the camp. The irony didn't escape me. For years, I had dreamed of my honeymoon with Richie spent in glorious Venice, and now, here I was, on an army issue blanket on a mountaintop. Richie would have been talking to me when he kissed me and touched me. Otto was silent, so involved in his lovemaking that he barely said a word. All the memories of my first and only love came rushing back to me, overpowering me. I did not feel anything with Otto, no matter how hard I tried. I closed my eyes and bit my lips while he made love to me. To bear it, I had to imagine he was Richie and even then I was more observer than participant. When we finished, I opened my eyes and looked up at Otto as he leaned down to kiss me. I saw in his eyes how much he loved me. Maybe he even loved me as much as Richie did.

Life went on. On the surface, I was smiling and pleasant, someone who passed for happy. Otto was so happy that he sometimes yelled out on the street that he loved his wife. It would embarrass me and I would think, why does he have to yell like a mad man? But I understood. Once, I, too, had wanted to tell the whole world I was in love.

chapter *Eighteen*

I was married, but I still felt like a child, especially surrounded as I was by my mother, sister and brother. When the chance came to move to Weilheim, where Otto had lived before, I jumped at it. I wanted my own home, and I wanted some distance from my family, much as I loved them. A few hundred miles would do it. Perhaps, I thought, with privacy I might achieve the intimacy with Otto that I didn't have now. At least I would be running my own home.

It was in Weilheim that my marriage really began. There I had to learn to cook and to do daily chores and, most of all, I had to learn to live with Otto. We were surrounded by Otto's friends, most of whom didn't like me because they felt I had tortured him during the first few months of our courtship. Even a picture Otto had of the two of us had been torn in half by one of them, so that I was missing from the picture. I realized I would have to prove to them that I was worthy of Otto.

Otto's friends were as zany and funny as he was. His friend Little George, who I had met at the Brauwastl Hotel, was a year younger and had a droll sense of humour, which was amazing considering he had survived the horrors of Auschwitz. Another George, a friend of both of ours, was also in Weilheim, but he had known me before he'd known Otto and I did not have to prove myself to him. Otto's friend Paul was a lifelong friend, the one he had gone through Auschwitz with, whose father had died in Otto's arms. The bond between Otto and Paul was like the bond between two brothers.

We lived on the top floor of an old Bavarian-style house owned by an 84-year-old German woman named Frau Marie, who was gruff but kind. There was no running water and no electricity, and the toilet was a small room off the kitchen with a seat with a hole in it. At night, I would have to walk down there in the dark. One particularly horrible night when I sat down on that bench I found hundreds of white maggots. I don't know how I managed not to scream. We washed in a large basin, with water which we hauled upstairs in buckets heated on the wood-burning stove. Fortunately, all our meals were at the hotel down the street and we were allowed to take baths there as well, which is what I did.

From the beginning, Otto was a very good husband. He would have brought the stars down from the sky if I had asked him to. As it was, he served me breakfast in bed every day – in a manner of speaking. He had promised, when we were engaged, that he would spoil me, even bringing me breakfast in bed, but I never dreamed he would try to fulfil this promise. When we lived in Weilheim, his job was to deliver bread from the bakery to the camp and to those refugees housed in private homes. The German government was made to pay all the expenses for housing refugees, and fresh bread was part of their obligation. Each morning, Otto had to get up very early, take his big four-wheeled cart to the bakery and bring back delicious fresh loaves for the camp. I would still be in bed when he made his deliveries. He would call to me through the open bedroom window, and then a warm loaf of bread would come sailing through to land on the bed. This was Otto's version of breakfast in bed.

Much as Otto loved me and secure as he was about his work abilities, he was very insecure in our relationship, and I knew I had done that to him. He had never really recovered from the loss of his mother and his sister, and he was not sure of my love. He had promised me that if I found Richie, he would let me go, and the threat of that was always in the back of his mind. One night when he had a nightmare – and like me he had nightmares on many nights over many years – I woke him and he told me the nightmare had been about Richie.

'What's the matter, Otto?' I asked softly, gently shaking him awake from his nightmare. He was crying and he said, 'Don't ever leave me. I am so alone.'

I was stunned and very frightened. 'But you said I could leave you if I ever found Richie.'

He didn't answer me, but just cried as I held him and tried to comfort him. 'I love you more than life itself, Baby,' he said over and over again.

I did not want to hear this. I wanted him to confirm his promise to me that he would let me go if I ever found Richie, but he never did. Still, even as Otto suffered, I continued to look for Richie. He was so much still a part of me that I could not stop. I felt sorry that this made Otto unhappy, but I could not help it and I would not give up my hope of finding Richie alive one day.

Because he was so insecure in our relationship, Otto was very jealous of anyone who even looked at me and would get into fights with them. I could not even go to a dance with him without his commenting on the men who were looking at me. After a while, he began to keep those thoughts to himself because I demanded that he not act like such an idiot.

In those first couple of years after the war, Otto was a very angry, violent young man. He had fist fights. He once even gave me a flat-handed push when I suggested that he hadn't been well brought up. His language was often coarse and crude, and it really embarrassed me. 'Were you raised by monkeys in the jungle?' I asked him. He moved so quickly that I didn't have time to react when suddenly he pushed me backwards, his palm on my chest. 'Don't you ever criticize my upbringing, because that is to criticize my mother, and I will never hear a word against her. She was an angel.'

Looking back, I realize that we were both still children, even though our childhoods had been taken from us by the war and by the Holocaust. Otto and his friends were still angry at the Germans who had done this to us. They told me a story once about a bar where Otto politely asked a girl who was with a German date if she wanted to dance. The fellow insulted Otto, calling him a dirty Jew. Otto waited until the fellow went to the bathroom and his companions were on the dance floor. Then Otto went over and quietly peed in his beer.

Once his morning job was done, our days were free and often we would go out looking at furniture. Once I told him how much I loved Oriental furniture and how I hoped to own some one day, and to buy it on a trip to China, since I had inherited my father's wanderlust.

The next day when I came home from an errand, I

gasped when I looked at our living-room furniture, which was owned, of course, by Frau Marie. In fact, the pieces were family heirlooms passed down from one generation to the next. In an effort to fulfil my wish for Oriental furniture, Otto had cut off most of the legs of the two-seater sofa, the table and four chairs. I can still hear Frau Marie's shrieks when she saw her mutilated furniture for the first time. 'What did I ever do to you that you should destroy my inheritance?' she wailed.

After the first couple of months, I developed a new confidence in myself as a married lady. I could function without my mother and could even cook – perhaps not as well as she could, for she was a truly wonderful cook, but I could prepare tasty meals and each day I experimented and learned something. Once, when I tried to cook soup, the beans were on the stove for hours but wouldn't get soft. Eventually, Frau Marie said she was running out of wood for the stove, and she slipped some white powder into the soup. I came back into the room as she was doing it, and I was sure she was poisoning us. I told Otto, who came running downstairs, shouting at her to explain her actions. The old woman looked terrified, and explained that she had merely added some bicarbonate of soda to make the soup cook faster. But I had not got over my mistrust of Germans, and I still refused to eat the soup and wouldn't let Otto eat it, either. Instead, we went over to the hotel for a group meal, where we knew the food hadn't been doctored.

Most of us had this abiding distrust of the Germans because of what had been done to us. I had one friend who was pregnant and refused to see a German doctor, even when she was about to deliver. Several of us dragged her to the local hospital, where they put her in a room, but every time a doctor came near her she would scream and say, 'Get that German doctor away from me. He will kill my baby.' Finally, she allowed us to bring a nurse into the room to advise us as we helped her deliver. My job was to hold her hands, and her nails cut into my hands so much that my palms looked as if they'd been clawed by a cat. When I told my mother I had witnessed childbirth, she said, 'The pain is awful, but God makes us forget it so that we have more children.'

My cooking experiments continued, and I was quite proud of each new accomplishment, wanting to show off for Otto's friends. When I had finally mastered dessert pancakes, I invited Little George and Paul over for dinner and served them the mouthwatering morsels. Chubby little Paul liked them so much that he ate and ate, finally lying on the floor as I dropped them into his mouth, like a sleek, contented seal.

Surprisingly, my mother respected my new-found independence and she never interfered in our affairs. She trusted Otto completely. Whatever Otto did was good enough for her, and Otto told her everything he did. He wrote her letters all the time telling her how happy he was with his little wife.

Our lives settled into a pleasant routine and day by day I was winning his friends over as they saw what good care I took of Otto, although it wasn't until we had our first child and two of his friends became his godfathers that they really accepted me without reservation. If the sex for me was still more a duty than a pleasure, I never spoke about it to anyone, and hoped Otto didn't notice.

Back in Wetzlar, my mother was coping as best she could. My sister Rose had taken a long time to get her strength back from the starvation, exhaustion and infections we had endured. For both of us, it took months after the liberation for our menstrual cycles to become normal. But of all of us, it was my little brother Larry who bore the brunt of the physical consequences of our ordeal. Only ten at the time of the march, he had basically been starving for two growth years of his life. He had also had a very high fever in the camp and after the war doctors surmised that he might have had a mild case of polio, which had caused some permanent curvature of his spine. At any rate, physically, he still looked much younger, was still frail and was still underweight for his size and age.

Emotionally, Larry seemed to have more scars as well. Even though my mother had tried to shield him as much as possible from the physical and mental hardships, carrying him for the march across Hungary, he had still seen and experienced things that would have killed the average ten-year-old. In fact, most children his age had not survived the hardships of the march and the camps, but then they hadn't had my mother to see them through. Larry was still suffering.

Otto and I would go to visit my family about once a month, bringing presents when we could. My brother and sister both loved Otto, which was ironic because when Rose first met Otto, she said to me, 'Where did you find that peasant?' She had thought him rude and crude. But now she loved him, and he treated them as if they were his brother and sister, too. I know this made a big difference in Larry's life, since he had lived so much of his childhood without an adult male figure in it. Otto was not a substitute for the father he had lost, but he was at least a big brother, and a funny, loving one at that, who made him laugh and taught him how to box. I did love Otto for that: for how he loved my family and honoured my mother. I could see what a good man he was and how genuine he was with his love and his feelings. But he also kept a lot inside and he was plagued by demons, as so many survivors were. I never felt that Otto was at peace, even when he was laughing – perhaps especially when he was laughing. But then I had my mask in place, too, so who was I to blame him?

I tried to live life the way my mother believed we should, to take what comes and make the best of it. Otto was a good man and a very good husband. Richie was still missing, perhaps dead. I had made the best of things, hadn't I?

A year went by very quickly. We were all going to America, but unfortunately not all of us were going at the same time. Otto's immigration papers, through the displaced persons' camp in Weilheim, came through in February 1948. As his wife, I could have elected to go with him, but my family's papers in Wetzlar had not yet come through. For all my newly won independence, I didn't feel right about leaving my mother behind with two children, one of whom was still frail. I decided I would wait and leave with her, never dreaming that it would be almost another year before I would be able to join Otto. On the other hand, I can't deny that the thought of being separated from him made me feel free, in a way that I hadn't felt since we'd married. A little voice inside me said, 'Perhaps he will meet someone else in America, someone who really loves him, and he will divorce me.' I liked that idea, but I never told anyone.

When Otto left, I moved back home with my family in the camp in Wetzlar. Meanwhile, Otto suffered terribly on the ship to America, being so seasick that he could barely move. Even so, he wrote every day of that journey and every day after he got to New York. I never seemed to answer him fast enough.

His arrival in New York was only the beginning of a

brand-new struggle for him. He and his friend Little George met up with another fellow named George, who they immediately dubbed Big George, and they decided to share an apartment so that they could pool their expenses. Little George was a tailor and Big George was a waiter, so they both made more money than Otto did in his first job cleaning tables in a café. In fact, Otto never had any money, because whatever he had left over after his expenses, he gave to me. I was always writing, asking for things I imagined he could get easily in America, never stopping to think of the cost or whether Otto could afford it. In a way, I think I was testing his love, waiting for him to say no to something, so that I could tell myself he didn't really love me all that much. But he never said no. I would ask for mayonnaise or caviar, and he would send it. Once he sent three blouses, all in the same style, from Woolworth's, one in pink, one in white, one in blue. He even bought me underpants, because you couldn't get any new clothing goods in Germany and, besides, we didn't have any money. We were totally dependent on the charity of the Americans and the Germans. I felt so starved for life's little luxuries and, fairly or unfairly, I expected Otto to provide them. It was only after I got to New York myself and realized what he had been earning and what his expenses had been that I understood what each of my luxuries had cost him.

While Otto was working hard to establish himself in New York, we were waiting for the American immigration authorities to allow my brother to emigrate. They kept examining him and telling us he was just too thin and frail to survive the trip to the United States.

We spent the rest of 1948 and the first two months of 1949 in the camp at Wetzlar. By that time, I was beginning to doubt that my life would ever have a new start. I had tried to use that time in Europe to find Richie, but with the same result. I could find no trace of him except for that ominous listing at Kassel, which said that he had died.

My mother did her best to fatten up my brother, who felt terrible that he was keeping us from going to America. Major Daniel helped with milk and eggs and all the rich food he could find for us. Eventually, Larry started to put on a few pounds.

We sailed for the United States in February 1949 and arrived on 14 March, a couple of weeks after my twentieth birthday. I still remember my first glimpse of the Statue of Liberty and the tall skyscrapers beyond. New York looked like a city filled with promise. Perhaps here I would finally be safe and happy.

chapter *Nineteen*

 As the boat docked, my eyes scanned the pier. I can't say I was sorry to leave the ship. The *SS Marine Shark* had originally been built by the army to transport 500 soldiers. In our case, it had been used to transport 1,000 refugees. The crossing had been crowded, and the accommodation less than luxurious, but everyone was filled with hope. The thought of coming to America was a very powerful one. So now, as I looked down at the faces on the pier, I felt ready to start my new life.

There, looking tall and handsome, was Otto, in an overcoat a few sizes too big. Next to him were my Aunt Rose and her husband, my Uncle Victor. Next to me, I heard my mother cry out as she saw her sister. We rushed down the gangway to greet them. My mother and Aunt Rose hugged for a long time, tears streaming down both their faces. We were crying, too, knowing how they must feel to be survivors of what had once been a large and loving family, so many of whom were now gone.

I ran to Otto and he opened his arms. 'I have missed you so much, Baby,' he whispered in my ear. I could feel the heat of his body and the intensity of what he was feeling by how tightly he held me, as if he wanted to fold my body into his. I forced myself to respond.

Once we had been through passport control, we were on our way, in two separate taxis – Otto, Uncle Victor, Larry and I were in one cab, and my mother, Aunt Rose and my sister in another. We took the cabs all the way to my aunt's small apartment in the Bronx, where we camped out for the first night. It was a one-bedroom apartment, but Aunt Rose had bought both a couch and a chair that opened into beds and for one night we were able to survive, even though it was packed with people. My mother, sister and brother went to stay with my Aunt Lina, I stayed with Aunt Rose and Otto went back to the apartment he shared with his two friends. Privacy did not exist for us, but it didn't matter just then, because there was so much to do to get settled.

On my first weekend in New York, Otto came to get me at my Aunt Rose's and took me back to his apartment, where he had made sure his friends would be out for the day. He made love to me once, and then again. Nothing felt different. I still felt like a truly displaced person in his arms.

The next week, we looked for jobs and an apartment that all of us could share. My mother, sister and I found jobs through the Joint Committee for Refugees. We went to work in a jewellery manufacturing firm owned by a German man named Weltner. The three of us worked side by side. My mother and my sister quickly began to design pieces in their spare time and eventually were given design assignments. The work paid by the piece, so you had to work quickly, and the money was

not generous, but at least we had jobs. And we needed
them, because we had found a one-bedroom apartment
to share in Manhattan's Yorkville section. By pooling our
money, we could just afford the $100-a-month rent plus
food, utilities and subway fare. There wasn't much left
over. My mother immediately enrolled Larry in school,
happy at least that her dream for him would be achieved
and that he would finish the education the war had interrupted.

Otto got a job in a leather goods factory, where he
worked long hours, but he seemed to love the work. On
the surface, he seemed all right but I soon learned that
underneath, his demons were still there. It was Aunt
Rose who realized, when Otto first came to New York,
how depressed he was. Perhaps because he had been all
alone, with just his two friends, it hit him all over again
that he had lost his entire family. He was terribly lonely.
Aunt Rose sensed that and immediately adopted Otto.
But she also realized that her affection and attention
alone weren't enough to help Otto with his problems.
She thought she had a solution, but she wasn't sure how
to get Otto to accept her help.

Aunt Rose had a friend who was a well-known
Freudian psychiatrist with a substantial private practice
at Bellevue Hospital. She asked this man to meet Otto
and talk to him to see if he could confront what was
troubling him.

Otto went to the man's apartment, at first only knowing that he was a friend of Aunt Rose and some kind of
medical doctor. Otto told me later that as they talked, he
found it odd that the man was asking him so many
questions about his thoughts and feelings, including what
he thought about Germans and Hungarians and
Americans. They even talked about Otto sending me all

those luxury items. The psychiatrist told him that if it made him feel better to send me these things, Otto should continue to do it, even though it was a financial sacrifice to him.

Otto eventually told this man about his feelings of loss and anger and depression. The doctor then told Otto he was a psychiatrist and could help him, and at first Otto insisted on paying him, but the doctor refused to take his money, saying that he was a friend as well as a therapist. Having him to talk to probably saved Otto's life. For years, he would go back to this man and bare his soul. It was the only place where Otto felt he could do this. And even with the therapy, Otto suffered from depression as well as the nightmares that plagued his sleep for many years and still haunt him, even now.

Otto and I fought all the time. Maybe it was the pressure of living on top of one another with very little privacy, or maybe it was my anger that in our year of separation he had not found someone else, and still wanted me. I, on the other hand, was still ready to end this marriage. In the meantime, Otto wanted us to get married again in New York. We'd been married by a rabbi in Wetzlar and had had a short civil service in Weilheim, but Otto claimed he wasn't sure that we were legally married in America.

'The wedding with the rabbi isn't a legal wedding,' he said, 'and we never got a certificate from Weilheim. It may be on file in their town hall, but we have no copy and therefore no proof of our legal marriage.'

I was all for keeping it that way. No legal marriage meant no divorce; all I would have to do would be to walk away. But Otto moved with typical speed and single-mindedness, aided and abetted by Aunt Rose. She found a judge who was willing to perform yet another marriage ceremony and even helped Otto find me a brand-new wedding ring, one that wasn't much better than the first one, since we still had no extra money. When I saw the new ring, I told Otto I didn't like it, hoping that that would delay any wedding. No such luck. Otto shrugged. 'It will have to do for now, because we're getting married today.'

I was in shock. Once again, events were speeding past me. This was my life, but I didn't feel I had any control over it. It was a sunny day in late April 1949 when we walked into the judge's chambers in Yonkers, New York, with Aunt Rose and Uncle Victor as witnesses.

'I don't want to do this,' I said to Otto as we sat there waiting for the judge. 'I don't think I want to be married to you any more.'

Before he could even reply, Aunt Rose jumped into the discussion. 'Would you stop throwing this boy around as if he's some kind of children's ball?'

I couldn't believe she would take his side, but just as I was about to say so, the judge appeared and asked, 'Who's to be married?' Otto raised his hand and pointed to both of us. 'Where are the witnesses?' the judge wanted to know, and Aunt Rose and Uncle Victor raised their hands. With that, the judge performed the ceremony before I could say or do anything. It took exactly three minutes. I was so mad and frustrated at once again being steamrollered by Otto and my family that when the judge handed me the marriage certificate, I tore it in half. Once again, Otto had got his way, and now I was surely trapped, married to Otto for ever in my new country which I had hoped would provide me with a second chance.

After the ceremony, Aunt Rose had a cake for our wedding – a strawberry whipped-cream cake – at her apartment. She invited my mother, my brother and my sister and Aunt Lina and Uncle Ignatz. They were all ecstatically happy, and I was angry. I stayed angry for two days.

We lived together as one big extended family for over a year in our tiny furnished one-bedroom apartment. Otto and I put a bed in the kitchen. Needless to say, we had little privacy, but in a way that suited me fine. But in other ways, the situation drove me crazy. We were crowded into this tiny space, and I could never rest because my brother played the radio constantly and my mother kept an eye on me all the time. Whenever I wanted to go somewhere, my mother would say, 'Wait for your husband to come home.' I couldn't go anywhere without him.

I wanted a husband who talked to me about everything, but all Otto really talked about was his work; otherwise, he was boring, a closed-up personality. My family was considerate, though. Every Saturday they all went out for a few hours and left Otto and me alone so that we could make love. I closed my eyes and remained as distant from his caresses as if I were viewing them from the moon instead of experiencing them first-hand. When we made love, I felt as if I didn't exist. And, although Otto didn't say anything – we never discussed it – I knew he could tell I was not responding and I knew that that made him angry. His solution was to work more hours, to make more money, to try to buy me more things, perhaps to buy the love he felt I wasn't giving him.

Some Saturdays we all went on long walks together, dressed in our best clothes to enjoy the lights of Times Square and window shopping on Fifth Avenue, where we longed for the things we still could not afford to buy. But

we could dream. Since Saturday was our sabbath and day
of rest, on Sunday we would go to the launderette and do
the laundry for the week. Otto was the perfect son-in-
law. When we went food shopping, he refused to let my
mother carry any packages at all.

'I can do it, Otto,' she would say.

But Otto would just smile as he reached over and
grabbed the packages. 'You have carried enough to last a
lifetime,' he would tell her.

I liked working at the jewellery company and it laid
the seeds for the serious jewellery designing I did years
later, but when a better-paying opportunity came along,
I left Weltner for a job in a factory that made expensive
handpainted scarves. I would paint the intricate designs
and sometimes create patterns of my own; and often
they would ask me to model the scarves for buyers.

I liked my job and had accepted my marriage, at least
for the moment, but I had a secret. I wasn't feeling well
and I realized I hadn't had my period for about four
months. Eventually I told Otto and my mother and they
immediately found me a Hungarian doctor to see. Otto
went with me on what turned out to be a long walk
there. I realized I might be pregnant, but when the doctor told me I was five or six months' pregnant, I was in
shock. First, it didn't make any sense. I hadn't been here
long enough to be that pregnant by Otto and I certainly
hadn't slept with anyone else, but the doctor was
adamant about how far gone I was. I couldn't help it, but
I started to cry. I had only been in America since March
and now the doctor was telling me I was going to give
birth in November or December. My last words to the
doctor were that he was wrong about my due date.

All the way home, I could see happiness in Otto's eyes.
'I have lost my family and now you are giving me a

new family, Baby, and that means all the world to me,'
Otto said, holding my hand as we walked home.

'Don't expect this baby so soon,' I told him sharply.
'There's no way this child will be an autumn baby.'

I worked at the scarf factory until my pregnancy
showed and then they told me I had to leave, because I
could no longer model scarves in the showroom. In
those days, pregnant women weren't allowed in the
workplace. But while the scarf factory wouldn't allow
me to work while I was pregnant, my old boss, Mr
Weltner, was happy to take me back at the jewellery factory and I was able to work there right up to the day
before I delivered.

One morning in the second week of December, I woke
up with labour pains. I walked to the doctor's office on
West 105th Street, twenty-three blocks north and ten
blocks west of where we lived on East 82nd. It was a
Sunday morning. When I asked the doctor what was
wrong with me, he examined me and told me I was two
centimetres dilated, at the beginning of labour, and I
should wait in his front office for an hour for the labour
to progress. I sat there in the front office and there was
no change, so finally he called me in and gave me an
injection to induce labour. I sat there for a few hours
more, and nothing happened, even though he gave me
more injections, eleven altogether. Then he sent me
home and told me he'd see me at the hospital later that
day.

Once again, I walked home from the doctor's office,
this time with no labour pains at all. The doctor kept calling through the afternoon and evening, which was no
easy task because we had no telephone in the apartment.
He would call one of our neighbours, who would have to

come and get us to talk on their telephone. Finally, he stopped calling and I went to sleep.

When I woke up the next morning, I felt just fine, so fine, in fact, that I decided to go to work. I worked for about another month, until 15 January, when I went into real labour. Again, it was a Sunday, and Otto took me to William Booth Memorial Hospital in Manhattan, a charity hospital, because we had no money to pay maternity fees. They put me in a labour room with another woman and after a while they asked Otto to leave, which made him very sad. He wanted to stay with me. By then, it was past midnight and I was screaming with pain; but the doctor told me he had to wait to deliver my child because the baby was in the breech position. I was in labour for what felt like an eternity, but finally at three o'clock in the morning, the doctor wheeled me into the delivery room. I begged him to give me something for the pain: I had wanted to have a natural childbirth, but the pain was too intense. He gave me something that put me out, but not enough. I felt the cut of the episiotomy and a hand up inside me turning the baby. After that my son came out fast, giving me immediate but momentary relief because the next thing I felt were the stitches.

But none of that mattered. I got my first glimpse of my son Robert and it was love at first sight. He was on the small side – only six pounds and one ounce, but then I was small and this was my first child. Much later, I was told that the doctor could have killed my baby with all those injections to induce labour.

I stayed in the hospital for a week and I was in a lot of pain from my stitches. Bobby cried a lot, and when I got home everyone pitched in to help take care of him. We had a bris, a ceremonial circumcision, for him, but I was not allowed to attend because it was the custom then that it was bad luck for the mother to be present. It was a small breakfast and we had placed an advertisement in the local Jewish newspaper in Yorkville inviting anyone from our community to attend. Otto was happy because he had begun the task of recreating the family he had lost. Already, he said, he could see his older brother in our son. I did a lot of complaining and a lot of crying. I was washing nappies all the time and taking care of a demanding infant, and I wasn't prepared for all that. I loved my job and wanted to go back to work, but I couldn't find anyone to take care of the baby during the day, so I stayed at home. I asked my mother to bring me piecework home from the factory and, at night, when others were there to help with Bobby, I did the work. During the day, my baby seemed to absorb every minute of my time.

A new baby changed life for all of us in that cramped apartment. Larry could no longer play the radio because there was no door between the kitchen, where the baby slept, and the living room, where the radio was. My sister, who had blossomed from a short, scrawny adolescent into a willowy young woman with a gorgeous figure, had started to date but now could no longer bring her dates home because we had nappies hanging everywhere. Bobby was a difficult baby – a finicky eater and a delicate sleeper who woke up often, cried and fussed a lot. And I was an inexperienced mother in an unhappy marriage trying to cope with all this. It was a nerve-racking situation for everyone.

It was ironic, in a way. Living in a concentration camp and then a displaced persons' camp we had had to learn to get along with strangers, but now we couldn't get on with each other living under one roof. We argued because I didn't clean the bathroom or didn't make dinner, a chore that had become my daily job and was beyond my limited culinary skills. Every argument seemed to need a mediator. We were at each other's throats.

Something had to change. When Bobby was about eight months old, none of us could stand it any more. Otto, Bobby and I took our own apartment upstairs, even though financially it was a strain for all of us, including my mother and sister. I felt guilty about leaving them, but I had no choice. I needed to have room to think and breathe. Besides, Otto and I were still fighting all the time, and it was difficult to have a fight when everybody took Otto's side.

Upstairs, we still fought, mostly about how much Otto worked. He worked twelve hours and more a day, and worked most Saturdays as well, leaving me alone with an infant in a fourth-floor flat with no lift. I would have to go down to the basement to wash the nappies and then come back up to hang them out to dry on the roof. And I had to take Bobby, in his pram, with me. It was impossible, and I resented being cooped up with a baby, cut off from the excitement of work or the possibility of making new friends.

What, I would ask myself as I rocked Bobby to sleep, had become of my life?

chapter *Twenty*

*W*e may have lived separately, but we were all still connected financially, with one bank account to support our two households. Whoever needed money took it out of the account. That arrangement created even more problems. After having had nothing, we all had our own dreams for that money. I wanted to save for an apartment of our own with our own furniture, my sister wanted clothes, my brother wanted a record player and my poor mother and Otto just wanted me to be happy. But where was my happiness? My baby was my only friend. And I took great advantage of that friendship by talking to him every day about how miserable my life had been and still was in some ways. Bobby just cooed and smiled at me, as if he was telling me that life was going to get better.

I may have been unhappy and I still longed for Richie, but I also wanted a better life for my new family. By the end of the year, I had saved enough money so that we

were able to get a fourth-floor furnished apartment in
the Bronx. It cost only $45 a month instead of the $100
we'd been paying on East 82nd Street. If I saved the difference, I would be able to afford a nice unfurnished
apartment and furniture of our own instead of the awful
mismatched castoffs that came with furnished apartments. True, we would have to live in the Bronx instead
of Manhattan, but we could have a better apartment and
that was more important.

Otto was working as hard as ever, although he now
tried not to work on Saturdays (except just before
Christmas when he would have to work Saturdays and
Sundays). He had taken a new job with two brothers who
had been salesmen for Buxton, and were starting up on
their own to create the Carter Leather Goods Company.
They were great salesmen, but knew nothing about
manufacturing, and that's where Otto came in. He was
hired to design and manufacture leather goods for them,
and he made the business very lucrative for them. He
worked day and night for them, set up the entire factory,
opened and closed it every night, and was the first one in
and the last one out. He took the job at the end of 1949
and worked there until 1955.

He was earning more money than he had at his last
job, but he was home even less and when he was he was
so exhausted that all he could do was sleep. We fought
the most during the years he worked for Carter because
he had no time for me and Bobby.

'I have nothing to do and no one to talk to,' I would say
over and over again.

Otto's solution was to buy us a television set for
Hanukkah that year. We were one of the first families in
our immigrant crowd to have one, and it cost an outrageous $500 dollars, which was all his bonus, but Otto

was extremely pleased with himself.

'Now you have company,' he told me proudly.

I just shook my head, but after a few months I had to admit that Otto was right to buy us a television. Bobby fell in love with it instantly, learning unaccented English and every commercial jingle on the air. His favourite was about Ajax, the foaming cleanser. And he loved to imitate Jackie Gleason saying '*And away we go!*' Perhaps it's even why Bobby is well-known comic Robert Schimmel today. He is a true baby boomer.

Television taught me English too, making me much more fluent than I had been, teaching me the slang and idiom of the language and helping me to build my vocabulary. On the other hand, the television was no substitute for human companionship, and I told Otto so. He would nod in understanding and still come home at eight o'clock at night to sit and fall asleep in front of the television. Desperate for some human contact, I would put Bobby to bed and then go shopping at night, leaving Otto to babysit our sleeping child. But it was no good. I would come home a couple of hours later and Otto would be sound asleep in his chair and baby Bobby would be sitting up watching television.

'How can I leave you with a sleeping baby and come home to find you sleeping and him watching television?' I would demand.

On such occasions Otto had the good grace to blush. 'I guess he can climb out of his cot,' he said. 'And he really likes television.'

From then on, I made Otto watch without the sound on so that Bobby wouldn't hear the television and climb out of his cot. It was a mad way to live. In an effort to get Otto to spend some time with his family, I demanded that he spend part of Saturday and Sunday with us. On

Saturday, he had to help me do the laundry, carting the nappies and the sheets and towels down four flights of stairs and walking four blocks to the launderette, where we sat with Bobby and watched everything tumbledry. It took hours, because we always had a couple of loads. On Sundays, I made him wear a jacket and tie to take Bobby and me for a walk, just as my father had done with us so many years ago in Budapest.

He never complained, but I never felt that he really enjoyed it. Otto lived inside himself, perhaps with his demons. Alone together at night, after dinner, we sat but didn't talk. I could hardly bear it. Each working day, Otto would leave at six o'clock in the morning, take two subways to his job on Broadway and 14th Street, and not come home at night until seven-thirty or eight o'clock at night. I felt as if I was dying from loneliness.

One day I told Otto that there was a Hungarian dance on and I wanted to go. Otto refused. He still hated the Hungarians as much as ever.

'If they had not allowed the Arrow Cross and the Nazis to do this to us, we would have been saved,' he would say over and over again. He would make jokes about the Hungarians. 'Do you know the favourite Hungarian recipe for chicken?' he would ask anyone who would listen. 'First you steal a chicken . . .'

But I still wanted to go. I loved the Hungarian songs and the gypsy music, and I was starved of the company of other fun-loving young people who spoke my language and knew my customs. Finally, Otto agreed to go, but we were still fighting about it in the car on the way there. I didn't care what he said. 'Look, I have to have some kind of a life apart from the baby,' I told him, but he just didn't understand. So he came to the dance but he was so cross with me that he refused to dance with me.

My sister Rose and her girlfriend had come along with us. They looked stunning in identically cut dresses, one in black and one in white. My sister's friend was a blonde, so she wore the black and my sister, a brunette, wore the white. They looked as stylized as two art deco figurines. I wore a simple, elegant black velvet suit.

The music began to play and my feet began to tap to the beat. My shoulders were swaying back and forth and I was singing along softly. But still Otto would not dance with me.

'All right,' I said, with a toss of my head, as I surveyed the room. I spotted a very good-looking man across the room and went up to him and asked him to dance with me. He gave me a big smile. 'It would be my pleasure.'

He was a smooth, natural dancer, as I was, and we moved across the floor, talking and smiling all the while. When the dance was over, this fellow, whose name was Jerry Horvath, asked me if I was with someone and I told him I was married to Otto. He looked a little disappointed that I was married, but he was thrilled that it was to Otto. He and Otto were good friends.

I gave him a speculative look. 'There is someone I would like you to meet,' I said, grabbing his hand and walking him over to my sister.

And that is how Rose met her husband Jerry, who is as devoted to her today as he was that night they first met in 1951. And he is as close and as good to me as a brother.

Jerry was an optician by trade, but he didn't want to remain one, so he went to hotel management school and ended up being manager of New York's Park Lane Hotel for twenty-five years, where he served as a right-hand manager to Leona Helmsley. They have one son, who is now a well-known blues guitarist who plays all over the world.

I knew as soon as I saw them together that there was
magic happening for them, and I felt both happy and sad.
I was happy for my sister, who had suffered so much in
her young life, but I was sad for myself because I had had
the magic once and now I'd lost it. My thoughts drifted
back to Budapest and the memory of Richie's first kiss. It
had felt so natural to feel his mouth against mine and I
remembered what he'd said to me that day. 'You are
mine, *kis pofa*, and nobody else is ever going to
experience this kind of kissing with either one of us.'

I closed my eyes, feeling suddenly faint from a
memory that was so strong. I had always loved Richie's
lips and I would touch them, tracing their line, after
every soul-searching kiss, as if to memorize the shape of
his mouth and carry it with me. I kept my eyes closed and
I could see us together; see Richie kissing my hand, then
biting off a piece of bread and sharing it by putting it into
my mouth. He was always so romantic. We'd even
invented our own secret language so that we could 'kiss'
without anyone knowing, even in a crowd. He would
wink at me and I would wink at him, and that meant
'kiss' in our private language.

I had to look away from the light shining in my sister's
eyes. Suddenly, the dance was no longer fun. I didn't
think I would ever have that kind of heartfelt fun again,
because my love had been taken from me. As the years
had gone by with no word from him, I couldn't help but
think that Richie truly was dead. Otherwise, surely he
would have found me by now, would have rescued me
from marriage to a man I did not love. I was very quiet
on the way home from the dance, and Otto didn't
question me because he was still cross. Good, I thought,
because at least he will not try to make love to me
tonight. I couldn't bear it.

*

Life went on. Otto continued to leave for work at dawn and return when it was dark. He dutifully helped me with the laundry and walked with me and Bobby in the park, but that was the extent of our life. I had no friends, no one to talk to about how isolated I felt and how desperately unhappy I was. I tried to just go along day by day, to tell myself that I was very lucky, that I had nothing to complain about. We bought some furniture, with a loan from Otto's boss as a down payment. I was acquiring some of the things I wanted, but I still felt empty inside. Otto and I were living together, but our lives were not one.

I was dragging the pram back up the fourth flight of stairs one day, Bobby cradled in my other arm, when I just couldn't stand it any more. 'This is not a life,' I said to myself. 'I want a life.'

I called a Hungarian man who I was friendly with – he loved America so much that he had enlisted in the American army – and asked him if he would drive me to my mother's. It was 1952. By this time, my mother and Larry had moved to Sunnyside in Queens. I packed everything I owned into a suitcase and brought along all Bobby's stuff as well, and met this man at my front door. He was kind enough to drive me from the Bronx to Queens. It was already dark by the time I arrived at my mother's front door. When she opened it and saw me standing there with a suitcase in one hand and Bobby in the other, she said, 'What are you doing here?'

I held myself rigidly straight and looked right at her, two five-foot tall women eye to eye. 'I can't take it any more,' I said. 'I can't stand the loneliness. I have no friends to talk to. All I have in my life is Bobby, who I love with all my heart. But it is not enough.'

My mother looked at me as if I had lost my mind. I can see now that a thousand things must have been running through her head – that she had a small apartment, that I was a married lady and belonged at home with my husband, that she didn't quite know what to do.

'If I could stay here for tonight, we could see what will happen tomorrow,' I said hopefully.

But my mother shook her head. 'How could you do this? Do you realize that when Otto gets home and you and Bobby are gone he will go mad with worry? You don't even have a phone so that we can call him and tell him where you are. This is an impossible situation.'

I stared at my mother, who had never let me down in all my life. But I felt now as if she was letting me down, as if she no longer loved me or my child, which was ridiculous because I knew she doted on Bobby.

'You must go home now, before he worries too much,' she said, handing me the bus fare. So I walked to the bus with Bobby in one hand and my suitcase in the other, and rode home to my apartment in the Bronx. I simply had nowhere else to go.

By the time I got there, it was after eleven o'clock and I had to knock on the door for Otto to let me in, because I had left my key behind, since I hadn't been planning to come back.

The first thing I saw was Otto's tired, frantic face. 'Where were you?'

I moved past him and put my exhausted son in his cot before coming back into the living room.

'I left you today, Otto. I took Bobby and everything I owned and I went to my mother's.' I gave a tired little laugh. 'Only she didn't want me there. She sent me back home. On the bus. With my suitcase.' I poured myself a glass of water from a jug on the kitchen table and walked back into the living room. 'Maybe she would want you to live there – she loves you so much. Maybe you should go there and I should stay here with Bobby.'

Otto put his head in his hands, his shoulders shaking as he sat there. When he looked up at me, his eyes were bright with unshed tears. 'I don't know what you want from me, Baby. I do everything possible for you. I don't take holidays, I don't even take a day off. I work all the time to give you and Bobby a better life, but nothing is ever enough.'

I started to cry then. It was true. He worked hard for us, but the man himself remained hidden behind so many walls. But I knew the real truth was that I didn't love him in the way he wanted to be loved, and that wasn't his fault, it was mine.

I wiped my eyes and went over to him and put my arms around him. 'It will be all right, Otto, we will try again,' I said, smoothing his hair. 'But could you try to spend some more time with us?'

He promised, and for a while his weekends became more free, but soon he was back to his workaholic habits. I did what I had to do. I adjusted, and we went on.

Otto was moving up in his company and Bobby was a handful who kept me busy all the time. He had an extremely high energy level. I realize now that he was hyperactive, but then I had no frame of reference and just thought that's how all children behaved. I had to run to keep up with him, and I was exhausted by the end of each long day. By now we lived in a bigger, better apartment in the Bronx and all the furniture was our own. Otto was proving indispensable to his company and was moving further up in the management, although the pay rises and the share in the company that the two brothers had promised him had not materialized, and Otto would never demand them.

I became pregnant again and our daughter Sandy was born on 7 August 1954. I'll never forget the first time Otto saw her. He looked at her for a long time, and then I saw tears streaming down his cheeks. 'She is the image of my mother. Thank you, Baby, thank you, for giving me back another member of my family.'

I felt my heart soften towards him at that moment. I knew how much he suffered every day with his memories. And I knew what a good man he was, a loving, generous husband and father, and a loving son to my mother. All he wanted, I realized, was to be surrounded by the love of his wife and family. I vowed to myself that I would try to be better at giving him that.

My mother came to the hospital the next day, oohing and ahing over Sandy as she held Bobby by the hand. Somehow, she had managed to sneak him up for a visit, and even let him hold his baby sister, so long as he sat on the chair in the room and was very, very still.

'There were so many times when I thought I would never live to see my children grow up, that they would never survive to give me grandchildren. This is a joyous day,' my mother said, her eyes filling with tears. 'I thank God every day for all He has given me.' Then she straightened her spine and wiped her tears away. 'I'll come and take care of you when you get home,' she said.

What would I have done without my mother? She was such an independent woman, content in her apartment building in Sunnyside, where there were other Hungarian immigrants. She was involved in good works for her synagogue, she was still making and designing jewellery and she steadfastly refused to even consider dating anyone. 'After having known and loved your father, there could be no one else,' she would say matter-of-factly whenever the subject came up. She had found her kosher butcher and her good works and she was surrounded by her children and her grandchildren. What more could she want? Once again, her God had not let her down.

And then, one night, at the beginning of 1955, Otto got a phone call that changed our lives. The owner of Baronet, a leather goods company, wanted Otto to come and work for him in Reading, Pennsylvania. Otto didn't know what to do. He had worked for the two brothers for almost six years, but Baronet was offering a lot more money and the brothers hadn't kept all the promises they'd made to him. He went in and told them about the offer. At first, they thought he was just bluffing. Then, when they saw that he was serious, although he still hadn't told them it was a much bigger company, Baronet, that had made the offer, they offered him more money.

But this time, Otto stood up for himself. 'I am sorry, but that's not enough,' he told them. 'This new opportunity is a chance to better myself, to give more to my family.'

The brothers got angry. 'We've been so generous to you,' they told him. 'Why, we even gave you the keys to the factory.'

Otto had to laugh. They'd given him the keys because he always arrived before anyone else and left after they were all gone. He saw now what their problem was. They knew they would never find anyone who would work as hard for them. But Otto had made up his mind. He was going to Baronet. He came home that night and dropped the bombshell. He was to be the general manager of a factory, it was a big promotion, but we would have to move to Reading, Pennsylvania.

I was shocked. We had made a life in New York. Bobby had started school. I had made friends with other young mothers when Sandy was born. My sister, my mother, my brother, Aunt Rose and Uncle Victor were only a bus ride or subway ride away. How could I leave all this for the wilds of somewhere called Reading, Pennsylvania, where there might not be many Jews?

But there was no choice, really. We were going to Reading and that was that. What's more, Otto was going there first, to supervise the building of the factory. He took me out to Reading for a weekend and we found a house to rent. Then I went back to New York and packed up everything and made the move, two small children in tow. That move set the pattern for the rest of our married lives. I would do the packing and the moving, and Otto would work. And how he worked. He worked as hard as two men, but he never wanted to ask for more money or any extras. I managed the money for us, and I knew that we could do with more, and that he was worth more. I told his boss that when he talked to me about the move to Reading.

'You know, you are probably right, Betty,' his boss said to me. 'But it is for Otto, not you, to come to me and tell me what he needs.'

I nodded, but I hadn't finished yet. There was something else I wanted that I knew Otto would never ask for. 'Since we will be moving to a new place, I need a washing machine, a dryer, a new refrigerator and an antenna for our television.'

His boss, who was a German Jew, stared at me for a moment, then he smiled, shaking my hand. 'Done. I will give Otto a check for two thousand dollars. That ought to cover it, right, Betty?'

chapter $\mathcal{T}$wenty-one

$\mathcal{O}$ur first house in Reading was on the absolutely wrong end of town. What made it intolerable was that it was so near the railway tracks that I heard the trains going by all the time, and every time one went by it would trigger my memories of the deportations in Budapest. I could not bear it, and I could not sleep there. But I forced myself to be strong because at that time I had no choice about where we lived.

I immersed myself in being a mother. But I soon realized that the children wanted only my attention, because Otto was hardly ever there and hardly ever did anything with them. Finally, one day he took Sandy and Bobby skating on the nearby lake and they loved it. I was tempted to go with them, but I knew my skating far outshone his and I wanted this to be Otto's day with his children, when he was the hero daddy they looked up to.

Otto did such a good job for Baronet that year that his boss, who was a generous man, gave him a bonus of

$1,000 and then came back to him with a second cheque for another $1,000 later that day. 'This,' he told Otto, placing the cheque in his hand, 'is for all the extra effort you put in.'

When Otto came home that night, his face was radiant. He was so proud of those cheques and what they symbolized. He loved his work, he loved doing a good job and he loved being recognized for it. I praised him and gave him a hug and a kiss. I opened a savings account with those cheques.

'Soon we will be able to move to a better house, and get away from this horrible neighbourhood where the trains come through,' I told him.

By 1957, we had moved to a better neighbourhood in Reading, where we rented a two-bedroom apartment in a converted garage owned by a Reading millionaire.

Bobby was going to Hebrew school and Sandy was in nursery Sunday school at the synagogue. I had become very involved with B'nai B'rith, a Jewish organization which helps the needy and fights discrimination, and was even helping immigrant Jewish families to settle in Reading. When the Hungarian Revolt occurred in 1956, I made the three-hour drive to Camp Kilmer in New Jersey to meet refugees. I told Otto it was to help resettle some families, and it was. But I also went in the desperate hope that Richie might be among them. If he was still alive and still in Hungary, I could well imagine him rising up against the oppression of the Communist regime.

I searched every face, and even asked some discreet questions, but it was another dead end. It seemed that Richie Kovacs had vanished just as surely as my father had, and perhaps for the same reason. They were both dead, casualties of a world war, but somehow I still couldn't bring myself to believe it.

Most days, there wasn't time to think about what was missing in my life. On 24 June 1957, I gave birth to our third child, Jeffrey. I remember thinking, as I looked at my beautiful son, that now I would have absolutely no time to think of the past. There was only the present and my three young children who needed me, and the charity work I was doing.

I had also made a wonderful friend. Her name was Gerta and she was a Viennese Jewess married to a Czech Jew. They were very wealthy. Their family owned a company that manufactured men's socks. More importantly, Gerta and I understood each other. She, too, was a concentration camp survivor who had been first at Theriesenstadt and then at Dachau. Besides that, we had daughters the same age and my youngest son was the same age as her baby boy. We were a perfect fit. And, rich as they were, every Saturday night they would end up at our house for dinner. Otto still worked most Saturdays and was often tired on Saturday night, but even so he enjoyed their company, too. Gerta was like a sister to me.

One day Gerta came round, all excited, and told me they had bought a new house in the Pagoda section of Reading, the most exclusive and totally Gentile part of the city. The house was more than a house, it was a mansion, and Gerta wanted my help in furnishing and decorating it. I had developed an eye over the years, and was clever at designing curtains and other things. I decorated the house with as much loving care as if it was mine.

One morning we were sitting there, our children playing contentedly together in the garden where we could watch them through the huge windows. We made notes on what we still needed to buy and what lighting fixtures needed to be changed. Then Gerta asked me to go to the caterers with her to discuss the housewarming party she was planning.

'You are such a wonderful cook, Betty, and I want your advice on telling them what to serve.'

I smiled and scooped up my two kids while she scooped up hers and we drove over to the caterers, where we put together a fantastic menu. After we'd done all that I went back to her house for a cup of tea and a pastry before taking the kids home for a nap.

Gerta leaned across the table and touched my arm. 'Baby, there's just one thing. When you're at the house-warming party, don't talk about being Jewish. This is a very Gentile neighbourhood and we are not going to tell them we are Jewish.'

I was stunned that she could say such a thing. I jumped up, almost knocking over the fragile, nineteenth-century teacup in my anger. 'You don't have to worry about my saying anything to give your secret away because I won't be attending your party. As a matter of fact, I will never speak to you again.'

Gerta started to cry and grabbed my arm as I turned to leave. 'Please, Baby. You don't understand. I just want a peaceful life after all the horror I've been through. It is no one's business that we are Jewish.'

I looked at her and I tried to explain why I was so angry, but it was difficult, because I felt as if my heart was breaking at losing this friend over such a reason. 'Look, Gerta, you went through a concentration camp and so did I. I saw my best friend killed by a Jew hater. I promised myself then, when all the killing was going on, that I would never keep quiet about my religion.'

I pulled out my arm from under her clutching fingers. 'You are two-faced and I want nothing to do with you ever again.'

I grabbed my three children and left. I never spoke to her again after that, though she came over one day soon after to beg me to change my mind. On this subject, Otto and I were in total agreement. Never again, we said. And we did everything we could to raise our children without prejudice, to be colour-blind. Even in the days when we didn't have much, we helped other Jews who needed help and supported Jewish charities. I might have had my arguments with God, but I was Jewish to my very soul and proud of it, defiantly so.

I still managed the money, but I was pretty naïve. In Hungary, there was no such thing as a mortgage. If you wanted to buy a house, you paid for the whole thing in cash. At that rate, I had calculated it would take another twenty years of saving – since we lived virtually from pay cheque to pay cheque – to afford one. I really didn't understand American ways of doing things. But, thanks to some of the women friends I made at the Jewish Center, I learned that Otto and I could afford to buy a house. With a mortgage, we could afford one tomorrow, according to my friends. In 1958, in Reading, Pennsylvania, you could buy a very nice house for $19,000, with a deposit of only 10 per cent. I went home that night and explained it all to Otto and the next day he asked his boss to write a letter to the bank attesting to the fact that he had a steady job. We got the house.

I was fast becoming an accomplished cook. My mother had very kindly handwritten two cookbooks for me – one of main dishes, and one of her delectable pastries and baked goods. I called her whenever I needed more advice or inspiration and I made everything from scratch just as she had taught me. When she came to visit, we baked and cooked together; it was like a graduate

course in fine cuisine, but in a homemade way. Julia
Child could have shown me no more, although my
mother's recipes were decidedly Middle European
rather than French. I learned to make cookies and
strudel, light-as-air Viennese cakes and pastries, and
traditional Hungarian dishes such as her delicious
cholent. My mother drilled me on making stuffed cab-
bage. 'The secret,' she told me, 'is never to have to use a
toothpick to fasten them. It's all in the folding.' And she
patiently demonstrated it until I got it just right.

Pretty soon, everyone wanted to eat at my house, and
I grew to enjoy entertaining and learned to do it with
style.

For the ten years we lived in Reading, I filled my life
with my husband and children, my home and my volunteer work for B'nai B'rith. I also volunteered at a state
hospital for mentally retarded children and adults. Even
on Sundays, I would sometimes go there, leaving Otto
with the children. I also took painting lessons at the local
college. One of the things that still distressed me was
that the war had interrupted my education, and with my
hasty marriage and then having three children in seven
years, I had never completed it in America either. I had a
lot of creative energy and a lot of intellectual curiosity. I
loved to paint, but Otto refused to allow me to do it in
the house. He said he, who worked in a business filled
with noxious-smelling chemicals, couldn't stand the
smell of the oil paints. 'They give me a headache,' he said.

I continued to paint, using acrylics instead, but, to me,
they had no life to them, just like me. I did my job, I tried
to be a good wife and mother, but inside I was empty. I
had moved thousands of miles and light years away from
the laughing young girl whom Richie had called *kis pofa*.

But if I was a hollow shell, Otto had no time to notice.

Baronet was growing and he was growing with it. His boss asked him to open up a factory in Puerto Rico that would employ 1,800 people. As usual, Otto did a superb job and, as usual, family time was sacrificed. He travelled all the time, sometimes spending as much as six weeks at a time in Puerto Rico. I often felt as if I was raising the children alone, although sometimes we would go to Puerto Rico with Otto, on short trips during school holidays. He would be at the factory all day, of course, but the children and I would frolic on the beach and wait for Otto to finish work. At least I was travelling and, just as I knew I would, I loved it.

A few years later, we moved again. Baronet opened up another huge factory, this time in New Jersey, and Otto was now spending a lot of time in New York, supervising that operation. Eventually it made sense to move back to the New York area, but Otto was adamant that we should live in the suburbs, not the city. I agreed, upset as usual that I would be making this move alone again, this time with three children in tow, because Otto was needed in New York. What else was new?

At least we were able to househunt together. After looking at some older homes, we found a new development in Spring Valley, New York, where a developer was putting up custom-built houses for just $34,000. Otto and I had a terrible fight because he thought we couldn't afford it, but I insisted that we could and, in the end, he gave in.

It was 1964, and that four-bedroom colonial home was my dream house, what I had envisioned so many years ago. But I still wasn't happy with my life. I was happy with all except for the man I was sharing the dream with, but I tried not to think about it.

The move itself was horrendous. True, the company paid for it, but it was I who packed all the fragile antiques and collectibles I had managed to accumulate along the way, and I had to supervise every bit of the packing they did. I also had to sell the house and furnishings we didn't want to take with us, while at the same time make decisions on the house we were building and take care of three kids. This was a tough move for Bobby, who was a difficult child anyway, because he would have to transfer to a new school in the middle of secondary school. I ranted and raved at Otto, but he barely heard me. He had work to do.

I still longed for adults to share my life with, but after the disastrous end to the friendship with Gerta I held my secrets and my vulnerability close. It seemed a better strategy than risking such disappointment.

My baby brother Larry had grown up. He had lived at home with my mother until 1957, which made it hard for her to leave him and travel to visit me or my sister, because he expected her to keep house for him the way she always had. But in 1957, he fell in love with Eva, a beautiful Hungarian freedom fighter, who had fled Hungary after the thwarted revolt in 1956, and married her. They moved to California, which was a good thing for my mother because then she had Rose living near by and me in Reading, and she didn't have Larry to look after any more. My brother opened a jewellery store in Los Angeles and his wife became a property broker. My mother went out there every year at Christmastime to help run the shop and visit them.

I made the four-bedroom colonial home in Spring Valley a showhouse. I decorated it just the way I wanted it to be, and I luxuriated in the space. I got the children settled in school, even Bobby. If my marriage to Otto was no better, it was certainly no worse. And people who met us socially thought we were the perfect couple. Otto still didn't spend much time with the children. He never coached a ball team, he never took them out to the cinema or bowling, he never did the things all those sub-urban fathers were supposed to do, all those things I'd seen on television on those long nights when Otto was asleep and Bobby and I were alone. On the other hand, the children didn't complain about his lack of interest. They accepted us for who and what we were, even though we had never told them much about the shatter-ing events of the war and the Holocaust that had shaped us and, in some ways, warped us. Like so many sur-vivors, we couldn't talk about the past even though we lived with its aftermath every day.

We were good at pretending to be happy. But in the middle of the night, I would still wake to Otto's screams and he to mine. We continued to be haunted by the past. We didn't have the kind of healing love that could keep us happy in the present. When we were alone together, there were a lot of silences and they weren't comfortable ones. We both accommodated ourselves to the situation. Otto lost himself in his work. I lost myself in my children and in a new organization for me, Hadassah.

But it was not enough.

chapter *Twenty-two*

*B*ad things always seem to happen to me in March. On a sunny, warm day in March 1965, a day that felt more like spring than winter, I had a breakdown. I'd been sweeping up leaves in the garden, getting things ready for the spring. I had raked about ten bags full when all of a sudden I looked at them and it seemed as if there were hundreds of them. I threw the rake down and my heart was thundering in my chest. I felt such palpitations that I thought my heart would burst. Somehow, I managed to make it inside and call Otto at work.

'You must come home,' I said, barely able to speak, 'I think I am having a heart attack. You must take me to hospital.'

They kept me in hospital for a week. When I arrived my heart beat and blood pressure were very high. With medication, they were able to control both, but the doctor thought they were symptoms, not the cause of what had happened to me.

'Take Betty away somewhere for a rest and a holiday,' he told Otto. I would have preferred to go off by myself, to try to understand what had snapped inside me and caused me to have what the doctor called an anxiety attack of major proportions. I refused to consider that it was all the unresolved conflict inside me that had made me implode. I was not into self-exploration in those days; it was simply too painful. But although I would have preferred a solitary journey, the truth was that I had never travelled anywhere alone and wasn't about to start now, when I was hardly myself. Otto agreed to take me away. It was a measure of how worried he must have been, because it was the first time he ever took a holiday from his sacred work.

We decided to go to Florida. My Uncle Ignatz (whom I had met at Augsburg) had moved there when he retired and we thought we could visit him as well as rest and lie in the sun. My mother came up to Spring Valley to look after the children.

The day we left was as different from the day I had the attack as winter is to spring. The warm weather was gone and the cold was back with a vengeance. A heavy blanket of snow was falling as we sat on the runway at LaGuardia Airport, waiting to take off. While we waited the wings of the plane had to be constantly de-iced. I had told Otto before we got on the plane that I wasn't feeling very social, that I did not want to talk to other passengers. Otto is the type of person who talks to everyone, who gets to know strangers instantly. I had never been like that, and I certainly wasn't feeling like socializing now. I wanted to be by myself and keep to myself.

I was sitting there next to Otto, feeling numb as I looked out of the window at the ice and snow, and I remember thinking, God help me, 'I wish the plane would crash.' Then my life would be over and the pain I had been carrying around inside me would finally stop. I wanted my life to end because I was so unhappy, and it wasn't any one thing, it was the sum total of my life. That realization horrified me. I had the house of my dreams, I had my children, we had a nice comfortable life, and yet I wanted it all to end. Perhaps if I had had all these things with another man, it would have been enough. Perhaps it would have been if I had married Richie, I thought, who made me feel like a woman all the time. Otto never made me feel that way. Could that be, a little voice inside me asked, because I never let him make me feel like a woman? I had no answer. So once again I felt guilty, but I didn't think I could help myself. So it would have been easier to die. I was thirty-six years old.

Uncle Ignatz was waiting for us at the airport. 'You look terrible, Baby,' he said when he saw me. 'What happened to you?'

'I had a nervous breakdown,' I said wearily.

Uncle Ignatz looked at me long and hard. 'Nerves don't break,' he said firmly.

I felt guilty all over again. Uncle Ignatz had lost his wife and children to the Nazis and he had not had a breakdown. He had gone on. So what was wrong with me that I couldn't do the same?

Before we left the airport, a property developer came up to us and asked if we would like a free trip to St Petersburg in Florida. We were in Fort Lauderdale.

'You should go,' Uncle Ignatz said. 'These guys are selling condominiums there. They'll fly you there and back for free, put you up overnight, and wine and dine you. All you have to do is listen to their pitch about the condos.'

'Let's go,' Otto said. 'At least it will give us something to do while we are here.'

I didn't want to go, but Otto looked so eager I said yes. We scheduled the trip for the next day.

But when I woke up the next morning, I felt awful, my head heavy from the Valium I was taking to calm my nerves.

'I can't possibly go,' I told Otto.

He looked so disappointed, so I suggested that he call Uncle Ignatz and take him instead. It was six-thirty in the morning, but I knew my uncle would already be up: he was an early riser.

'Good idea,' Otto said, smiling. He made the phone call, asked Uncle Ignatz and was quiet for a couple of minutes, frowning as my uncle said something on the other end.

'Can he go?' I asked when Otto hung up the phone.

'It all depends on his pot roast,' Otto said, barely able to keep a straight face.

'What's pot roast got to do with it?' I asked.

Everything, it turned out. Uncle Ignatz had patiently explained to Otto that he had cooked a pot roast the morning before. Then we had arrived and bought him dinner last night, so he hadn't been able to eat the pot roast. If he went away with Otto overnight, he wouldn't be able to eat the pot roast for another two days, by which point it would be ruined, and he couldn't bear to waste it. He would only go along if he could give the pot roast away.

As soon as he got off the phone with Otto, Uncle Ignatz grabbed the pot roast from the refrigerator, heavy casserole and all, and, with only his trousers on, ran down the block to his best friend's house and knocked on the door. After several minutes, a voice yelled out from inside, 'Who's there and what do you want?'

'It's Iggy and I've got a pot roast for you,' my uncle replied.

The door opened and a large man appeared in the doorway, staring down at my dishevelled uncle and the heavy pot he was carrying. Uncle Ignatz had never seen the man before in his life.

'Are you some kind of lunatic?' the guy demanded before slamming the door in his face.

Uncle Ignatz looked up at the house number and realized he'd made a mistake and offered the pot roast to a total stranger. He collected himself, ran back up the block and finally hit the right doorbell. His friend was delighted to have the pot roast.

A few minutes later, the phone rang in our hotel room and Otto reached for it. 'Wonderful,' he said with a smile after listening for a couple of minutes. 'We're all set,' he told me. 'I'm meeting Uncle Ignatz at his house and we'll drive to the airport.'

The two of them sat in the departure lounge until the flight was called. The property developers called their names. 'Mr and Mrs Schimmel.' Otto and my uncle got up and started making their way to the lounge door.

'Excuse me,' the young woman representative said nervously. 'This trip is for husbands and wives only.' She was staring at them, the little old man and the tall, hand-some man he was with. 'You're not married, are you?' she asked uncertainly.

Otto was still laughing when he and Uncle Ignatz got back to our hotel room.

'But what about my pot roast?' Uncle Ignatz wailed. 'Now I have no lunch.'

'I'll buy you lunch,' Otto said, still trying to catch his breath – he was laughing so hard. I was laughing, too.

That was the high point of the trip. Otherwise, Florida was a disaster. We had a nice time with Uncle Ignatz, who was very happy to see us, apart from losing his pot roast.

But Otto was like a caged animal. I could see it by the look on his face and by the way he paced up and down the soft carpeting of our hotel room. His mind was back at work. He was here because the doctor had ordered it, but he didn't want a holiday. He wanted his life back, and he wanted me to be the same old Betty who had made the house run and had taken care of the children. He loved me, but he didn't want our lives disrupted. And, underneath the annoyance and the irritation, I could tell that he was scared. I could see that he was thinking, 'What if the old Betty never returns?'

So I sat there for a couple of days in the hot Florida sun and on the third day I looked up at Otto, held out my hand and said, 'I'm better now. Let's go home.'

He looked so relieved that I wanted to laugh, but I didn't. 'Are you sure, Baby?' he asked.

I just nodded, and that was enough. He began neatly, meticulously, packing his bag. He asked me to call the airlines and we were on a plane that afternoon. My crisis was over, or so I said.

My mother looked at me closely when we walked through the door of our home, then she took me in her arms and hugged me, before studying me again. 'You are all right now, Baby?'

I nodded. I felt slightly ashamed in front of my mother, who had never weakened, even in the face of Eichmann, the SS and the death camp. What must she think of her pampered daughter in her luxurious house who broke down over raking some leaves?

But she never said anything about it, never criticized me. Instead, she took me aside and told me that while we were away, Bobby had hidden a bottle from our drinks cupboard in an umbrella stand near the door, ready to take it out with him when his friends picked him up. My mother had seen him do it, waited for him to leave the room and then had simply returned the bottle to its rightful place without ever saying a word to him about it.

I tried not to sigh. Bobby was the one who was always testing the limits. But maybe it wasn't all his fault. Maybe it was because his father worked all the time and I was locked inside myself. Maybe he just needed more attention. I vowed then I would do better. I would throw myself into my family and into good works, and I would succeed and survive.

For the next three months, I was a zombie. I was dutifully taking the heavy dose of Valium the doctor had prescribed for me and it was making me so groggy that I could barely function. One morning I got up and simply threw the pills away. They were not the answer. My family needed me and I needed a focus for my energies.

Hadassah was part of my new resolve. I moved up within the organization, beginning as membership chairman. Then I ran their auctions for them and became a major fundraiser before being elected president, receiving many awards along the way for raising both money and awareness of the Jewish cause.

The children were much older now and I had a lot more free time. I used it to take courses in ceramics and painting at New York's New School for Social Research. I was good at painting, but it was my sister Rose who had a major art talent. Tragically, the war curtailed the fulfilment of her enormous potential which could be seen in the drawings she did in childhood. But she became a wonderful jewellery designer and made a good living from it. I painted quite a lot as the children were growing up, and I arranged art and ceramics classes for my daughter Sandy, who had a fantastic talent, as well as the more traditional ballet lessons. Sandy and I would sit side by side, I at my big easel and she at her smaller one, using acrylics so that Otto wouldn't get a headache. Today, Sandy is still an excellent painter who does beautiful portraits, so I suppose I was able to pass along to her my love of art.

In fact, all our children love the arts. Bobby is a comic, Sandy is an artist as well as a public relations expert and Jeffrey is a writer. Of course, the writing genes may well have come from Otto's family. His Hungarian cousin Hattie has written a number of popular children's books.

I had been president of Hadassah for two years in 1973 when they asked me to run for president of the New York State region. But I couldn't accept. We were moving once again.

A business friend introduced Otto to a man who needed a partner who was an expert in manufacturing small leather goods. He wanted to start a new company to be based in Phoenix, Arizona. By this time Bobby and Sandy were at university. Otto went on ahead to Phoenix, immersed in this new business venture, while I stayed behind to sell the house, pack us up and get us moved with only Jeff, still at secondary school, to help me.

I was horrified at first that we would be moving so far away. My mother was getting older, the two older children were in the east, and I had never been to Arizona. But Otto assured me that we would use the opportunity to travel all over the state and even throughout the west. That appealed to my sense of adventure.

I flew out to Phoenix and we bought a brand-new house that I really didn't like, but Otto didn't have the time to look with me for the older house with some character that I had been hoping to find. Once again, I was angry at him for not taking time with things I felt were important in life. He was still as preoccupied as ever with work. Bobby used to joke that 'Dad gets orgasmic whenever he walks into a leather goods store.' And it was true; the business was his passion.

I had seen pictures of the desert, of course, but nothing had prepared me for its stark beauty, for the drama of its naked, jagged hills and tall prickly cacti outlined against the sky like nature's sculptures. And there was something in the air there that made me feel peaceful, even on a hurried trip to buy a house. Otto was right about one thing: I really did want to see the rest of this interesting, intriguing state that was to be my new home.

We bought a house that wasn't yet built in one of the new developments that were springing up all over Phoenix in the 1970s. I knew we could afford a bigger, better house, but Otto was nervous about going into business for himself and insisted that this house was all we could afford. All our married life, Otto had been very generous with me in terms of buying me something right then — a television in 1949, furniture, pieces of jewellery. But he was always afraid of long-term financial commitments and would fight me on what he thought was a big mortgage. With all his success — and by the time he left Baronet he was vice-president — he was still afraid that somehow he would not be able to make the monthly payments.

'Look, Otto,' I said on the morning when we had to make a final decision about the house, 'we'll make a nice profit on the house in Spring Valley and we have no other major purchases to make. There's no furniture we have to buy or appliances. So we can afford to buy a better house out here. Besides, Arizona is growing. It will be a good investment.'

But Otto just shook his head, with that stubborn look on his face I recognized. Where I reached for the next plateau, Otto desperately clung to the one he had just landed on. With all his success, Otto could not picture himself living any better.

'This house is good enough for me, Baby,' he said.

I took a deep breath and let it go. I was tired of fighting about the kind of house we could afford. 'All right,' I said, 'but at least pay the extra money to upgrade the carpet and get the best you can.' And I showed him what I had in mind before flying back to Spring Valley and the packing crates.

When I arrived in Phoenix with Jeff a couple of months later, I gasped when I walked into my new house. Otto had paid more for the carpeting, but he had chosen the style himself. I was stuck with room after room of white shag carpeting that I hated on sight and I knew, given Otto's fears, that it would take me years to replace.

'Why would you buy such a thing?' I said in a rage, all my anger at the move, his not being there to help and our disagreement about the kind of house we should buy coming together in my reaction to the ghastly carpeting.

Otto looked stunned. 'But I thought you would like this better. It looked elegant to me.'

I closed my eyes. That had always been the problem. Otto's taste and mine did not come together. He would always choose the showy piece over the subtle one. I knew that he had grown up differently from the way I had. My parents had always had excellent taste and, even when on the run during the war, had bought good things. Richie had in fact given me a graduate course in fine furniture, art and china as we visited the antiques shops of Budapest all those years ago. And with whatever artist's sensibility I had, I took these choices seriously. What I lived surrounded by affected my mood and my outlook. But none of this was the same for Otto. In leather goods, he thought about each and every tiny detail, but his aesthetic sense in other areas was just not there. Once again, I felt our differences and what they had cost me over the years. Then I shook myself. My mother would be ashamed of me. Here I was, with a generous husband who had always been a good provider, three lovely children and a new home in a growing city. What right did I have to be angry about carpeting? I smiled at Otto. 'It will be all right,' I said, gesturing towards the carpeting, while vowing to myself never to look down.

When Sandy and Bobby came home from college, they fell in love with their new state. They explored the desert and loved the climate. Jeff too, always an easy child, adapted to his new life and his new school.

Although I missed the culture of New York, I found myself enjoying Arizona, but I think that had a lot to do with my mother coming out for a long visit. We moved there in August 1973 and my mother arrived for Thanksgiving and stayed until 1 April of the next year.

It was a wonderful visit. One morning, after Otto had left for work and Jeff had left for school, my mother came into my bedroom. 'Look out of the the window, Baby. Look at the hot air balloons rising over the desert.'

I sat up in bed and looked out of the window at the whimsical yet majestic sight of five large colourful balloons lifting off into the bright blue sky, leaving all ties to earth behind. It was beautiful.

'Come,' I said to my mother, holding the covers open. 'Lie here with me and we'll watch the balloons.'

And we did, snuggled close as we used to when she

kept us safe from harm on all those bitter cold nights of the march and beyond. All my life, my mother had been my rock and my compass, my friend and adviser. She was tiny physically but she was such a giant in every other way, especially in her capacity to love and to believe. And she had taught me that family was of the highest value. She had done that by example, even mothering Otto so that he felt he had a mother figure in his life. My children adored her and respected her, too.

How could I have been so lucky, I thought, to have a mother like this, and to still have her now, all these years later?

She was retired now, but that didn't mean she did nothing. She was constantly in motion, working for the poor of her synagogue, seeing her friends, acting as a mother figure to many other refugees who sought her counsel. She went faithfully to temple, and travelled to see her children, who were now spread out across the country. She had even gone to Israel two years before with a friend, and she'd brought back a tiny bag of sand from Jerusalem.

The most amazing thing about her was that she still had the curiosity and the energy of a young woman, even though she was by then sixty-nine years old, and had survived the horrors of the war and the devastating loss of her beloved husband. Her hair was grey now and very long, but she wore it in a soft chignon, her still slender body ramrod straight after all these years.

Plenty of men had looked at her over the years, because she was a beautiful woman inside and out, but she just wasn't interested. She had loved my father and she had lost him. A few times after the war I caught her crying when she knew he wasn't ever coming back, but when I asked her what the tears were for, she would say,

'Just for everyone. For mankind.' But I knew they were for my father. I had cried some of those myself, and my sister Rose still cried for him.

As mother kept a kosher home, when she came to visit me I had to buy kosher meat. Although I did not keep kosher with two sets of dishes, I did keep a separate set of glass dishes for her so that she could eat at our house and still keep kosher. My mother was always a woman of principle, but she was never without wisdom or humour. She went through life issuing sayings as if they were maxims, which of course some of them were. 'Be careful what you wish for, because you might get it and find you're not happy with it,' she'd warn us. Or, when a friend of ours behaved badly, she'd shake her head and say: 'From a dog you cannot make bacon.' Or, 'Don't walk backwards,' her way of saying never look back. And she never did. She was the type of person who accepted things. She never fought – except for her children.

So now, as we lay cuddled together in my bed, I said to her, 'You know, the life I am living is a lie. I didn't love Otto when I married him and I still don't love him enough.'

My mother looked at me calmly, stroking my hair back from my face as if I was once again her little girl instead of a forty-five-year-old mother of three. 'Now that is a lie,' she said firmly. 'You do love Otto, but you still have Richie on your mind.'

I didn't agree with her then, but she was right.

It was beautiful in Arizona and I wanted my mother to see everything. We took her to the Grand Canyon, Sedona and the Painted Desert. She was amazed at the size of the Grand Canyon and she called Sedona a very spiritual place, a natural temple. Every weekend, we went somewhere different. I had just taken a job with a travel agency, ready, now that the children were older, to satisfy my wanderlust. On days when I worked, my mother would walk to the grocer's and come home and make dinner for us. The whole family loved having my mother there. She was never a problem, never in the way. And she still cooked like an angel.

When we were alone, we even talked a little about the past, something my mother did not like to do. And we talked about how life had turned out.

'It must have been difficult for you to move so far away, Baby,' she said to me one day as we sat outside in the early morning, sipping our coffee. 'But it is a good move and a way of bettering yourselves. This is a good opportunity for Otto.'

I nodded.

She smiled at me. 'Otto has not disappointed me,' she said. 'He has made you an excellent husband and is a good father.'

I kept on smiling, but inside I thought, 'How would you know? You've suffered quietly all these years, missing my father, but all you knew how to do was suffer quietly. You've never talked about how much you miss him, or how you cope with the loneliness.' I didn't say any of this. My mother was a proud and in some ways solitary woman and she wanted to carry her own burdens.

'Otto is a good man,' I agreed.

I could tell that my mother wanted to hear more, that she was hoping that I would finally say how much I loved him, but I could not. Richie was still in my thoughts; I could still see his face in my mind as if it was yesterday. But I couldn't burden my mother with this; I couldn't let her see my suffering and I knew if we talked about him, even now, I would cry.

Instead, we talked about going back to Budapest together. It was something I felt I could do now, and she wanted to go with me.

'Next year,' she said, patting my hand.

During my mother's long visit, my sister and her husband, and my brother and his wife came to visit, too. Once again we were all together, this time in Arizona, with Otto enjoying it too because he knew my mother loved and accepted him as much as she accepted her own children — in some ways, more so, because the two of them were confidantes. Who knows what secrets they kept?

We had a happy reunion and I could see from my mother's face how delighted she was that we were all together again. But it was to be for the last time.

My mother was to go back in early April to help celebrate my sister's birthday. Her husband Jerry was now a partner in the exclusive Tamcrest Country Club in New Jersey and had planned a lavish surprise party there for Rose. Before she left we went shopping together for a formal dress for her to wear and found a beautiful long gown at Goldwater's department store. That night, we took her to a cowboy restaurant called Pinnacle Peak for dinner. Keeping kosher as usual, she had salad and beans cooked in water and a baked potato. We looked out at the night sky and the lights over Phoenix. It was a beautiful day, already late spring in Arizona. The African daisies were in bloom and the cacti were in flower. It was almost as if Arizona was celebrating my mother's presence.

When we got home that night, my mother felt very sick. She told me she had a terrible stomach ache.

'I'm not surprised,' I said. 'You ate all that salad and beans cooked only in water, and that's full of gas. You are suffering from it now.'

She didn't answer me, but I could see from the look on her face that something was wrong. I couldn't imagine what. Over the years, she had developed problems with asthma and emphysema, a legacy of the war years and the acrid smoke in Mauthausen. But since she'd been with us in Arizona, where the air was so pure, she hadn't even had to take her asthma medicine.

'You will be fine by tomorrow,' I told her, kissing her goodnight.

A week later when she got back home, she went to the doctor. She hadn't been feeling well for a long time, but had told no one. My mother was always fiercely independent and she hated being ill. But this time, she couldn't ignore her symptoms or the pain.

Without even doing a biopsy, the doctor told my mother: 'You have colon cancer.'

My sister was with her, and she said my mother closed her eyes for a moment and then asked calmly, 'What does that mean?'

'We will have to operate,' the doctor explained, 'and we have several options. We could simply remove the tumour if the cancer is contained within it; we could remove some of your intestines; or we could remove more of your intestines and give you a colostomy.'

My mother nodded, thinking it over. 'You can operate and you can take some of my intestines, but no colostomy because that is unnatural. I will not do anything that is unnatural to stay alive.'

As it turned out, when they operated, they simply removed the tumour. They didn't give her much hope at all.

I flew east to be with my mother while she was in the hospital. They kept her there for about three weeks. When she was ready to go home, Rose took over. A few

months passed, the summer was almost over and Rose
and Jerry took my mother on holiday with them to the
Catskills.

I picked up the phone one morning in early
September and heard my mother's voice. 'Hello, Baby,'
she said, but I didn't like the way she sounded.

'Is everything all right, Mama?'

There was a slight pause. 'I don't know,' she said. 'I
have this terrible pain in my back, a pain such as I've
never had before, and I feel cold all the time.'

I felt a chill myself, even though it was over a hundred
degrees in Phoenix. 'Maybe you are feeling cold because
you are anaemic, as the doctor explained to you.'

'Maybe,' she said, but I could tell she didn't believe it.
I didn't know what to believe myself, or what to do.

'Why don't you tell Rose, and she and Jerry could
take you back to your doctor?'

'I'll think about it,' my mother said. 'We're only here
for another two weeks and then we're going home.
Maybe I'll wait until then.'

And that's what she did. I don't think she ever even
told Rose about her new symptoms, probably because
she didn't want them to interrupt their holiday or maybe
because she just didn't want to face bad news.

When she went to the doctor, he immediately put her
into hospital and, apart from a week when she was well
enough to go home, she never left the hospital again.

We were all there while she was in the hospital for the
last time. We didn't know then that when she went home
for a week, she got everything ready for her death. She
laid out the dress she was to be buried in and had sewn
her own plain muslin shroud. She wrote a letter to all of
us telling us what to do when she died. She was to be
buried in her own plot she had bought years ago, at

Pinelawn Cemetery on Long Island. We had all bought
adjacent plots there, too. My mother was our family, and
that of our spouses too: both Otto and Jerry were the
only ones in their immediate families who had survived
the Holocaust, and Larry's wife had fled Hungary.

Meanwhile, we all tried to keep her spirits up and we
all tried to say our individual goodbyes.

Once again, my mother amazed us. There she was
weak, dying, lying in bed with all these tubes and, when
they lifted her up to change the bed, she began her
stretching exercises. 'So that I will be strong enough to
go home,' she explained as we looked on, wide-eyed.

But this time, even stretching exercises couldn't save
my brave mother. God took her gently and peacefully.
She died on 24 October 1974.

When we went to her apartment, we found a letter
addressed 'to my three children'. It was five pages long,
a combination of my mother's love and her practicality.
As usual, her last thoughts were for us:

> I know I am dying. Do not change any of the plans I
> have laid out here for my funeral. I want it to be dig-
> nified and in keeping with Jewish tradition. I want the
> simplest coffin and I want to be dressed in the dress
> that is put aside in my closet and then shriven in the
> muslin shroud that I made myself. It is in a bag in the
> cupboard. Also, I want to be buried with the little bag
> of sand I brought back from Jerusalem.
>
> Always remember that I love you. I want each of
> you to love one another all the time as much as I love
> you, and you must never let each other down. If one
> needs something, then the others should help.
> Mama.

*

We wept then, because we knew, all of us, even Otto, maybe especially Otto, that we had lost the one person in the world who loved us unconditionally, who had kept us safe and put us first, who had filled our lives with certainty and security even in the midst of war. I could not imagine my life without her. My mother was as constant as the sun, and as important in our lives. Now she was gone, and things seemed suddenly very black.

We buried her the next day, a beautiful, brilliant October day that was too sunny for a funeral, but perhaps God was smiling because one of His truly chosen ones had returned home to Him.

As we flew back home, I made myself a vow. I would do myself what my mother and I had talked about doing the spring before. She had said it was time we went back to Hungary, that now we were ready to face all the memories, good and bad. Now I would do it in memory of her.

chapter Twenty-three

'I can't believe this,' I said and threw up my hands. 'You said you would go with me to Budapest, and now you won't go.'

Otto just hung his head.

I suppose I shouldn't have been surprised. Work had always come first. He had never taken time off for family holidays, so why should this one be different? Except this trip *was* different. This wasn't just another holiday, it was a trip back in time. I was going back to Budapest, just as I'd told my mother I would, and I wanted Otto with me.

Now he said we'd have to reschedule or he would have to stay behind, because of yet another business crisis which only he could solve.

I shook my head. 'I will not wait for a better time to go,' I told him. 'I have waited long enough.'

'Then why don't you take Sandy with you, as a graduation present?'

That made me smile. Sandy and I had had a difficult

few years, as many mothers and their teenaged daughters have, and perhaps this trip would be a way for us to
become closer. 'Good idea, Otto. Now you can stay here
and work in peace, and I can go to Budapest.'

I was still working for a travel agency and I had made
all the arrangements. It was June 1975 and Hungary
remained a Communist country. I had to admit to myself
that I felt some fear in going back, but I wanted to do it,
for myself, for my mother, and for Sandy, so that she
could see our past.

I was totally unprepared for the paralysing fear I felt
once we arrived in Budapest. Now we know much about
post-traumatic stress syndrome, but in 1975 it was not a
well-known psychological condition. All I knew was that
I was terrified, and I couldn't get over it.

The first problem was our hotel. It faced the railway
station, which brought back all the memories of deportations during the war. I started to cry and I told Sandy I
simply could not bring myself to leave the hotel room.
Poor Sandy, I thought. She begged me to go out with her.
After a couple of days, I managed to get our hotel reservation switched to the Intercontinental in the centre of
the city and far enough from the station. But even in a
new hotel, I could not force myself to go out.

Old friends of mine and Otto's came to see us at the
hotel. They, too, tried to persuade me to leave the building and rediscover the city I had once called home.

Today Budapest has rediscovered its beauty, artistry
and energy. But in 1975 it still suffered under the
oppression of its Communist government. The buildings
looked run down and the people looked defeated. They
looked afraid, too, which only fed my fear. Hotel rooms
and even tables in the coffee shop and restaurants were
bugged with listening devices. The manager of one, who

happened to be somebody I knew as a child, told me not to sit at a certain table. I found out later it was because of suspected listening devices planted there. This was such a strong reminder of the Nazis and the Arrow Cross. Only the names had changed. What if they decided to arrest me? I had no idea what they would arrest me for, but the thought took hold and I couldn't shake it off. Sandy thought I was losing my mind, and I couldn't really disagree with her.

Finally, after the fifth day, I took hold of myself. I had to get out. I wanted to share the city with my only daughter, the city that had held such vivid memories of hope and love.

We started walking. One of the first places we visited was the home of the mother of one of Richie's fellow musicians. She threw her arms around me and hugged me close. 'It's Baby,' she said. 'And you look wonderful.' At forty-six, I was still pretty and slender, my dark hair shoulder length.

Sandy examined pictures on the woman's piano. 'Who are those boys?' she asked, holding up a picture of Richie and the three other boys from his band.

'This boy is my son and that's your mother's boyfriend with the two other members of their band,' she said. 'How they loved each other. I remember catching them a couple of times kissing in the hallway.' She laughed and hugged me again.

I felt as if I was floating, just seeing Richie's picture and hearing her talk about him. I had no pictures of Richie, so for all those years I had only been able to see his face in my mind.

'Have you seen Richie?' I managed to ask. But she hadn't. Another dead end.

We stayed for some tea, and when we left, Sandy had

a thousand questions about Richie and me. Somehow, my having had a boyfriend I had loved and lost made me more human to her, perhaps more sympathetic.

'I loved Richie with all my heart,' I told her. We continued through the streets of Budapest and I showed her the building I had lived in. We took a tram and then walked the rest of the way to the boathouse, where I told her about one of our favourite spots. I took her to the Castle Hill, up the winding pavement to see my name and Richie's still carved in the stone wall. I cried when I told her about him, and how we had parted that day so long ago.

'Poor Mum,' Sandy said, her arm encircling my shoulder.

That night, we had dinner with a close friend of Otto's from Auschwitz, a man named Janos. Janos was from a wealthy family and was a great actor, director and drama teacher, as well as an art collector. His wife Violet was also an actress and the two of them were a wonderful complement to each other. I looked forward to getting to know Janos better, and Sandy was eager to talk to him about the state of the arts in Hungary.

I felt preoccupied when they arrived. The day had been filled with memories and with such strong feelings that I had kept inside for so long. The whole evening, it was an effort to compose myself after seeing that picture of Richie and his friends. The flood of memories would not stop.

Janos and Violet picked us up and drove us to the restaurant. Imagine my shock when Janos pulled his car up to the Hotel Royale. I couldn't get out. 'My God, why did you bring me here?' I asked.

'Is something wrong?' he asked politely. 'This place is

still elegant and the food is very good, and who would
not want to come here at least once?'

'It's fine,' I said, getting a grip of myself as I climbed
out of the back seat with Sandy. 'It's just that I have such
memories of this place.' I didn't tell them that years ago
I had dreamed of marrying Richie here.

Sandy nudged me and whispered. 'Is this the hotel
where Richie used to play at the tea dances?' I nodded,
my eyes trying to take everything in all at once, my heart
beating fast as I saw the familiar entrance and the dining
room beyond. The Hotel Royale. Was all this part of a
dream that had begun earlier today? It all felt unreal.
Then I began to feel a wave of tension and expectation
that I could not account for. Of course, I kept all this to
myself.

Janos led us into the dining room, following the *maitre
d'* to our table. The room still retained its elegance,
although it was somewhat shabby now, as so many places
were under the Communists. I sighed. What a waste, I
thought, for so much beauty to be so ignored.

The dinner conversation was lively, and a trio of gypsy
violinists circled the room, playing romantic songs from
my childhood that made my eyes fill with tears.

'How was your day?' Janos asked.

We told him about visiting my old friend's mother and
about seeing pictures of Richie when he was a teenager.
I described our walk and my conversation with Sandy
about Richie. Up to this time, I had never told anyone
but Otto about my first love. I had stored it away all these
years as a sacred treasure in a private place in my heart.

It was about eight-thirty when we started to eat and,
as I looked around, I suddenly froze. I felt as if I had died
that second and everything had stopped.

'What's the matter?' Sandy asked.

I tried to focus on her, but my thoughts were in total chaos. 'Why do you ask?'

'Because you're so pale,' she said.

I raised my hand to my hair and realized it was shaking. I lowered it to my lap. 'That's Richie over there, with his back to us, eating dinner.'

Sandy looked over and saw what I saw: the back of a man's head and neck as he sat eating dinner with a woman and child who could have been his wife and daughter. The man could have been anyone.

Sandy shook her head at me. 'Mum, come on, pull yourself together. That's not really Richie. You're just under the influence of the day. It's nothing more than the power of suggestion, or maybe wishful thinking.'

Janos and Violet were riveted by what was going on, by the intensity they could feel coming from me and from the situation, as if they were spectators at a play. Years later, I asked them what they felt that night and they said it was a tension so electric it had weight.

I turned to Sandy. 'That is Richie. I sat behind him in gym lessons every day for years and I would know the back of his neck anywhere.'

We sent the waiter over to ask the man whether he was Richie Kovacs. The waiter came back quickly and said no, the man was not Richie Kovacs. I was still not convinced. Strong-willed as I am, I was not ready to give up. My heart was pounding so hard and fast I knew, after all these years, that I had to know the truth.

I said to Violet, 'Come for a walk with me. Let's go down the staircase that passes in front of his table. Maybe he'll look up as we walk by. Maybe he'll see me or at least I'll be able to see his face clearly.'

So we went for a stroll and, as we neared his table, Violet and I began laughing and talking loudly, hoping to attract his attention, but he never looked up. I returned to the table feeling frustrated, and a little annoyed at Sandy, who had rubbed her two fingers together as if to say, 'Shame, shame.' Sandy acted as if Violet and I had been engaging in some meaningless charade instead of trying to identify the most important person from my past.

We finished our dinner, but before we could leave, Sandy turned to me. 'Are you just going to leave without finding out for sure whether or not it's him?'

I took a deep breath before I answered her. 'No,' I said. 'I'm going over there.'

My legs shook so badly that the steps seemed to take for ever. I could barely breathe. Finally I was right behind him. I leaned over the banister of the staircase and put my hand on his shoulder and said, 'I am sorry to bother you, but I think we know each other.'

He looked up and seemed frozen for an instant, then he jumped up and pulled me down the five steps that separated us and hugged me so close I thought my body would merge with his. We both cried and he touched my face and said over and over again, '*Kis pofa, kis pofa.*'

Neither of us could do more than touch each other's faces for a few minutes. It was like so many of the dreams I had had over the years, only this time it was real. He was real. Then I stepped back. 'I'm sorry I embraced you in front of your wife,' I said.

But he smiled and answered. 'She is not my wife. I just arrived in Budapest today. Her husband is a colleague of mine and they took me out to the theatre. Then we had planned to go on to dinner, but he was called away on an emergency – he's a doctor. But he insisted that we go on to dinner anyway.'

With that, Richie turned and explained the situation

to them, and excused himself, asking the wife if she could find her own taxi. 'I really apologize and I'll pay the bill if you wouldn't mind finding your own way home.'

She smiled and reassured him that that was just fine. Then she turned and smiled at me as well. I smiled back. Right then, I would have smiled at anyone, I was so happy, so euphoric, so filled with joy, with life.

I looked up at Richie as we walked back to my table, hand in hand. He was still as tall and handsome as ever, his dark hair edged with grey at the temples, his blue eyes as bright and compelling as ever behind wire-rimmed glasses. 'I came here tonight looking for my youth, although I didn't think I'd find it. But I have,' Richie said, looking dazed.

When we got back to the table, I simply introduced him, and he sat down, still holding my hand. 'Forgive me, please forgive me,' he said to everyone, 'but my heart is beating so fast I think I'm going to be sick.' I held his hand tightly, as if I never wanted to let it go, and I didn't. But I was also very aware that I had my child with me, and that she was witnessing all of this, and it made me self-conscious and conflicted.

'Why did you tell the waiter you weren't Richie Kovacs?' I asked him.

He smiled at me. 'I did some work for the Underground even after the war and before I left Hungary, and I thought the Communists might be looking for me. That's why I changed my name after the war. It's now Carpenter, a nice American name with no past.'

I had so many questions to ask him, but this was clearly not the place to do so.

Richie and I wanted to go outside and talk, but Janos said he would drive us back to the hotel and then we

could catch up uninterrupted. We all jammed into Janos'
tiny car. I was sitting in the middle in the back seat, with
Sandy on one side of me and Richie on the other.

It only took a few minutes to get back to the hotel.
When we got out of the car, we said goodbye to Janos
and Violet, and then I took Richie up to the room I was
sharing with Sandy. At that point, we still didn't know
anything about each other's situation.

I always travel with pictures of my family and there, on
the bedside table, were pictures of me and Otto and
Bobby and Sandy and Jeff. He looked at them silently for
a long time.

'I have no sons, only daughters,' he said. 'No one to
carry on my name.'

'But you changed your name, so what difference does
it make?' I asked sharply.

He seemed surprised at the hint of sarcasm in my
voice. Then he turned to Sandy and asked: 'Would you
mind if I took your mother for a walk?'

'Richie and I would like to be alone for a while,' I
added gently.

She looked from my face to his, and I could see how
upset and confused she was at what was happening. She
had always just thought of me as her mother, as her
father's wife. She had always felt that Otto pampered me
and catered to me and sometimes said, 'Why do you
deserve to be treated so well by Daddy?'

Now, in the space of a day, she was seeing me in a
different way. She stood and faced us both coolly. 'I'll go
with you. I'm not going to leave you alone.'

Richie still looked dazed and a little desperate. I was
beginning to feel desperate myself. It was after ten, and
we were scheduled to leave Budapest the next morning.

'I am only here for tonight,' I told him in Hungarian.

'That cannot be,' he said, and I saw him trying to work out what to do.

I just nodded, tears filling my eyes at the irony of our situation. 'But it is. We have to leave before any offices are open and you know, in such a controlled regime, you cannot simply stay longer without extending your visa.'

Richie looked as if he would cry again. 'How can fate have played this kind of trick on us? I've just arrived for a conference on biochemistry. I'm to give a lecture tomorrow.'

Sandy's eyes darted back and forth between us, trying to figure out what was being said. Whatever she saw in our faces made up her mind. She was not leaving. Richie studied her and could see her determination. We had walked back through the lobby by now and out of the front door. He smiled faintly as he grabbed my hand and hers.

'Let's walk,' he said. I could feel his hand shaking in mine as we strolled down the street, Sandy on one side of him, me on the other. He must have been staring at Sandy, because she suddenly said to him angrily: 'Don't look at me. I don't look anything like my mother. I look like my father.'

I saw him squeeze her hand and smile at her. 'I am staring because you are a very pretty girl and because you are Baby's daughter and I wanted to look at you.'

Sandy wasn't pacified. 'I can tell you one thing,' she said. 'My father would never be out walking the streets with someone who wasn't his wife. My mother is his whole world and he would do anything for her.'

Richie said nothing in response. What could he say?

So we kept walking and I realized as we negotiated the streets and made the turns that we were going to Richie's house. It was a walk I had made so many times before, his hand holding mine, that I almost broke down. He had only daughters, he had said, which meant he was married, too. What an impossible situation.

When we got to his house, the letters of his family's company still faintly outlined against the brick façade of the building, Richie broke down. 'Do you remember when I kissed you at the door, and my mother opened it and we both fell into the entrance hall, and my mother couldn't stop laughing? Do you remember how many times I walked you home, from my house to your house?'

He kept talking, the words flowing out of him in a steady stream as Sandy stood there, watching us like some kind of sentry. She couldn't understand Hungarian, so she had no idea what was being said, but she didn't need any language to understand the intensity of what was taking place, and I could see she was terrified.

But Richie didn't even notice, and I barely did — we were so caught up in each other, the love as strong inside me as it had been the day I last left him on the Castle Hill.

As if he could read my mind, Richie pulled out his wallet and reached into it, handing me a small picture of myself at fifteen. 'Look, here is the only picture I have left of you and I have carried it around with me since we were separated on the day Budapest was bombed. I have looked at this picture a thousand times, each time hoping that we would meet again. And now, we have a sign. God wanted us to meet again. He brought us both here to Budapest, both of us for the very first time since the war. This was meant to be, we are meant to be. And now that I have found you, I will never let you go.'

I tried to answer him as best I could, with my daughter standing there. I struggled to stay calm, but inside I was screaming. I wanted only this man, and to forget everything else, all my obligations, all I had become. I just wanted him so desperately, the way I always had. But life was never that simple, at least not for me.

'Look, my darling,' I said to him. 'My daughter's standing here. I can't make a choice like this in a minute. We will talk tonight and discover what has happened to both of us over the last thirty years.'

He nodded slowly. 'Does it hurt you as much as it hurts me to remember all we have lost?'

I felt the tears filling my eyes. Oh God, this was so painful. 'Yes, of course, but we should try not to torture ourselves with the past.' I had been doing that for thirty years, but I couldn't tell him that; I couldn't add my pain to all the pain he had been carrying around. 'I am just so happy that you are alive, because I thought you were dead, and I am so happy that we have met again, because now I know you are all right and I can go on with my life.'

'No,' he shouted, his voice choked with pain.

I saw Sandy flinch and I knew that she was close to breaking. She was only a 21-year-old girl. Much as she thought she was a sophisticated adult who understood all life's mysteries because she had taken a degree in psychology, I knew that nothing had prepared her for a moment like this, and it wasn't fair to her.

'All these things are for us to discuss privately, not in front of others,' I said to Richie, and I could see him visibly take control of himself before he nodded his agreement.

We walked back to the hotel, and I asked Sandy to go upstairs and start packing while Richie and I had a drink in the bar.

Richie sat down on a bar stool, cradled his head in his hands. 'I can't believe how you fucked up my life,' he said.

Richie had always been polite and refined, his words chosen carefully.

It was the most shocking thing Richie could ever have said to me, because it meant that he was telling the absolute, awful truth, and it had been wrenched from the depths of his soul.

'Why did you get married so soon after the war?' he asked, staring at me, anger behind the glint in his penetrating blue eyes. 'I waited fifteen years to get married. I looked for you for fifteen years, all over Europe, even in the US. I was in New York in 1950 and I saw an announcement for a bris for a son born to a Betty Schimmel, born Betty Markowitz, and I thought it might be you. I went to the apartment, but a tall blond man who was there, who looked like a leftover from the Hitler youth, insisted there was no one there by that name, and, when I persisted, he shoved me down the stairs.'

Now it was my turn to be shocked. Otto had lied to me, had betrayed me, all those years ago when Bobby was born. He had known since 1950 that Richie was alive. Richie had been at my front door and Otto had sent him away, even though he had promised me he would let me go if Richie ever came back. I could have had my life back. I had been only twenty-one. Still a child. I could hear only the roaring in my ears and I thought I might be physically sick from the pain. Otto, the man who was supposed to have been my protector, had tormented me all these years by keeping such a secret. I would kill him, or I would leave him.

As the news sunk in, I heard Richie still talking. 'I even went back there again, but you had moved away.'

Now I understood why Otto was so eager to leave Manhattan and why Reading had looked so good to him. Part of his mission had been to keep me from ever finding Richie again. I tried to push all that out of my mind.

I wanted to know what had happened to Richie after the war and I wanted to tell him why I had got married so quickly.

'I thought you were dead,' I told him quietly. 'After we were taken, we were marched across Hungary in a death march that killed most of us. You remember Violet, beautiful Violet? She was killed during the first week of the march, shot to death in front of us. The horrors never stopped. We were imprisoned in Mauthausen. I was so sick with typhoid fever they thought I would die.'

Tears rolled down Richie's face as he listened, his hand caressing mine, his voice whispering, 'My poor darling, my poor *kis pofa*,' as I told him all that had happened to us.

'After the war, I didn't want to live because I couldn't find you. I went from camp to camp looking for you, checking each and every file card made by the Red Cross, HIAS [a Jewish Refugee organization] and ORT [a Jewish trade organization]. And then, one day, more than a year after the war at a displaced persons' camp called Kassel in Germany, I found your name listed among the dead, and that's the only time I ever found your name or ever heard anything about you.'

Richie leaned over and cupped my face in his hands, then kissed me gently on the lips. 'I am so sorry for all that you have suffered, my darling Baby.'

I couldn't stop myself then; tears were streaming down my face and I could feel a sob rising in my throat. Richie threw down some money and said, 'Let's get out of here.'

We walked out of the hotel and down the street. As soon as we were out of sight of the hotel, Richie pulled me up against the wall of a building and kissed me the way he used to, a soul-shattering kiss that told me who and what I was and all that was important in my life.

Ever. I never wanted the kiss to end, because in it I found all the answers, no more questions, no more hurt, no more anger. And I could tell he wanted to lose himself in just this, too, our perfect love that needed no words and no name.

But after a long time, when my legs were shaking and I thought I would die, he pulled gently away and wiped my cheeks with his thumb. I realized then that I was crying, crying as we kissed for all that had been and all that could never be.

'Let's walk, *kis pofa*, and I will tell you what happened to me after we were separated.' He wrapped his arm around mine and drew me close to his side, his head leaning down for a moment to rest gently on the top of my head.

'We were taken out of our house that day, too,' he explained, as we strolled along the banks of the Danube. 'We were sent to another Jewish house in another district. I was still working for the Underground, taking guns over to Buda in a wagon, taking messages from one part of the city to another, even out into the countryside. We knew the war would be over soon, but we didn't know whether we could survive until then. The killing turned into a massacre in the ghetto.'

He shook his head, as if trying to rid himself of the awful memories. I knew those feelings. I raised my head up to his and stood on tiptoe to give him a kiss, and he clung to me.

'I went crazy when I got to your house the next day and you were gone,' he said, the pain so vivid in his voice that it was like a living thing. 'All the neighbours could tell me was that you had been taken, with every other Jew from that house, but nobody knew where. I sat down on the front steps and I cried and cried. Then I went to

every Jewish house I knew of, but I couldn't find you.' He
leaned down to kiss my eyelids.

'I was reckless. I didn't care what happened to me
then, which was good, I suppose, because the Arrow
Cross came and took me and any other able-bodied men
they could find to a forced labour camp. And that's where
I was for the rest of the war. It was six or seven months
before I was allowed out of the displaced persons' camp
and could get back to Budapest, and it took about that
long for my mother to get back into our old apartment.'

I nodded. So that is why my letter went unanswered.
He wasn't there when I sent it. Even if I had made it back
to Budapest after the war, I wouldn't have found him
there.

'I went back to university in Hungary for a while, but
then I left and went to Austria, because the authorities
told me that that was where your group had been taken
during deportation. I went to three or four of the big
camps there, looking for you.'

I nodded. 'By then, we had been taken to a camp in
Germany.' How cruel fate was, I thought, preferring not
to blame God again, as I had during the Holocaust. I had
imbued my Jewish faith in my children, and become so
involved in Judaism that I no longer felt I could blame
God, but blaming fate felt safe, and I had to blame someone – Hitler, Eichmann, Otto, someone. But the thought
of Otto as an enemy was too hard to bear. I couldn't
think about that.

'I finished my studies at the Sorbonne, while I continued to look for you in Europe. They took me in, as
they did many refugees whose lives had been disrupted,'
Richie said. 'I knew I could never go back to live in
Hungary with the Communists in place, but my poor
mother was still there. I emigrated to Canada, went to

Montreal, and from there, after a year or two, I was able to bring my mother over.

'I was teaching biochemistry by then, but I was still searching for you, I could not believe you were gone, and yet I couldn't find a trace, except for that time in New York.'

He saw me close my eyes.

'That was you, wasn't it? And the Hitler youth who threw me down the stairs, that was your husband?'

I nodded, trying to find the right words. 'Otto was a victim himself,' I said softly. 'He lost his entire family – his mother, his sister, his grandmother – at Auschwitz. His brother died in the ghetto. When he met me, he fell in love with me and pursued me. But he also fell in love with my family. And he wanted desperately for the two of us to reproduce his own family. When you found me, that was the bris of our first-born son, Bobby.'

'Did you love him?' Richie asked me, and I could hear the pain in his voice.

I shook my head, wondering why everything tonight felt like a betrayal. 'No, and he knew it. He knew that I loved you and he promised me that if I ever found you, he would let me go.' There, the words were out, and I heard Richie gasp, because he now knew what I did – that Otto had lied and with his lying had kept us apart and ruined both our lives.

Richie's voice hardened. 'Will he be sorry enough to let you go? We can start again,' he told me. 'I will leave my wife. Even after fifteen years, when I married her, I told her if I ever found you I would leave her.'

I looked up at him, and I was so confused. 'Do you love your wife?'

He hesitated. 'After you, there was no love that touched me in that same way. I feel love and affection for her, I love our two daughters and I would feel bad about leaving them, even though I would always provide for all of them; but God meant us to be together, Baby, and we have suffered enough.'

'Is she Jewish?' I asked.

He closed his eyes. 'Yes, and she's a very good woman.'

'Look,' I said to him, 'I don't know what I am going to do. I have to have time to make my decision. You don't know how I prayed for you every night, how I wanted you near me. And I have had visions of you returning to me. I have loved you all these years, but now I don't know what I am going to do. The feeling is the same as it was, I still want to be with you, but at this moment I can't make a decision. Please understand this involves a family, not only for me, but for you. We have to think about this.'

He stood there looking at me, seeing our past as well as our present in my eyes. 'God made this happen to us tonight, Baby, and He is telling us something. We are going to start a life together. I love my children, too, as much as you do, but we belong together. Finding you again after all these years is a miracle. And I want you just as much as I did thirty-one years ago. This was meant to be.'

I was shaking. I knew that he was right, that we belonged together, but not after I had committed myself to another man. I had children and so did he. We would need more time to see whether we truly felt the same way that we did before. Yet here we were now as adults and as parents and we were still professing love for one another, just the way we had when we were teenagers. I could not fathom it. I kept looking at him in disbelief. I still could not believe that he was here in front of me.

Richie held me, and his kisses took me straight to heaven. Then I thought about saying goodbye tomorrow and I went into shock. How could all this happen so quickly?

Never before had I seen the Danube as I was seeing it now. The lights of the little boats played on the waves as Richie and I walked hand in hand, kissing again and again. I wanted to stay like this for the rest of my life. But I knew that this night had to end, that I couldn't just stay on in Hungary without a visa.

I had to face my daughter and tell her the whole story – how I had searched and searched for Richie, how I had met her father, how he had promised me he would let me go if I ever found Richie again. But how could I tell her the truth – that I still loved this man? I knew I had to make a decision. I went through it again and again, what I would tell Sandy, how I would tell her.

Our steps took us across one of the beautiful suspension bridges spanning the Danube. Up ahead of us was the serpentine walk to the Castle Hill. Richie pulled me up the hill until we found our old spot.

'You see,' he said, pointing to the heart he had carved into the wall so long ago, 'it is still there, just like our love.' We kissed again and again, until my head was spinning.

'You see how our mouths and our bodies still fit together so well?' Richie asked. 'I told you we were meant to be.'

I nodded, smiling up at him, but inside I was in complete turmoil.

What were we going to do? How could we measure our happiness against the lives of so many others? I looked up at the midnight sky. Clouds had hidden the moon and I felt the first few drops of warm rain begin to fall.

'Let's go somewhere where we can talk and stay dry,' Richie said, guiding me across a wide boulevard and down a side street.

In a few minutes, we were in the rented apartment he had been given for the length of his stay in Budapest. Richie closed the door and took me in his arms again, not even bothering to turn on the light. I felt his lips hot against mine, I felt the shape of those lips that had been the first to ever kiss me, and I was lost. I felt Richie pressed against me, the lights of Budapest illuminated in the window behind us. How handsome he was, and how dear his face was to me. I felt his hands move from my neck down to my breasts, touching them softly through the thin silk of my dress. I shuddered. I had not felt desire like this for all the years of my marriage. I had not felt desire like this since the last time Richie had touched me this way.

'So beautiful,' he murmured, as he caressed me. I knew I would never feel better than this, lighter than this, as if suddenly all the weight of the past, all the pain, had lifted, and there was only this man, my own true love, and this moment, and what we felt for each other. I wanted him so much. And I was terrified.

'We have to go back,' I said, pulling away. 'It's so late and I have to leave in the morning.'

I went over to stand by the window, to compose myself, but Richie came up behind me and encircled me with his arms. 'Don't go yet. I've just found you and I've been starving for you all these years,' he said, kissing me down the side of my neck.

I melted in his arms, leaning back against him, wishing I could stay this way for ever.

He turned me around and kissed me deeply, his hands circling my back and feeling for the zipper at the back of my dress. I felt the first pull as the zipper started to come down. I wanted this moment more than I had wanted anything in my life, but I didn't feel I had the right to it. Not now. At least, not yet. I pushed against his chest and stepped back, my entire body shaking.

'We have to stop,' I told him. 'You take me back to the hotel or I'll take a taxi back.'

Richie looked at me for a long moment with all the pain from his past, all the love and longing he felt now. But he didn't force me and he didn't push me.

'All right,' he said quietly, 'I'll take you back.'

As we walked the long blocks to the hotel, the warm rain continued to fall. It felt light and pleasant, but Richie took off his jacket and put it over my shoulders. We walked slowly, as if we never wanted to reach the hotel. I told him about Otto and what he did, and he told me he was a professor at a major American university.

'Your husband probably earns a lot more than I do,' he said. 'University professors don't make all that much. I'm not going to be able to give you as much as your husband has.'

I stopped and faced him. 'Don't assume we are going to get together. This has hit me like a bolt of lightning. I need time to think.'

Richie cupped my face in his hands. 'This was meant to be. We were brought together for a reason. Do you know that every year I still remember your birthday? Did you know that one of my daughters was born on the same day, 1 March, and every time we celebrate I think about you?'

I closed my eyes against the joy and the pain. 'Let me tell you one thing,' I said softly to him. 'There are things that money can buy and there are things beyond price. What you give me is beyond price and is all I ever wanted. I would live in a shack with you if I had to.'

His eyes shone like the sun. 'I told you this didn't just happen,' he said. 'It happened for a reason. We can't change the past, but we can change the future, and we are going to change the future.'

How I wanted to believe it was possible, but I didn't answer, because I didn't know whether I could walk away from the man who had been my husband for twenty-eight years, who was the father of my children.

'This is not something we should decide in a moment,' I told him again.

'I can understand that, but know this, Baby. The love I have for you has always been with me and will be with me until the end of time.'

I cried then, because I had heard the words I had longed to hear for all those lonely years when I had lost him, lost my own true love.

Gently, Richie turned me to him and kissed each one of my tears away, catching them as they rolled down my cheeks. 'I love you now as I loved you then. Nothing has changed,' he said. 'I longed for you and wanted you to be near me. Now, tonight, my prayers have been answered and I will not give you up. Please stay with me.'

It was so terribly tempting, but it was impossible.

'I cannot stay now, but we will make arrangements to meet again,' I told him. 'Then we will make a final decision. I love you and I want to be with you, but right now I can't make this decision. Please, let's wait until I feel comfortable and stable.'

As we walked, Richie pressured me to answer him, but I resisted.

'At least give me a few hours,' I said. 'I will meet you at our place on the Castle Hill before we have to leave for the airport.'

I don't know why, but I lied to him about where we were going. We were going by train, not plane, to Vienna, before going on to Paris. Perhaps I wanted to make sure Richie couldn't follow me unless I wanted him to. Or perhaps I knew that if he came to the train station, I could never say goodbye to him and I would have to stay.

We were still walking back to the hotel. He had one arm over my shoulder and he turned to me and said, 'Look, I'm a respectable man and mature. I am very serious about our meeting, that it was meant to be. I want you enough to leave my wife and children for you. I know what it takes for you to leave your husband and children, but life has been unfair to us. It has robbed us of our happiness, and we have the right to that.'

I knew that Richie was speaking the truth, but I couldn't say anything that would commit me to this course. At least, not yet.

'We have to know each other better,' I said at last. 'A lot of time has passed since we have been together and this is an enormous decision that affects many people. We would be tearing apart two families.'

He kissed me again and all reason fled. I was terrified that I would not be able to withstand the force of our love and that I would just react, do what made me feel good without thinking of all of those I loved, all those my mother had asked me on her deathbed to put first.

By this time, we were at the hotel. As we walked into the lobby, I saw Sandy and she was hysterical.

'Where have you been?' she asked angrily. 'I was about to call the police.'

I shuddered. The last thing you should do in a Communist country is call the police. My worst nightmares could have come true and we would have found ourselves in a cell somewhere.

'I am here now, there is nothing to be upset about,' I said as calmly as I could. 'Wait here for a minute.'

Then I walked Richie outside and kissed him again as if I could give him my soul with it.

'You will hear from me in the morning,' I said. 'Meet me at eight at our spot on the Castle Hill.'

His eyes searched mine. 'I love you, Baby, I have always loved you and I will always love you. We have given enough to the past. The future – what's left of it – belongs to us.'

I smiled up at him, tears brimming in my eyes. 'I love you with all my heart, my darling. I will see you in the morning.' And then I turned and ran into the hotel.

Sandy was still standing there. 'Are you aware that it's three in the morning?'

I didn't answer, simply nodded and walked past her to the lift.

chapter *T*wenty-four

*W*hen I reached our room, all hell broke loose. I became hysterical, screaming and crying out in pain. I could tell I was frightening Sandy, but I couldn't help myself. So much had happened to me, and I wasn't sure I could cope with any of it. I wanted to get out all those suppressed feelings inside me, the things I had kept locked in for all those years, the things that had given me headaches and heart palpitations and high blood pressure. And I wanted to tell Otto what he had done to me when he hadn't told me that Richie had come to claim me.

I went downstairs to the telephone booth in the lobby and called Otto, not wanting Sandy to hear the conversation. He sounded worried when he answered the phone and the operator told him he had a call from Mrs Schimmel in Hungary, but when he heard my voice, I could feel him smiling through the phone.

'How are my darling wife and my beautiful daughter? All is well?' he asked.

'All is not well,' I answered. 'Your daughter is packing and crying and I am so angry with you that I could kill you if you were here.'

There was a stunned silence on the other end of the phone. I went on ruthlessly, 'I met Richie here in Budapest at the Hotel Royale. He told me that he'd found me in New York in 1950 but that you sent him away.'

I heard Otto's gasp, all those thousands of miles away.

'Please forgive me,' he said, and I could hear that he was crying. 'I couldn't let you go. I couldn't let my son go. I had already lost so much – everyone I had ever loved. I could not lose you, too, Baby, I couldn't.'

The pain was pounding in my head now. 'How could you? How could you steal my life that way? How could you let me think all those years that Richie was dead? My love was not yours to keep. You promised you would let me go.' I was sobbing now, clutching the receiver and crying deep, gasping sobs that felt as if they would rip open my chest.

I yelled at him, becoming uncontrollable. I cried out loud in the telephone booth. People had gathered outside, looking in at the crazy woman on the telephone, but I didn't care. I had held this in for so many years, and now I just had to let it out.

'Shame on you, Otto. You promised me freedom, but you withheld it from me. When Richie found me, you chased him away. You made two lost souls wander in the world without a reason to go on. Only our children gave me any reason at all to go on.'

I knew I was saying things that hurt him, but he had hurt me so deeply that I didn't know whether I would ever recover. I kept on talking, saying everything I had to say.

'My children kept my soul alive within me. I gave you

back the family that you had lost. I paid for Hitler's sins against you with my life. You can only say that you are sorry? That's all you can say?'

'Baby, let's talk,' Otto pleaded. 'I love you. You must forgive me.'

'I can never forgive you,' I shouted, and hung up.

I was crying and shaking, beside myself, as I ran back upstairs and threw a suitcase on the bed and began packing.

'Mama, maybe you'd better sit down and get calm,' Sandy said.

I gave her a hug. 'Go to bed, Sandy, and get some rest. As it is, you will be exhausted tomorrow.'

Miraculously, she did as I asked, and she was asleep in a few minutes. I was still crying, my brain numb from it.

An hour later, I felt an almost eerie calm. I had looked deep inside myself and made a decision. My whole life had led me to this moment. I prayed I was right. I sat down and wrote the most difficult letter I've ever had to write. I still don't know how my fingers found the power to pen the words:

My Darling,
You are my first love and the love of my heart, and what we have together will always live on within me. But that was the past and this is the present, and in the present we both have other lives, other obligations that we must honour. I cannot go with you, and I am afraid to meet you again, for fear that I would not have the strength to do what I know is right. Now, just knowing that you are alive, I think I can go on and that my life will be different. You must go on, too. I can't leave my children, but our love will live for ever.

Forgive me that it is these few lines that will be waiting for you instead of me. Goodbye, my love.
Kis pofa.

I placed the note in a hotel envelope and sealed it.
Then I threw on a sweater and ran the couple of blocks
to the bridge and over it, and up the long winding walkway in the dark until I reached our place on the Castle
Hill. I stuck the note into the wall, in a place next to the
heart Richie had carved for us so long ago. I took a
moment to trace its outline and the words within it:
'Richie and Baby for ever.' Then I turned and ran back
down the hill before I collapsed against the cold stone
wall.

When I reached the hotel room, I finished packing,
moving like a robot from the chest of drawers and the
cupboard to my suitcases, seeing nothing. I could not
sleep. When I went to lie down, all I could see was
Richie's face and the pain I knew would be there when I
didn't come to him the next morning. The anger I felt
toward Otto threatened to consume me, and I ranted at
the fate that had been so cruel to Richie and to me. I
tried using the Transcendental Meditation techniques
Otto and I had learned the year before to ease our stress
and our nightmares, but I couldn't concentrate well
enough to put myself into a soothing trance. The last
hours with Richie kept playing over and over again in my
mind, like a film. I could not look ahead to the rest of my
life. It seemed too hopelessly grey, without shape or
colour, without the love of my life beside me. How was
I ever going to live without him?

The next morning, Sandy looked at me as if she
thought that I would break. The train journey to Vienna
lasted two and a half hours, and I cried all the way. Sandy

slept on and off, but I couldn't even close my eyes because every time I did, I saw Richie. I glanced at my watch. He must be reading my note by now, I thought. I knew that he would feel angry and betrayed, and that he would try to find me. But I knew he wouldn't succeed. He knew my married name, but I hadn't told him where we lived and I didn't leave him an address or telephone number. I knew the hotel would tell him nothing: the Communists never gave out personal information about guests unless it was to the secret police.

Once again, I lost my love.

When we arrived in Vienna, we took a taxi to the Intercontinental Hotel and I told Sandy I was going to sleep. I was totally exhausted, physically and emotionally. We had a prepaid tour of the city and I encouraged Sandy to go on alone. While she toured Vienna, I stayed in the hotel room and cried.

At dinnertime, Sandy came back to the room and we had dinner together in the hotel restaurant. I knew I looked terrible, my eyes all red from crying, my hair a mess, and I hadn't even bothered to put on make-up.

'What's the matter with you?' Sandy asked. 'Why are you crying like this? So you met your ex. That's not a reason to carry on like this. Get yourself together. Let's enjoy our dinner and by tomorrow you'll feel fine.'

I looked across the table at this lovely young woman who was my daughter, and realized how innocent she was. At twenty-one, she had never been in love the way I had been; she had not experienced all the horrors I had lived through or the pain I had suffered. She still didn't know that her father had lied to me — a betrayal so massive that it made our marriage a mockery. I knew that I would have to face him when I got home, that we would have fights such as we had never had before. She does not know what awaits me, but I do, I thought.

I tried to smile at her. I knew she was only trying to help, to show that she understood my pain.

When we went back upstairs, she told me, 'Why don't you take a pill so that you can sleep?'

Because of the nightmares and the headaches I some-times suffered, my doctor had prescribed some mild sleeping pills. I took one of those now, and it worked. I slept.

The next morning, we flew out of Vienna to Paris. When we arrived at the Intercontinental Hotel, Otto was waiting for us in the lobby. I couldn't believe it. The very sight of him rekindled my anger. He couldn't even wait until I got home to talk to me. I started to walk past him, but he grabbed my arm.

'We need to talk,' he said.

I looked at him through narrowed eyes, my suspicion on the rise. I knew Otto would try to 'handle' me, the way he always did.

'This had better be good,' I said as I continued walk-ing.

As I took a second look at him, shock penetrated my anger. I had never seen Otto look like this. He was pale, so pale he looked like death. He was more pale than he had been when I first met him when he had just got out of Auschwitz. His hair was a mess, he hadn't shaved and his eyes were sunken. I realized he must have flown all night to meet me here. I told myself that I didn't care. How he looked and felt was no concern of mine. Hadn't he lied to me and cheated me out of happiness? Besides, I hadn't slept much either and it was his fault.

We got to our room and Sandy left us alone, mur-muring something about getting a bite to eat and going to see the Eiffel Tower while we worked this out.

I turned to face him, the good husband who had always taken such excellent care of me, who would have given me anything, or so he said, except my happiness, which he had withheld from me. I was so angry that I was shaking.

Otto looked like a ghost. He wanted to touch me but I pushed his hand away.

'Don't touch me,' I said. 'I will calm down and then you and I will talk.'

Otto was quiet, but I was not. I was pacing the room, saying over and over again, 'You had no right. You promised you would let me go. You had no right.'

Otto said nothing, and that got me even more angry. I walked over to him and shook him by the shoulders. 'Why did you do this to me? He was looking for me, he found me, and then you sent him away. I will never forgive you for that.'

Still Otto said nothing, and I sat there, wondering what I was going to do. There was not only no way for Richie to get in touch with me: but I did not know how to get in touch with him in Budapest, either. Perhaps the university there could get in touch with him, but the telephones in Hungary were a nightmare. It would be difficult.

Then I heard Otto clear his throat. 'Just listen, Baby,' he said.

'It had better be good,' I said again, turning to face him, 'because I am tired of your lies and you have lied to me for years. I lived on the memories of a dead man, because I believed that Richie was dead and you let me believe that.'

Otto looked straight at me, and I saw pain and love in his eyes. 'Just listen to what I have to say, Baby. That's all

I ask. Then, after I'm finished, you can do whatever you
want. If you want to leave me, you are free to go.'

I sat down on the couch, trying not to feel sorry for
him. When he spoke, he barely had any voice. He was
hoarse, from crying, I guessed. It was pitiful to see him
that way. He had always been a strong man who talked
fast and talked a lot. It was hard to believe that this man
was that man I had known, and it was equally hard to
believe that a man could fall apart so quickly.

He sat down opposite me, in one of the armchairs. He
was trembling, and he insisted on holding my hand as he
told me what had happened on that morning in January
1950.

'We were having the bris, and this young, handsome
man came to the door, asking for someone named Baby
or Betty. I didn't know what to say, but I found myself
saying no, there was no one here by that name. I was
trembling like I am now when I asked him who he was.'
Otto shuddered. 'He told me he was Richie Kovacs and
that he was looking for his lost love from Budapest.
When he had read about the bris in the local Jewish
newspaper, he had hoped that the woman who had given
birth was his old girlfriend. He told me he had been
looking for her since liberation and he had been all over
Europe and now America trying to find her.

'The room started to spin for me then,' Otto continued, 'and without even thinking, I pushed him out of
the way and shut the door in his face, saying no one by
that name lives here. When he knocked on the door
again, I told him to go away – that this was the celebration of my son's birth and he was intruding.'

Otto looked over at me. I was sitting there, one hand
still in his, the other clenched in my lap. I wanted to slap
him, to punch him, to make him feel the pain that I was

feeling. But I knew he already felt the pain, far more than any slap or punch could inflict.

'From that day on, I had to live with the knowledge that he was alive,' Otto continued. 'I thought that I would die then and there. I could not go back into the living room and say a word to anyone, I was so distraught. You were so tired and had just given birth, but I had seen a look of love in your eyes when you looked at Bobby that I had never seen when you looked at me. I knew you didn't love me in the way you loved Richie, and I thought I would lose you if I told you the truth. So I kept quiet and it ate at my guts, because I never wanted to lie to you, but the circumstances demanded that I lie to you. Then it was too late to correct it. He was gone and I had sent him away and there was no going back.' Otto ran his fingers through his uncombed hair, then squeezed my hand.

'Please forgive me. I love you more than life itself. Without you there is no life for me. I want to be your husband and the father of our three children. I beg you to come home with me. Let's go to a counsellor to try to save our marriage.'

I started to yell at him, all the pent-up rage unleashing as I faced the full knowledge of his deception and betrayal.

'You had no right to do that,' I shouted. 'My life has been so miserable, not knowing whether Richie was alive or dead. Why would you want to live with me if I love someone else?'

The moment those words were out of my mouth, I was sorry I'd said them, even though they might be true. He was in such bad shape and he was so vulnerable that I should never have said that.

Otto looked down at the floor, as if trying to absorb

the blow. 'But it is enough for me if I love you, Baby,' he said quietly. 'If you are there when I come home from work, it makes my day worthwhile. We can make it, Baby, you will see.' And then he broke down and cried. 'Don't leave me, Baby. I've already suffered so much for what I did, and life would end for me if you left me.'

My heart broke for this big man who sat there crying, this man who loved me so much, who had always loved me. How could I, after twenty-eight years of marriage, leave him? And yet my life had just been turned upside down. I had found Richie again, who also loved me and had never stopped loving me, as I had never stopped loving him. But I could not think of only myself, or even Richie, in the face of Otto's pain.

I realized that my husband had suffered so much in his life, and that there was no reason for him to suffer any longer. I walked over to him and touched his shoulder. 'Everything will be all right,' I said.

He took my hand and kissed it, and pulled me down to him on the couch and kissed me. That was the first kiss that made me feel like Otto's real wife. I kissed him back. The kisses became more heated and before we knew it, we were making love as we'd never made love before. I felt a greater excitement and involvement in it than I had ever felt before, and a completion I had never imagined. When it was over, I felt that this was truly the first time we had consummated our marriage as husband and wife, after twenty-eight years of sleeping together. For all those years, it was as if I had been an instrument and Otto had played me, but I had few strong feelings about it. This time, I was a willing and very satisfied participant. I was beginning to see my husband through new eyes. Why this should be happening after I had just met Richie again, I had no idea.

By the time Sandy returned, we were sitting side by side on the couch, holding hands and talking. Sandy looked so relieved to see us happy together that I almost laughed out loud. We told her we would explain everything to her later, and she seemed relieved, even happy, not to have to hear any details right then.

'Would you like me to bring you up a snack or order up room service?' she asked.

Otto and I looked at each other. 'No,' we both said at once. 'Let's go downstairs and get a snack together,' I suggested. I realized then that I hadn't eaten anything since dinner the night I'd met Richie. No wonder I was so hysterical. No food, no sleep, but plenty of shock. I went to comb my hair and put on some lipstick.

After our dinner, the three of us walked the streets of Paris together, window shopping. Under the Communist rule, there had been nothing to see in the shop windows of Budapest, but Paris was another story.

Otto turned to me. 'Let me buy you something to remember the day by,' he said.

I could hardly believe my ears. 'It's not necessary. I don't think I'll ever forget this day,' I answered, my voice laced with sarcasm.

Otto wisely ignored the comment. We walked for hours, Sandy walking a little bit ahead of us, so that we were able to talk. I told Otto that we would have to talk more openly in the future, to share our feelings and our souls. He agreed, but I knew that on that day he would have agreed to anything.

We stayed in Paris for another two days, exhausted by the sightseeing we did from morning until night. Otto didn't leave me alone for a second, which was good, in a way, because it gave me no time to think. It was when we were going to the airport that I began to cry.

The taxi driver, who had no idea what the matter was, said, 'It's OK, lady, you'll get over it, don't worry.'

For a minute, I thought maybe he knew something I didn't, but then I remembered that Paris is a city for lovers and that he must have seen more than his share of tears.

We had to wait hours for our flight out, and I told Otto and Sandy that I wanted to be alone for a while to meditate. They left me and I went into a meditative trance so deep that I awoke only when Otto shook me gently and told me it was time to board the plane.

We found our seats and I settled down next to Sandy. I was thinking of Richie. I closed my eyes and I could see him just as he had been five days ago. I longed for him, and wished that I could be with him again.

The plane to New York arrived late. As soon as we disembarked, Otto started running for the plane to Phoenix, but I just stood there. 'I am not going back to Phoenix right away,' I announced. 'I'm going to stay in New York for a few days.'

Otto looked at me with surprise in his eyes, but I was adamant.

'Then I will stay too,' he said.

'Please don't,' I said. 'I will go and visit my sister and be home in a few days.'

With that, I said goodbye to him. Sandy was going back to the town where her university was and one of her friends had come to the airport to pick her up. Otto ran for the Phoenix flight and I got myself a taxi. As I drove into Manhattan, I thought about whether I could tell Rose that I had found Richie.

By the time I got to Rose's apartment, it was dinnertime. She was absolutely delighted to see me. Once dinner was over, I helped her make up the bed in the spare room and she wanted to know all about my trip.

'You know,' I said, 'I'm really tired tonight. Why don't I tell you all about it tomorrow?'

I went to bed, hoping that my dreams would be filled with Richie. Instead, I fell into a sleep so deep it was dreamless and before I knew it it was morning.

My sister couldn't wait to hear about my trip. I told her the food was inexpensive and good, the hotel was nice, and yes, I had seen our old house and some of our old friends as well as friends and relatives of Otto's.

My sister couldn't have been nicer or kinder or more interested in me and what had happened, but I found her attention suffocating, and realized that I needed some time to be alone, truly alone. So I lied to her, so as not to hurt her feelings, and told her I was going home that day. As soon as I left her apartment, I checked into the Hilton Hotel. I stayed there for another day and night so that I could cry. I had been ashamed to cry in front of my sister but, in the antiseptic privacy of my hotel room, I allowed myself to howl with grief. I screamed into my pillow for hours. When I had no more strength left, I fell asleep.

The next day, I made a flight reservation to go home. I called Otto from Kennedy airport and told him the time of my arrival.

He was there at Phoenix airport, waiting for me. He kissed me hello and asked where I had been for the last day. Rose had called last night wanting to make sure I had made it home all right and, of course, I hadn't been there.

'I checked into a hotel for a day because Rose was asking me too many questions about my trip and I just didn't want to answer them,' I told him.

He accepted that and didn't ask me any more questions, which I was glad of, because it meant that I didn't have to lie or withhold the truth from him.

When we got home, he had dinner waiting and the table set. He made a great show of serving me and then sat down opposite me, the light from the candles he had lit shimmering on his face. He asked for my hand and I reached across the table and placed my hand in his. He looked into my eyes and said, 'You don't know how lucky you are. You found that someone you loved was alive. I wish I could find somebody in my family alive who I thought was dead.' And then he kissed my hand.

That night, we made love again. I felt I had been liberated from the heavy burden of my belief that Richie was dead.

I was very restless in the days and months to come. I wanted to get away all the time, to see parts of Arizona I hadn't yet seen, but I didn't want Otto to come with me.

'I want to air my head out,' I told him, and watched him laugh at my fractured English, a legacy of having Hungarian as my first language, a language Otto and I generally spoke when we didn't want the children to understand what we were saying.

I travelled through Arizona on my own. I stopped wherever I wanted, and continued on when I felt like it. I called home and Otto would always ask, 'When are you coming home?'

'I don't know,' I told him honestly. 'When I calm down a little bit.'

The first trip took ten days. I drove all over the state, sometimes in dangerous places, but mostly I just wanted to meditate outdoors. When I came home, I was calmer, and I had a new acceptance of my fate as it had been given to me.

chapter *T*wenty-five

*M*y life was as before, and yet nothing was ever completely the same after that meeting with Richie. I still cooked and baked, and sometimes I worked as a travel agent. I took as many trips as I could. I went to Mexico City, and to the Caribbean, and I did it all alone. I could not yet completely make peace with Otto and, sorry as I was for him, I still needed to take off on my own. I would just go off for a day or two, drive into the desert, stay at a roadside motel and come home. Otto never said a word. He didn't dare.

One day, Sandy called me and told me she had looked up Richie in *Who's Who in America* and found where he was teaching. I stored the information away. A couple of months later, when no one was at home, I picked up the phone and called the university. I don't want to mention its name, because Richie deserves his privacy. The operator put me through to the Science Department, which in turn put me through to someone else and then

again to another exchange. Finally, as I was about to give
up, I heard Richie's voice. 'Hello?'

I froze. What could I say? That I wanted to be his
friend? We felt too much for each other for that. Could
we all play cards together, Richie and I and Otto and
Richie's wife? Of course not. So what did I want from
him? I did not know.

'Hello. Is anybody there?'

I held on to the receiver for one long minute, drinking in the sound of his voice saying even such mundane
things. Then I gently replaced the receiver. There was
nothing I could say to him, although my heart wanted to.

A year later, I decided to go back to Hungary, but this
time Otto wouldn't hear of my going alone. We went
together, but we went our separate ways. Otto spent
most of his time visiting his aunt, who was his mother's
sister, and I wandered the streets of Budapest like a lost
soul, hoping to run into more people from my past, but
seeing no one I knew. I even went to neighbours and
asked them if my father had ever returned, looking for us
after the war. I knew that it was many years since the
liberation, but I still believed that someone somewhere
might know something. After all, I had found Richie after
all those years. But this time there were only dead ends.

I wandered the streets of the ghetto and tried to
remember where we had been taken, which house they
had put us in. It was a very trying time for me. I had
ghosts with me for company. I met Otto at night, but by
day I haunted the Castle Hill where I used to go with
Richie. That was the only place where I felt his presence,
and I could touch the carving with our names within it.
The first time I went back alone and touched it I wanted
to die. I wanted him so much, and the feeling was so
powerful that I could practically smell his distinctive

smell. Where is he? I thought of him every minute. It was as if I was under a spell, and I could not seem to free myself, although I have to admit I didn't really try. I had no power over the feeling; it had power over me.

That night, I went back to the hotel and had dinner with Otto as usual, but I was so restless I could not sit still. In Budapest I was always looking for Richie. In a way, I couldn't wait to leave the city and end the torture. In a few days we left for Spain and the island of Majorca. The world returned to normal, or at least to what was normal for me.

Otto and I smiled at each other and treated each other kindly, but there was no new openness between us and we never did see a counsellor. Otto didn't want to. But one thing did change. Now Otto took holidays with me. It was progress.

Over the next few years, I travelled to many different places, including Australia, where I looked up my old friend Fery, who had first introduced me to Otto. I'd learned that he had a shop in Sydney and I decided to surprise him there. I stood outside the shop window, looking in while he served customers. I saw him looking back at me and soon he came out and said, 'Do I know you?'

When I told him who I was, he threw his arms around me and said, 'I can't believe it's you, Baby, after all these years.'

We had a great time. He took me to see Otto's aunt and the next night he took me to a Jewish club, where I met several more friends from my past who had also emigrated to Australia. They all told me I should come back and bring Otto, so that we could get together for a celebration of life.

Two years later, we did just that. Otto and I flew from

Los Angeles and our son, Jeff, who came to see us off, teased me about it.

'Travelling again?' he asked.

'I've become a globetrotter just like my father,' I told him.

In 1982, I fulfilled another dream and travelled to China, going deep into the heart of the country, following the silk road all the way to Xian, before taking a boat down the Yangtze Kiang for ten days.

Otto went to Hong Kong regularly to have leather goods made, and often I went with him. We also went to Tahiti and a lot of other exotic places I'd only read or dreamed about before. I began to keep a travel diary of my journeys, just for myself, so that I could read it years later when I could no longer travel any further than my armchair.

I had brought back an idea from my native Hungary that was turning into a lucrative business for me. The Hungarians are known for their beautiful embroidery work on linens. I bought an embroidery machine in Phoenix, made up a few samples and took them around to the shops. By the end of a week, I had so many orders that the room where I worked was filled with them. Bullock's, Sakowitz, Goldwater's – they all wanted my embroidery. Eventually, when, even going without eating and sleeping, I couldn't get the work done on my own, I had to hire a couple of other women to help me. After a few years, I'd had enough of it and sold it for a healthy profit. I also went back to an old love – designing jewellery – and made some unusual pieces.

In the meantime, a lot was happening in our children's lives, and not all of it good. Bobby had married a young woman named Vickie, with a heart of gold, from a family where the father was very anti-Semitic. They went into mourning when she married Bobby, especially her father. None of the family came to the wedding except for two of her three sisters. We gave them the wedding. But Vickie embraced Judaism, even converting. Bobby and Vickie had four children. Their daughter Jessica developed juvenile diabetes at the age of sixteen but copes well with it and, at twenty-one, plans to be a doctor so that she can help others with the problem. Their middle child, Derek, tragically developed cancer, which the doctors told them would kill him within eighteen months. My son and daughter-in-law were deeply shocked, so we helped them take care of Derek and Jessica and then little Aliyah, when she came along. Derek survived for eight years, not eighteen months, but how he suffered. And we suffered with him – so much so that, at the end, all I could do was pray for his death so that this sweet, smart, beautiful little boy would be at peace and out of pain, safe and loved in the hands of God. When Derek died in December 1992, Vickie was very depressed, and we all rallied to help support her and Bobby, Jessica and Aliyah. Now Bobby and Vickie have had another son, named Jacob Isaac after my father and Otto's, a delightful baby to carry on the Schimmel name.

Sandy had become engaged to a wonderful and giving young man who, tragically, was killed by mistake by police while he was trying to help an older man who had been knifed by a younger man. The police shot before asking questions and he died instantly. Sandy told me then that now she finally understood what I had gone through over Richie. She ended up marrying one of her brother Jeff's friends, who had started out consoling her and fell in love with her. Sadly, the marriage ended in divorce. I love helping to look after Sandy's beautiful daughter Alexsandra.

Jeffrey also got married, to a girl named Gloria, a pretty little woman who immediately converted to Judaism. Conversion was never something we required or ever even mentioned; both daughters-in-law just wanted to do it. Their beautiful daughter Sarah is named after Otto's mother.

In February 1993, I was diagnosed with breast cancer and had to have a breast removed. The entire family came to the hospital the night before the surgery and I told them all how much I loved them.

My children are my proudest achievement, but my love for Otto also fills me with peace and pride. We did not have an easy road and for many years I mistreated him because I was so unhappy. But now we have been married for more than fifty years. We have shared life and death together.

I wanted to make it up to Otto for all the years that I had mistreated him. While he showered me with love, I took it as my due and never thought to give it back. Even at times when I wanted to love him, I felt that there was a demon holding me back from doing so. Even when we travelled together, we were a loving couple in public, but as soon as we were alone, Otto would stop talking and I would either suddenly become tired or develop a headache.

But Otto was patient and never demanded more from me. I suppose he knew it was something I would have to come to in my own time. And I did. One day I realized that I enjoyed Otto's attention, that it was a matter not of suffocation, but of love and protection. I wanted to be free and loving, too. I did not want to be trapped in a body that had no feeling or love for this man. I did love him. My mother was right. I promised myself then that I would love and honour Otto every day for the rest of our lives together.

My children still do not know how loveless much of my marriage was, and my grandchildren have no idea. In fact, it makes me very proud that my granddaughter Jessica wants to have a marriage 'just like Grandma and Grandpa's.'

My home is a peaceful place now for both of us. Otto still works, but now he comes home for lunch and he stops working early in the afternoon so that we can go to the cinema. Together, through the Phoenix Holocaust Survivors Organization, we speak to schools all over Arizona about our experiences. Nothing means more to me than the hundreds of letters I have received from schoolchildren telling me that, thanks to our talk, they will never forget the lessons of the Holocaust.

A day still does not go by when I don't think of Richie, and his love will live on in my heart until there is no longer breath in my body. But what I learned is that I had love enough for two, and was lucky enough, in the midst of a cruel world war and an even crueller Holocaust, to find two such good men who loved me.

I suppose my mother was right again. God has truly watched over her family.

Otto and me on our fiftieth wedding anniversary cruise in 1997.
(Courtesy of the author)

Authors' Note

In order to protect the privacy of several persons pseudonyms have been used. The name 'Richie Kovacs' is one. All other names are real.

For perspective and background on the Holocaust in Hungary, the authors used the two-volume *The Politics of Genocide: the Holocaust in Hungary* by Columbia Professor Emeritus Randolph I. Braham (Columbia University Press, 1994). His insights and information helped to illuminate the period.

Scribner

Man is Wolf to Man
Surviving Stalin's Gulag
Janusz Bardach and Kathleen Gleeson

When Janusz Bardach, a young Polish Jew, fled the
Nazis to join the Red Army, he found himself
enmeshed in the dangerous world of Stalinist
Russia. Falling foul of the regime, he was sent to
Kolyma, the harshest of all the Siberian gulags. In
his highly acclaimed memoir, Janusz Bardach
describes the terror and cruelty, the near-
starvation, the back-breaking physical labour and
the constant threat of death which accompanied
prison life. It is a moving testament to one man's
courage and the strength of the human spirit.

'I simply could not put it down . . . it expresses a
deep humanity and it takes the reader into an
extraordinary world with great force'
Adam Hochschild

'This outstanding description of the past at the
same time represents hope for a better future'
Simon Wiesenthal

ISBN 0 684 84047 2
PRICE £7.99

POCKET
B O O K S

I HAVE LIVED A
THOUSAND YEARS

GROWING UP IN THE HOLOCAUST
Livia Bitton-Jackson

'This is the story that Anne Frank was
never able to tell'
Jewish Chronicle

'A compelling, unforgettable read'
Kati Nicholl, *Daily Express*

This is the memoir of Elli Friedmann, who was just
thirteen years old when the Nazis invaded
Hungary. It describes her descent into the hell of
Auschwitz in intimate, excruciating detail,
recounts what it was like to be one of the few
teenage inmates and tells of the miraculous twists
of fate that helped her survive against all odds.

I Have Lived a Thouand Years is a searing story of
cruelty and suffering, but at the same time one of
hope, faith, perseverance and love.

ISBN 0 7434 0875 6
PRICE £5.99

**SIMON &
SCHUSTER**

'Colonel' Cody and the Flying Cathedral
The Amazing Adventures of the Cowboy who Conquered Britain's Skies
Garry Jenkins

In an age of flamboyant pioneers, 'Colonel' Cody cut one of the most colourful and controversial figures. His early years in America saw him on the same cattle trails as Wyatt Earp, and competing with the legendary Annie Oakley for the title of King of the Wild West sharpshooters. His life in Britain was no less impressive, his fame reaching its apex when he pioneered powered flight. A passionate kite-builder and flyer, he fought a bitter battle to become the first man to fly in England. Now Garry Jenkins brings this monumental figure and his amazing adventures back to vivid life in a bitter-sweet memoir of a career without parallel.

ISBN 0 684 86025 2

PRICE £14.99

**SIMON &
SCHUSTER**

LIPSTICK
Jessica Pallingston

This is the book that speaks to and satisfies your
lipstick fetish. At various times throughout the
ages lipstick has been illegal, a power symbol, a
medicine, a secret weapon, a potent image of
femininity, and the one cosmetic women won't go
without. This book is filled with quirky,
fascinating, and unusual facts on the history,
culture and lore of lipstick, as well as:

- How cosmetic companies name lipsticks
- Quotes from a wide array of famous people about
  their lipstick
- Great tips on the art and application of lipstick
- Details on what your lipstick shape says about
  you
- Exactly how the opposite sex views lipstick

This is a playful, affectionate look at lipstick, the
emotionally charged cosmetic that has fascinated
women – and lured men – for thousands of years.

ISBN 0 684 85870 3
PRICE £12.99

POCKET
B O O K S

KAY ALLENBAUGH

CHOCOLATE FOR A WOMAN'S HEART
PRICE £6.99
ISBN 0 671 03740 4

CHOCOLATE FOR A MOTHER'S HEART
PRICE £6.99
ISBN 0 671 03741 2

CHOCOLATE FOR A WOMAN'S SOUL
PRICE £6.99
ISBN 0 7434 0830 6

CHOCOLATE FOR A LOVER'S HEART
PRICE £6.99
ISBN 0 671 03742 0

Like the finest chocolate, these inspiring tales will
boost your spirits, lift your heart, and soothe your
soul. A rich, soulful celebration of womanhood,
one that any woman – mother, daughter, sister,
bestfriend or lover – will enjoy.

**SIMON &
SCHUSTER**

These books and other **Simon & Schuster** titles are available from your book shop or can be ordered direct from the publisher.

☐ 0 684 84047 2 **Man is Wolf to Man** – Janusz Bardach £7.99
☐ 0 7434 0875 6 **I Have Lived a Thousand Years** – Livia Bitten-Jackson £5.99
☐ 0 684 86025 2 **'Colonel' Cody & the Flying Cathedral**– Garry Jenkins £14.99
☐ 0 684 85870 3 **Lipstick** – Jessica Pallingston £12.99
☐ 0 671 03740 4 **Chocolate for a Woman's Heart** – Kay Allenbaugh £6.99
☐ 0 671 03741 2 **Chocolate for a Mother's Heart** – Kay Allenbaugh £6.99
☐ 0 671 03742 0 **Chocolate for a Lover's Heart** – Kay Allenbaugh £6.99
☐ 0 7434 0830 6 **Chocolate for a Woman's Soul** – Kay Allenbaugh £6.99

Please send cheque or postal order for the value of the book, free postage and packing within the UK; OVERSEAS including Republic of Ireland £1 per book.

OR: Please debit this amount from my:

VISA/ACCESS/MASTERCARD ....

CARD NO: ....

EXPIRY DATE ....

AMOUNT £ ....

NAME..

ADDRESS ....

....

SIGNATURE ....

Send orders to SIMON & SCHUSTER CASH SALES
PO Box 29, Douglas, Isle of Man, IM99 1BQ
Tel: 01624 675137, Fax 01624 670923
www.bookpost.co.uk
Please allow 14 days for delivery.
Prices and availability subject to change without notice.